AF600254

DEFINING THE MODERN MUSEUM

A Case Study of the Challenges of Exchange

Defining the Modern Museum

A Case Study of the Challenges of Exchange

LIANNE McTAVISH

UNIVERSITY OF TORONTO PRESS
Toronto Buffalo London

Toronto Buffalo London
www.utppublishing.com

ISBN 978-1-4426-4443-4

Library and Archives Canada Cataloguing in Publication

McTavish, Lianne
Defining the modern museum : a case study of the challenges of exchange / Lianne McTavish.

(Cultural spaces)
Includes bibliographical references and index.
ISBN 978-1-4426-4443-4

1. New Brunswick Museum – Case studies. 2. Museums – Case studies. 3. Museum techniques – Case studies. I. Title. II. Series: Cultural spaces

AM21.N4M37 2013 069.09715'1 C2012-906128-X

University of Toronto Press acknowledges the financial assistance to its publishing program of the Canada Council for the Arts and the Ontario Arts Council.

Canada Council for the Arts
Conseil des Arts du Canada

ONTARIO ARTS COUNCIL
CONSEIL DES ARTS DE L'ONTARIO
50 YEARS OF ONTARIO GOVERNMENT SUPPORT OF THE ARTS
50 ANS DE SOUTIEN DU GOUVERNEMENT DE L'ONTARIO AUX ARTS

This book has been published with the help of a grant from the Canadian Federation for the Humanities and Social Sciences, through the Awards to Scholarly Publications Program, using funds provided by the Social Sciences and Humanities Research Council of Canada.

University of Toronto Press acknowledges the financial support of the Government of Canada through the Canada Book Fund for its publishing activities.

For my former colleagues in the Department of History at the University of New Brunswick

Contents

Illustrations

Acknowledgments

I began researching museums as a graduate student in the 1990s, continued to pursue an interest in critical museum theory as a professor in the Department of History at the University of New Brunswick between 1996 and 2007, and finally completed this project while in my current position at the University of Alberta. I therefore have many people and institutions to thank, without being able to name them all here. Funding was generously provided by a standard research grant from the Social Sciences and Humanities Research Council of Canada (2001–5) and an award from the Killam Research Fund at the University of Alberta (2008). Research assistants at the University of New Brunswick included Matthew Ware and Dallas Guenther, and with Joshua Dickison I co-published 'William MacIntosh, Natural History and the Professionalization of the New Brunswick Museum, 1898–1940,' in the September 2007 issue of *Acadiensis: Journal of the History of the Atlantic Region*. That same year, Shawna Stairs Quinn and I launched 'Progress and Permanence: Women and the New Brunswick Museum, 1880–1980,' a website about female donors to the New Brunswick Museum and its precursors (www.unbf.ca/womenandmuseum). I am grateful to Margaret Conrad for her timely support of this interactive resource.

The editors of the *Canadian Historical Review* have kindly granted me permission to republish my 2006 article 'Learning to See in New Brunswick, 1862–1929' as chapter 2 of the present volume. Although I produced other articles from my extensive archival research, including 'What's Old Is New Again: The Reconvergence of Libraries, Archives and Museums in the Digital Age,' co-authored with library and information studies expert Lisa Given (now at the Charles Sturt University, Wagga Wagga, Australia) in the January 2010 issue of the *Library Quar-*

terly, none of them substantially repeats the final contents of this book. I would like to thank the anonymous referees of the manuscript and recognize both the skill and good humour of Siobhan McMenemy, my editor at University of Toronto Press.

Numerous archivists, librarians, and curators provided adept assistance, including those at the Nova Scotia Archives and Record Management, Museum of Natural History in Halifax, Miramichi Natural History Museum, Provincial Archives of New Brunswick, University of New Brunswick Archives, New Brunswick Legislative Library, McGill University Library Rare Books and Special Collections, McCord Museum Archives and Documentation Centre, Library and Archives of the Royal Ontario Museum, National Archives of Canada, Provincial Archives of Manitoba, Manitoba Legislative Library, City Archives of Vancouver, Vancouver Museum, British Columbia Archives, Royal British Columbia Museum, Archives of the Newark Museum, Metropolitan Museum of Art in New York, Field Museum in Chicago, and Guildhall Library in London. Archivist Cyndie Campbell at the National Gallery of Canada Library and Archives deserves special mention, as does the entire staff of the New Brunswick Museum, the institution that provided the primary case study for this book. I am grateful to Felicity Osepchook, Janet Bishop, and Jennifer Longon in the Archives and Research Library, particularly for their permission to reproduce many photographs. I was also aided by the New Brunswick Museum's CEO, Jane Fullerton, and such talented curators as Stephen Clayden, Gary Hughes, Peter Larocque, Donald McAlpine, and Randall Miller. Andrea Kirkpatrick, former curator of Canadian and international art, was my lifeline while writing this book, enabling access to documents, objects, and storage areas at the New Brunswick Museum.

My wonderful colleagues in the Department of History at the University of New Brunswick taught me to love working in both the archives and the province, and I dedicate this book to all of them. Early chapter drafts were read by Gail Campbell, David Frank, Bill Parenteau, Steven Turner, and Beverly Lemire, who is now also at the University of Alberta. More polished versions of the chapters in this book were critiqued by the fabulous women in my writing group at the University of Alberta, namely, Liz Czach, Liza Piper, Julie Rak, and Anne Whitelaw (now at Concordia University). I am lucky to have found equally supportive colleagues in the Department of Art and Design at the University of Alberta, above all its efficient and resourceful former Chair, Betsy Boone. I should also highlight the innovative scholarship of Ruth Phillips, as well as the work of performance artist Judy Freya Sibayan, for providing me with continual inspiration.

My academic and personal life has been further enriched by a broad circle of friends and family, including my community at the gym, where I did much of my thinking. In the end, however, I owe my greatest debt to my steadfast partner of twenty-four years, Lee Spence, for without him I am nothing.

DEFINING THE MODERN MUSEUM

A Case Study of the Challenges of Exchange

Introduction: The Impossible Museum

The modern museum does not exist. It is a mythical entity that has never been achieved. The museum cannot be situated in a single location or explained with reference to a linear, historical narrative, but it remains a powerful idea. Since the late nineteenth century, educators, reformers, collectors, curators, scholars, and patrons, among many others, have imagined the perfect museum, attempting to define it. The impossibility of realizing their goal may have motivated its continual pursuit. The plans of museum builders have sometimes existed in a fleeting manner on paper or in words, or have taken a more concrete form in relation to specific things, places, and people before being discarded, improved, or reinvented.

I participate in this process even as I strive to recognize it. After researching a number of Canadian, American, and French museums and visiting many institutions, I have come to embrace the museum as a process – an elusive set of actions that is continually performed but never in exactly the same way. This process can include brainstorming, writing mandates, baking, collecting objects, hiking, exchanging specimens, fundraising, lobbying governments, hosting parties, reading, wooing the public, renovating, or cleaning. It occurs in relation to a range of economic, social, and political circumstances, as well as to other equally elusive institutions, such as schools, libraries, and social clubs. The museum appears in unstable and temporary ways within a network of connections, remaining both incomplete and alluring.

This unsettling understanding of the museum has been embraced by other scholars. Those participating in 'The Relational Museum,' a project undertaken between 2002 and 2006 at the Pitt Rivers Museum in Oxford, for example, concluded that the museum is 'the least moored, stable, or pre-constituted entity imaginable.'[1] Drawing on a digital database of the archaeological and anthropological artifacts in the collections, they systematically analysed the relationships formed from 1884 to 1945 between the museum and the wider world. Emphasizing the agency of the material objects, the researchers at the Pitt Rivers Museum considered how its collections had created relationships between people, but also realized that people themselves had become connected by means of the objects. The results published in 2007 undermined any sense of the museum as a container for valuable items, or as a powerful entity that had imposed particular ideas on a vulnerable public. The research team affirmed that the museum was a shifting set of people and things, constantly brought into being through the actions of anthropologists and mediated by the material world.[2] The boundaries of the Pitt Rivers Museum were ultimately extended to include multiple locations around the world, blurring distinctions between its interior and exterior.

The study undertaken in 'The Relational Museum' is laudable because it refused to generalize about 'the' museum, and focused on one particular – albeit very important and well known – museum. The empirical methodology employed by researchers was enabled by the unusually thorough digital database of the hundreds of thousands of objects in the collections. Using statistical data as well as archival records, scholars had remained flexible, following the threads of connected places, people, and objects, while realizing that visitors, donors, and museum administrators had experienced, and continue to experience, the Pitt Rivers Museum in diverse ways. At once historically grounded and attuned to the present, this project in many ways offers a model able to inspire future research on museums.

My own research, also launched in 2002, proceeded rather differently. It was driven by critical museum theory, particularly the revisionary accounts of the museum produced during the last thirty years by art historians, sociologists, anthropologists, historians, and curators. Most early scholarship was concerned with undermining the museum's status as a neutral or inherently valuable institution, linking it with elitism, power, and the promotion of particular political agendas.[3] The most damning critiques of the modern museum focused on the anthropological exhibitions formed during the height of colonial expansion, with scholars charging that these displays removed both peoples and ethnographic objects from their original contexts to re-signify them in the interests of Western viewers.[4] During the 1990s, some scholars began addressing the generative as well as the oppressive potential of museums, noting how the institutions had long been open to a plurality of experiences and interpretations, and were not monolithic entities impervious to change.[5] More recently, a number of authors, including historian Steven Conn, have adopted a more defensive tone to argue explicitly in favour of museums, asserting that the earlier critical accounts are rife with 'museophobia.'[6] James Cuno, director of the Art Institute of Chicago, reaffirms what he considers the traditional values of the museum, calling for the return of its authority and ability to deliver wondrous experiences to visitors.[7] Other writers endorse a different albeit equally positive vision of museums, contending that the institutions have always responded dynamically to changing circumstances and the needs of visitors.[8] Former museum director Robert R. Janes claims that during our currently troubled times these flexible institutions are 'needed now more than ever before,' while Danielle Rice, director of the Delaware Art Museum, concludes that the complexity of museums and 'their ability to change according to shifting social needs ... insures their status as symbols of democratic civilization.'[9]

My approach was informed by the full range of critical museum theory – in the chapters that follow, I consider how the modern museum could be simultaneously constraining and enabling to various groups, especially middle-class women. I nevertheless grew increasingly dissatisfied with much theoretical writing on museums, including my own early work, finding it too generalizing. Some studies are quite abstract, referring more to museum ideals than to actual museum practices.[10] Others make broad arguments about the history and function of museums based exclusively on the interpretation of one kind of institution, usually art galleries, without exploring their distinction from, for example, natural history or anthropological museums.[11] A significant proportion of museum scholarship focuses on national, urban museums and controversial exhibitions, overlooking the important differences of smaller, less central institutions.[12] Furthermore, even many recent publications in the field retain a standard narrative of the development of museums, implying that they were powerful organizations primarily devoted to amassing and exhibiting objects during the nineteenth and early twentieth century, which became subject to debate, commercial interests, and a demanding public only within the past fifty years or so.[13] This historical overview allows museum critics to highlight the changing status of material collections, curatorship, corporate involvement, and the public in contemporary institutions. Eilean Hooper-Greenhill, for example, praises what she calls the emerging 'post-museum,' which, in contrast to the authoritative collecting and exhibiting practices of the modernist museum, is based on mutuality, diversity, experience, ephemeral forms of culture, and local interests that can be addressed in such popular sites as pubs and shops.[14] Others see the decline of the modern museum in negative terms, decrying its loss of authority and defilement by a commercialized kind of 'info-tainment' that panders to the whims of the public while undermining the value of material collections and the recognition of specialist curators.[15] Information studies scholars Juris Dilevko and Lisa Gottlieb insist that the intensified commodification of museums hinders their distinctive educational role by linking them with the kinds of entertainment offered by shopping malls, movie theatres, and theme parks.[16]

I decided to engage with this literature without producing another chronological narrative of the museum's triumph or decline by undertaking archival research at a single institution, namely, the New Brunswick Museum in Saint John, New Brunswick. By selecting a museum with diverse collections first amassed during the 1860s, I strove to emphasize the specific and local concerns of an organization that had not previously received intensive scrutiny, and was neither national in scope nor an art gallery. All the same, at first I worried that this institution, located in a small industrial city on the east coast of Canada, would provide little more than an eclectic case study. Examining it would no doubt reveal a complicated story of development, as well as the colourful personalities of those who founded and funded it. Yet I presumed that an account of the New Brunswick Museum would produce idiosyncratic details able to embellish but not to challenge the standard theories about the history and role of Western museums. I expected the usual themes to emerge, with documents revealing the ways in which upper-middle-class patrons strove to establish themselves while disciplining the lower orders, white settlers shaped their self-image by collecting objects made by colonial 'others,' administrators continually lobbied for increased government support, and marketers gradually commodified the museum in the absence of such support.

As I launched my research, however, I was led away from the museum as a building or a collection managed by individuals, toward other organizations and countries, as well as such themes as gift giving and gendered identity. I found that the New Brunswick Museum and its precursors had attracted diverse donors who were not exclusively from the elite classes, featured women as important contributors, produced innovative loan programs, fostered broadly international visions, struggled to professionalize staff members, and undergone varying degrees of commodification since the nineteenth century. Such information is in dialogue with the important work of historian Kate Hill, which analyses such previously neglected municipal organizations as the Liverpool Museum.[17] She argues that scholars have typically emphasized national museums, stressing their modernity, efficiency, and progressiveness, thereby simplifying our understanding of the museum project. Different places have in fact produced very different museums. Hill contends that smaller, regional institutions often continued to use sensational methods of display, endeavoured to build a professional identity for curators, and relied on volunteer societies long after larger museums had embraced both rationalization and professionalization.

Defining the Modern Museum: A Case Study of the Challenges of Exchange is similarly designed to 'provincialize' the museum, insisting on the positive aspects of this term. As a modifier, the word *provincial* usually refers to a limited point of view or lack of sophistication. My alternative understanding of its active form is inspired by Dipesh Chakrabarty's book *Provincializing Europe: Postcolonial Thought and Historical Difference*, published in 2000.[18] Chakrabarty systematically reveals the Eurocentric underpinnings of historicism, showing that Europe is an imaginary figure, generalized from accounts of European history. Instead of starting with this monolithic conception of Europe, his goal is to explore the undemocratic foundations of democracy by writing into 'the history of modernity the ambivalences, contradictions, the use of force, and the tragedies and ironies that attend it.'[19] Although I have a similar understanding of the imaginary, impossible museum, my work ultimately diverges from that of Chakrabarty more than it coincides with it, for I do not consider subaltern histories or contribute to the practice of postcolonial theory. I nevertheless similarly emphasize plurality, challenging both unifying histories of the museum and the European as well as the American dominance of critical museum theory by focusing on what might be considered a marginal Canadian institution. The New Brunswick Museum literally is a provincial museum, charged with representing New Brunswick. I therefore consider the shifting conceptions of this particular province in the chapters that follow, even as my interest in the local inevitably expands out to global concerns – concerns always perceived from a particular place and time. The resulting book explores the spaces between the New Brunswick Museum and other entities, at odds with most published accounts of museums which emphasize their collecting practices, exhibition spaces, architectural plans, public programs, directors, patrons, or visitors. Though in dialogue with this literature, my chapters instead address, among other things, how loaned and donated objects moved out of the museum, how the institution was linked with a range of organizations, including schools, libraries, and government agencies, and how different groups of people negotiated the right to stage their identities in relation to it.

My efforts to decentre understandings of the museum and critical museum theory were enabled by the archival research I undertook at the New Brunswick Museum. For the first time in my career, I read accession records, personal letters, and minute books, focusing on details and dates. I was simultaneously drawn away from New Brunswick, ultimately working in various archives across Canada and the United States, reading about such unexpected topics as nineteenth-century geology, the history of Chinese dress, and the establishment of public libraries. An archival approach to my case study brought me both closer to and farther from the New Brunswick Museum, changing my outlook on museums and critical museum theory.

I perhaps inevitably succumbed to what philosopher Jacques Derrida calls archive fever.[20] While sitting at the same desk everyday in the archives of the New Brunswick Museum, wearing the requisite white gloves, I began to imagine that I was the first person ever to have read the private letters and handwritten minutes being delivered to me. I felt that I had a special acquaintance with such historical figures as Alice Lusk Webster, founder of the museum's Art Department during the 1930s, especially after 'discovering' a stash of her letters to C.T. Currelly, director of the Royal Ontario Museum of Archaeology in Toronto – documents previously unknown to curators at the New Brunswick Museum. I became fascinated with bizarre details, revelling in descriptions of an early collection which had included a 'singular substance found on the snow after a fire at Gagetown, New Brunswick' and a bladder stone extracted from 'Mr. McG.'[21] I had never before contemplated having a complete and specialized knowledge of any subject. Yet after reading the contents of the archives in their entirety, poking through boxes of uncatalogued files, and even undertaking a clandestine visit to one of the backroom storage areas, I fancied that I had attained an unrivalled understanding of the origins of the New Brunswick Museum.

Once the fever broke, I had to admit that the records I had been consulting were for the most part carefully selected and arranged to produce a particular image of the New Brunswick Museum. The material was classified to highlight specific organizations and individual patrons. The archives supported research on the rich history of the institution, but were less forthcoming about controversies or anything particularly recent, both to protect the privacy of persons still living and to shield the museum from negative publicity. My research was therefore essentially limited to the period before 1950, and my ultimate decision to emphasize the Natural History Society of New Brunswick – founded in 1862 and one of the most important precursors of the New Brunswick Museum – was no accident. It was dictated by the archival holdings made available to me. Drawing on a body of theory that approaches archives as knowledge-producing entities rather than neutral collections of historical facts, I came to recognize that archives make some histories visible while excluding others.[22] I found little trace, for example, of the voices of the Aboriginal peoples whose objects were included in the collections of the New Brunswick Museum and its predecessors. I tried to move past the confines of the archives by reading 'against the grain' for less obvious material involving women and articulations of 'race,' as well as by relying on other kinds of records and published sources. At the same time, I attempted to recognize how my own interests have informed both what is featured and what is forgotten in the chapters that follow.

My view of the New Brunswick Museum was certainly shaped by the assistance I received from its generous staff, rendering me sympathetic to the realities of working in the institution. I became aware of the extensive intellectual and physical labour involved in museum work, as well as the ways in which long-term plans could be thwarted by economic and political pressures. My understanding of the New Brunswick Museum as a complex entity that has always been open to diversity and debate thus reinforces those more positive accounts of early museums, but I do not wish to defend the institution in a way that might ultimately reconfirm rather than question its authority. According to cultural theorist Ben Dibley, even the most perceptive and critical interpretations of museums, including the well-known analyses by Tony Bennett and James Clifford, reinforce stereotypical claims about the democratic potential of the institution, offering advice about how to improve and make it more inclusive.[23] Dibley implies that these and other critical studies are tacitly committed to recreating the impossibly perfect museum. My goal, however, is in keeping with the advice offered by curator and cultural historian Andrea Witcomb, who suggests that 'rather than seeing the range of changes that are currently

1.1 Exterior of the New Brunswick Museum (est. 1929), Douglas Avenue location, Saint John, opened 1933. X11448 [1]. Courtesy of the New Brunswick Museum, Saint John, New Brunswick.

occurring as the destruction of museums, it may be useful to pause for a moment and revisit the past.'[24] In the end, *Defining the Modern Museum* reconsiders the past in order to offer a broader range of ways to think about museums in the present.

The New Brunswick Museum

When driving south into Saint John to view the exhibits at the New Brunswick Museum, visitors pass by the old museum building, constructed during the early 1930s. Situated at the edge of the city, the imposing structure features a neo-classical facade with columns and broad steps (figure 1.1). This building continues to house the archives of the museum and to store its impressive collections, including rare masks

I.2 Façade of the New Brunswick Museum, Market Square, Saint John. The relocated exhibition spaces officially opened in this commercial centre in 1996. NBM–F3–44. Courtesy of the New Brunswick Museum, Saint John, New Brunswick.

from Easter Island, large Japanese vases, portraits of ships launched from the Saint John harbour, and thousands of local geological specimens. The official exhibition spaces of the New Brunswick Museum, however, have been relocated. In 1996, the museum officially opened in a downtown shopping mall, a move designed both to provide more space for displays and to revitalize the harbourfront area. Once visitors enter the Market Square commercial centre, they walk by various shops before arriving at a food court. There, next to a Tim Hortons concession stand, looms the three-storey painted facade of the New Brunswick Museum (figure I.2). After passing through its doors, visitors encounter displays that emphasize the province's economic history in terms of lumber harvesting and coastal fishing, the natural history of the region, and its artistic production.

This glimpse of the 1930s building in its setting reveals much about both the museum and Saint John. The east coast industrial city flourished throughout the nineteenth and into the early twentieth century, fuelled by manufacturing, lumber mills, and ship building. During the 1920s a handful of citizens, including doctors, teachers, business owners, and, notably, the lieutenant-governor of New Brunswick, lobbied for the construction of a provincial institution that would enhance the stature of Saint John. Their optimistic vision of the city was not unreasonable. Despite suffering a more intense economic decline than the one generally occurring throughout Canada at the time, Saint John was an active port city – in both summer and winter – and its inhabitants proudly recalled that it had been the fourth largest city in North America during the mid-nineteenth century.[25] The economic prospects of Saint John have fluctuated since then, and though the city remains a centre for oil refining and some manufacturing, it is now largely in post-industrial decline, with a population of only 125,000 people. The deteriorating 1930s building points to the fading glory of the city, even as it continues to function as a site of civic concern. The newer location downtown – part of a broader effort to provide an attractive destination for tourists – offers a rather different picture of the identity of Saint John, as it struggles to diversify its economy and temper its industrial reputation. The exhibition spaces within the shopping mall also allude to the changing status of modern museums in Western culture, as these institutions are increasingly expected to attract a wide public while turning a profit. In September of 2006, administrators announced a plan to create yet another 'new vision for the New Brunswick Museum' by revitalizing the 1930s building and enhancing its storage capacity, though the official exhibition spaces will remain downtown.[26] The continued transformation of this edifice provides one indication of the ways in which the past, present, and future of the New Brunswick Museum are continually reshaped.

The museum's official website draws attention to the rich history of the institution, proclaiming that it is the 'oldest continuing museum' in Canada.[27] Though established in 1929 and officially opened in 1934, the New Brunswick Museum was constructed from an amalgamation of earlier collections, including those of the Gesner Museum (1842–6), the Mechanics' Institute Museum (1846–90), and the Museum of the Natural History Society of New Brunswick (1862–1932). In 1842, the medical doctor and provincial geologist Abraham Gesner exhibited his collection of minerals, rocks, and stuffed mammals in one room of the Mechanics' Institute, an organization devoted to educating working men, located in downtown Saint John.[28] Stating that he wanted to encourage the study of the natural history of New Brunswick and his native Nova Scotia and 'satisfy the curiosity of strangers,' Gesner took out an advertisement in a local newspaper that announced: 'Specimens belonging to the Animal, Vegetable and Mineral Kingdoms, Fossils, Relics, Works of Art, Ancient Books and Papers, Models, Inventions, Domestic Manufactures, and Curiosities of All Kinds, will be thankfully received. The objects of Natural History of New Brunswick and Nova Scotia will be exchanged for those of Foreign Countries.'[29] Surviving catalogues show that Gesner amassed an expansive international collection that nevertheless featured geological specimens from his native Nova Scotia as well as New Brunswick. His efforts to profit financially from the exchange and display of his objects were less successful, and in 1846 the collections were seized by creditors who donated them to the Mechanics' Institute. This organization had already accumulated its own natural history specimens, as well as Chinese, Indian, and other objects donated by seafaring men returning to the port city of Saint John from various 'exotic' locations.[30]

The most important precursor of the New Brunswick Museum was the Natural History Society of New Brunswick. During the first meeting of the Society in 1862, its forty-three male founders – including George F. Matthew, a customs clerk and amateur geologist, LeBaron Botsford, a medical doctor, and Charles Frederick Hartt, a geology student – affirmed that residents as well as visitors should engage in 'seeing and studying [the] natural objects and productions' of New Brunswick.[31] These early members immediately constructed a public museum in a room rented from the Mechanics' Institute, and by 1864 it contained 10,000 minerals and fossils, 2,000 marine invertebrates, 750 insects, 500 plants, and 30 stuffed birds.[32] In 1890 the Mechanics' Institute closed, and for a mere $200 the Natural History Society acquired its collections – which included the specimens originally amassed by Gesner – moving them to more expansive lodgings. According to early members of the Society, the public display of these objects contributed both to the dissemination of useful knowledge and the promotion of New Brunswick's natural resources, especially its mineral deposits.[33] This conflation of museums and industrial expansion was commonplace during the Victorian era, when exhibitions were meant to stimulate the economy as well as the mind.[34]

The Museum of the Natural History Society was nevertheless quite innovative, acting as a site for the development of educational programming. William MacIntosh (1867–1950), the self-trained entomologist who served as its curator from 1898 to 1932, and then became the first director of the New Brunswick Museum, created what would now be called outreach programs, loaning objects, posters, and educational notes to New Brunswick schools in the late nineteenth century. By 1907, MacIntosh was preparing small collections of native insects and fossils for the use of public schools throughout the province, and in 1915 a total of 274 specimens were loaned, with a further 57 objects or collections of objects given to schools outright.[35] Historian Eileen Mak argues that Canadian museums followed the British trend by eschewing or ignoring educational programming for children until the 1930s and 1940s.[36] The Museum of the Natural History Society was delivering educational material to school children long before that, however, and this work was internationally recognized, influencing the programming of other North American museums.[37]

By 1881 women were allowed to join the Natural History Society as associate members, and they outnumbered male participants by the early twentieth century, making substantial financial and material contributions to the society's museum.[38] During the late nineteenth century, the Ladies' Auxiliary organized tea rooms and bazaars to fund the educational and social activities of the Natural History Society, while providing the public face of the institution.[39] In 1906, female members devoted themselves to raising money for the purchase of a new building to house the expanding Museum of the Natural History Society. An Auxiliary member, Catharine Murdock, paid off the substantial mortgage on this building in 1909, by leaving over $4,000 to the Natural History Society in her will.[40] As this generosity was scarcely recognized by the male members in the minutes of their meetings, the ladies were prompted to purchase for the rooms of the Society a beautiful oak lectern fitted with a brass plaque inscribed with the words: 'In living memory of Catherine Murdock, St. John, NB 1910, presented by the ladies of the N.H.S.'[41] The members of the Ladies' Auxiliary of the Natural History Society found multiple ways of making their presence known, by giving public lectures, commissioning newspaper reports of their activities, and donating valuable objects to the museum.[42]

Women arguably became more prominent once the New Brunswick Museum was established as a provincial institution. Despite providing funds for the impressive 1930s building, the local and provincial governments in New Brunswick offered little continuous financial support, compelling the museum to rely on wealthy patrons.[43] Dr John

Clarence (J.C.) Webster (1863–1950) and his wife, Alice Lusk Webster (1880–1953), were the most prominent benefactors, and both played a significant role in defining the institution. Dr Webster was born in Shediac, New Brunswick, and trained as an obstetrician in Scotland before conducting a successful practice in Chicago for over twenty years.[44] While living in the United States, he and his wife became connoisseurs of Asian art, fraternizing with other noted collectors, including Ernest F. Fenollosa, curator of the Department of Oriental Art at the Boston Museum of Fine Arts from 1890 to 1896.[45] When ill health prompted Dr Webster to retire to his hometown in 1919, he pursued his interest in Canadian history, focusing on the life of the eighteenth-century British general James Wolfe and, more locally, the history of the Acadians. He was the driving force behind the creation of museums at both Fort Beauséjour and Louisbourg, but the New Brunswick Museum was one of his greatest passions. After helping to found the provincial museum in 1929, he served as vice-president of its board and acted as honorary curator of Canadian history until his death in 1950.

Named honorary curator of the newly created Art Department, Lusk Webster began moving Egyptian, Asian, and European art objects into the New Brunswick Museum in 1934. From a wealthy family in New York, she was a well-travelled woman who had been educated in France, specializing in art history.[46] Lusk Webster was committed to the museum, for she funded the Art Department with her own money, donated many items from her personal collections, and physically installed most of the exhibitions. She also employed inventive strategies to acquire what she hoped would be a representative display of international culture. Approaching her well-heeled contacts in New York, she scavenged anything valuable as well as cast-off items such as broken porcelain, which she carefully reassembled and put on display.[47] Lusk Webster additionally drew on her connections with those in the museum world, especially her friendship with C.T. Currelly at the Royal Ontario Museum of Archaeology. In 1934, she offered his museum seventeen fine Japanese paintings owned by her and her husband in exchange for a substantial number of objects, including Chinese porcelain, which were given as a gift in kind to the New Brunswick Museum. The resulting influx of Asian art caused members of the Natural History Society – many of whom were appointed to the board of the New Brunswick Museum – great anxiety, for such objects had previously been considered mere 'curios' secondary to specimens related to the natural history of New Brunswick.[48]

Lusk Webster was ultimately able to insist that her understanding of culture was more important than specimens of natural history, given her pedigree, wealth, and marriage to a powerful man. Yet Lusk Webster's status within the New Brunswick Museum was undermined by a gendered hierarchy that devalued women. Her voice is less dominant in the archival sources than that of her husband, and some of her important accomplishments – including a major acquisition of British-Roman and early English material from the Guildhall Museum in London in 1940 – have been erased from the official narratives of the New Brunswick Museum.[49] In that sense, she did not fare much better than the Auxiliary members of the Natural History Society, women who contributed substantially to the organization even as they were denied full membership. During the 1940s, Lusk Webster attempted to professionalize her Art Department, meeting with resistance from MacIntosh as well as the board of directors, another example of the ongoing struggles that shaped the early New Brunswick Museum.[50]

Although this survey provides some background information about the New Brunswick Museum, the broader discussions that follow are more thematic than chronological or biographical. This museum provides an ideal launching point for my investigations partly because it is arguably a natural history, anthropological, historical, fine art, and children's museum all at once. Recalling the cabinets of wonder that flourished in sixteenth- and seventeenth-century Europe, it accommodates a wide range of specimens, including minerals, fossils, taxidermied marine animals, Aboriginal objects, European paintings, and Asian ceramics.[51] The New Brunswick Museum has never had a single, strictly regional, identity. Since the middle of the nineteenth century, administrators of the early collections interacted with institutions in Britain, Australia, the United States, China, Japan, and the rest of Canada. The collections of the New Brunswick Museum and its precursors have often been in transition, moving from the basement of a public school, to a neo-classical building in the suburbs, and then a downtown commercial centre.[52] Archival documents reveal the unstable location of the institution, while indicating that it has always existed in a transitional state in the ambitions, negotiations, and diagrams of museum planners. Instead of a limited study of a single institution, the following chapters offer a wide-ranging account of how historically specific articulations of place, land, vision, gender, class, and identity have informed modern museums, ultimately both expanding and undermining current conceptions of the museum.

Chapter Overviews

The first chapter, 'Exchanging Values in the Nineteenth-Century Museum Marketplace,' considers how the international trade of objects between museums constructed a web of social, cultural, and economic meanings. Administrators of the Museum of the Natural History Society sent mineral and geological specimens to similar societies in the United States, Europe, Australia, and New Zealand, receiving such 'exotic' items as Peruvian pottery and Japanese bird skins in return. Though objects were thereby acquired by the New Brunswick society, expanding the collections was not the ultimate aim of these negotiations. I contend that exchange itself was the goal, drawing on the anthropologist Arjun Appadurai's claim that 'exchange is not a by-product of the mutual valuation of objects, but its source.'[53] Members of the fledgling Natural History Society of New Brunswick sent out mineral gift-sets in order to position themselves in relation to a host of other societies, establishing their identity and legitimacy, while promoting New Brunswick as a unique geological area rich in mineral wealth. By analysing a series of negotiations between the Museum of the Natural History Society and the Field Columbian Museum in Chicago during the late nineteenth century, I insist that exchanges between museums were neither straightforward gift giving without social expectations, nor capitalist endeavours aimed to produce profit. The mineral and geological samples sent out by the Natural History Society became worthy of collection and display only after they had been evaluated in terms of other, mostly foreign, objects. The museum marketplace thus transformed the status of both the material objects and the people who exchanged them, an emphasis that challenges more conventional notions of the museum as a site of preservation. The spaces inside the museum building lose their primacy in this interpretation, with the 'museum' understood to encompass the relationships developed by means of the circulation of objects between organized social groups.

Chapter 2, 'Learning to See: Vision, Visuality, and Material Culture, 1862–1929,' explores looking as an historically, regionally, and culturally specific act by examining the visual training promoted by the Natural History Society of New Brunswick. The pedagogical efforts of members of the Society extended beyond the walls of their museum to include camping trips, a school loan program, and even a train filled with displays that travelled throughout the province. In keeping with the first chapter, this discussion emphasizes the circulation of objects and the continual reproduction of their meanings. The educational activities promoted by the Natural History Society had specific visual goals; they were meant to give residents of New Brunswick a newfound appreciation of their region, equipping them simultaneously with a love of nature and an eye for economic opportunity. According to pedagogues, learning to see properly would produce both entrepreneurial citizens and an ideal image of New Brunswick. Understanding this historical conception of vision can shed light, I conclude, on the past as well as the present. During the late nineteenth and early twentieth century, visual training was considered both useful and entertaining, but today some critics condemn attempts to appeal to the public, deriding the displays offered in contemporary museums as mere spectacle. Though these critics argue that the educational mandate of museums has declined in recent years, I contend that it is really the status of vision that has deteriorated. Museum critics risk ignoring the historical goals of early museum builders and reinforcing a denigrated understanding of vision when they dismiss current museum exhibitions as superficial.

The third chapter, 'Offering Orientalism: Women and the Gift Economy of the Museum, 1880–1940,' returns to the theme of exchange by analysing how gift giving allowed female volunteers to reshape both the Museum of the Natural History Society and its successor, the New Brunswick Museum. In some ways, examining the position of women in relation to these organizations produces a familiar story of women's struggle for power and authority within male-dominated institutions. Yet this narrative is too limiting, for a number of women devised strategies of self-representation that were ultimately enabled by the gift economy of the museums. While some female associate members of the Natural History Society donated natural history specimens to the collections, ensuring that their names would be recorded in official accession records, Alice Lusk Webster exploited her international connections to secure valuable artworks for permanent display in the New Brunswick Museum. Echoing historian Jordanna Bailkin's claims, this chapter shows how the modern museum acted 'both as a compensatory institution for women – a cultural offering for the denial of political rights – and as a central force in the creation of female political identity.'[54] Moving beyond this necessary affirmation of women's contributions to museums, I also consider how the women deployed the culture of 'others' in order to improve their own status. Both the members of the Ladies' Auxiliary and Lusk Webster collected, displayed, and dispersed objects of Asian origin, insisting on their right to participate in the colonial project of the museum. Focusing on Chinese objects, in particular, I compare and contrast how the Auxiliary members and the honorary curator engaged with shifting Western understandings of Asian culture to produce their own gendered and class-specific versions of the museum.

Chapter 4, 'Libraries and Museums: Shifting Relationships, 1830–1940,' compares the Natural History Society of New Brunswick with other societies featuring natural history established in Montreal (1827), Winnipeg (1879), and Vancouver (1894). Members of these organizations were linked through the exchange of letters, bulletins, and specimens, sharing fundamentally similar understandings of nature, the value of visual training, and the economic function of museums. In this chapter I focus, however, on how each society associated material objects with written words. To differing degrees, these regional organizations created libraries along with collections of specimens, arguing that reading and looking were complementary educational activities. Yet during the early twentieth century, local governments, often aided by the Carnegie Corporation of New York, increasingly funded the construction of separate library buildings, distinguishing them from museums. My comparison of these societies explores the changing connections between museums and libraries, highlighting their diverse regional articulations while also considering such issues as the differing participation of women, the role of exchange, collecting policies, and understandings of the public within each society. Tempering my emphasis on the Natural History Society of New Brunswick in the previous chapters, chapter 4 expands to consider how societies that might seem fundamentally the same in fact diverged significantly, preventing me from drawing general conclusions from my primary case study.

In chapter 5, 'Gendered Professionals: Debating the Ideal Museum Worker during the 1930s and 1940s,' I continue to explore the gendered museum in relation to professionalization, a theme suggested by chapter 4's analysis of the increasing distinctions made between museum and library work. Chapter 5 compares Alice Lusk Webster's efforts to professionalize the New Brunswick Museum with those of her husband, J.C. Webster. Although apparently united in their efforts to hire highly educated personnel and improve the culture of New Brunswick, Lusk Webster and her husband pursued different methods. J.C. Webster sought to replace the director of the New Brunswick Museum, the long-time curator of the Museum of the Natural History Society of New Brunswick, William MacIntosh, with an historian equipped with a

PhD. He endorsed the efforts of the Carnegie Corporation of New York, which had created a Canadian Museums Committee during the 1930s in the hopes of professionalizing the staff of Canadian institutions, then still largely made up of self-trained personnel such as MacIntosh. Members of this committee, which included Webster himself, usually sent promising candidates for museum work to train at major institutions in London, England, or Ottawa. Lusk Webster was similarly eager to hire a professional curator to run her Art Department, enrolling her female protégé in the apprenticeship program at the Newark Museum, a decision decried by some of her male colleagues. Begun in 1925 by the museum's founder, John Cotton Dana, the apprenticeship program strove to equip an intelligent workforce with an array of practical skills that could transform 'gloomy' museums into useful institutions that provided concrete benefits to society.[55] In direct opposition to the type of education promoted by members of the Canadian Museums Committee, Dana eschewed specialization in favour of an adaptable and largely female workforce. This comparison of the professionalizing efforts made by Lusk Webster and J.C. Webster draws attention to historical disagreements about what constituted a professional, how museum workers should be trained, and what kind of work they should perform. These ongoing controversies were informed by gender to a degree not previously recognized, and my exploration of them continues to reveal the museum as an arena that was perpetually under reconstruction. Chapter 5 concludes by considering how current debates about the identity of curators both intersect with and diverge from these earlier discussions.

In the end, the five chapters of this book are unified as much by their emphasis on movement as by their discussion of the New Brunswick Museum and its precursors. The objects collected by the New Brunswick organizations were constantly transported around the province and exchanged with the wider world. The staff of these museums not only travelled widely, but were trained throughout Europe and North America. The exhibition spaces of the museums were equally unsettled, moving from place to place throughout the city, depending on the shifting ambitions of museum administrators. Thus, even as my book appears to undertake a detailed case study of the development of one particular institution, it undermines monolithic understandings of the modern museum. The dispersed museum reappears in discussions of the culture of geology, the school loan program, popularity of Chinese textiles, the creation of Carnegie libraries, and the increasing status of credentials.

Conclusions

This book was written primarily as an intervention in critical museum theory, addressing many of the issues currently of interest to its practitioners: the historical function and definition of the museum, its commodification and globalization, the role of the museum in shaping social identities, the apparent tension between entertaining and educational exhibitions, and the professionalization of museum workers. It nevertheless also draws from and contributes to a host of other scholarly domains, including library and information studies, gender studies, sociology, women's studies, anthropology, visual culture studies, and history. In terms of this last scholarly field, my approach draws more from cultural than social history. For the most part, I have not provided detailed descriptions of the social world of either individual museum builders or various members of Canadian natural history and other societies, nor have I recounted their biographies in detail. Instead my focus is on how particular people and groups of people both articulated their identities and became visible in relation to the museum. The concept of the museum therefore remains central to this inquiry, acting as a guiding principle, even as I endeavour to displace and dissolve it. Perhaps I was ultimately unable to avoid the allure of the impossible museum, despite my best efforts.

Chapter One

Exchanging Values in the Nineteenth-Century Museum Marketplace

Every year scholars and tourists from around the world visit New Brunswick to explore its geological formations, especially those dating from the Devonian and Cambrian periods. In 1997, an international research team led by Dr Randall Miller, curator of geology and paleontology at the New Brunswick Museum, discovered a 409-million-year-old shark fossil (*Doliodus prolematicus*), the oldest in the world, in the Devonian-age rocks of northern New Brunswick.[1] Miller has also provided educational tours to amateurs, taking them to the Fern Ledges, a fossil-rich area of black shale and sandstone stretching along the Bay of Fundy near Saint John.[2] In keeping with his long-standing commitment to sustainable geological tourism, Miller encouraged the New Brunswick government's recent acknowledgment of the importance of fossil preservation in the revised Heritage Conservation Act, which now requires a permit for fossil collecting.[3] According to Dr Miller, 'The rocks in the Saint John area alone record about a billion years of earth history. There are fascinating rock formations and sites that are significant in understanding the fossil record of life.'[4] This increasing recognition of the heritage status of fossils ultimately led to the foundation in October 2010 of the Stonehammer Geopark, located in the greater Saint John area, as the first and only North American member of the Global Geoparks Network.[5]

Attempts to raise the profile of geology in New Brunswick date from the nineteenth century, though the strategies have changed. When the Natural History Society of New Brunswick was founded in 1862, its male members – business owners, doctors, customs officials, and teachers, among others – insisted that their organization should both foster science in New Brunswick and develop its natural resources, especially those 'vast and varied deposits of mineral wealth in which our Province abounds.'[6] They sought to accomplish these utilitarian goals by collecting specimens to display in a public museum in Saint John, and by publishing their research in scholarly venues read by other natural history enthusiasts. Their most important method, however, involved the art of exchange. The early founders of the Natural History Society arranged New Brunswick minerals and fossils into 'gift-sets,' mailing them to other societies and museums in the hope of receiving valuable items in return. In 1896, for example, the society sent a number of Devonian fossil biota – from what was later called the Pennsylvanian Lancaster or Fern Ledges Formation – to the Field Columbian Museum, and obtained a return gift of twenty-three pieces of 'Indian pottery' previously exhibited at the Chicago World's Fair in 1893. A subsequent letter from the Field Columbian Museum requested the 'further exchange of like courtesies,' implying that the trade was a civilized event unsullied by references to money.[7] Yet members of the Natural History Society exchanged objects in order to increase the economic and cultural value of their province's natural resources.

This chapter analyses what I call the museum marketplace of the nineteenth century, considering how the international trade of objects between museums constructed a web of social, cultural, and economic meanings. My interest is not in how the objects were originally collected or acquired – a topic studied by others, particularly in relation to the 'scramble' for African goods by European colonizers – but rather in how they were transferred between institutions after having entered collections.[8] Exchanging specimens or 'curios' produced obligations that tied museums together, making them dependent on each other for creating both their collections and their identities. The practice of trading specimens between collectors or donating them to museums was long-standing, and in 1800 naturalist Georges Cuvier argued that 'this reciprocal exchange of information is perhaps the most noble and interesting commerce that men can have.'[9] In contrast to Cuvier's evaluation, historian Simon Knell describes the esteem and recognition that individuals sought in return for their 'selfless' donations of geological specimens to museums, while historian Martin Rudwick compares object exchanges to the economy of 'a street market,' noting that both parties are concerned with the relative values of the bartered items.[10] To my knowledge, however, the market between museums has not been analysed in a detailed case study. By focusing on the Natural History Society of New Brunswick, I examine the ways in which values were negotiated during such exchanges, as well as those situations when expectations were not met, and gifts were underappreciated. My approach is informed by anthropological theories, including the productive work of Marcel Mauss, and some of the responses to his study of gift exchange in the non-Western world.[11] Though most of the institutions involved in exchanging objects with the Natural History Society were Western, the trades included ethnographic objects. Numerous scholars have examined the power relations involved as Western museums misrepresented or appropriated the products of an 'other' culture.[12] Thinking in terms of gift exchange adds another dimension to this discussion, for members of the Natural History Society initiated such exchanges to associate their own products with foreign material. Non-Western objects such as the Peruvian pottery sent to the Society's museum were not considered second-rate but actually set the standard used to assess the samples that had been forwarded from New Brunswick.

Members of the Natural History Society put their geological specimens into circulation to transform them into currency. In keeping with their efforts to industrialize New Brunswick, members of the Natural History Society wished to commodify the fossil and mineral samples they sent as gifts to museums around the world. They hoped to turn them into desirable objects by means of exchange, thereby presenting New Brunswick as an area both rich in natural resources and based on an impressive geological foundation. The society's museum played a crucial role in this process because it provided temporary storage for the specimens meant to be shipped to other museums around the world. Although some scholars contend that the primary purpose of modern museums was to preserve and display objects, in this case the museum of the Natural History Society of New Brunswick also acted like a warehouse and transfer point. Cultural critic Wolfgang Ernst has examined how the digitization of contemporary collections encourages museums to function as temporary rather than permanent storage containers, facilitating immediate access to the collections in keeping with the consumer demands of late capitalism.[13] My study of the museum marketplace suggests that these institutions already enabled the creation of commodities during the nineteenth century, a time when museums were embedded in economic and industrial interests.

The following discussion of the international exchange of specimens additionally challenges established theories of collecting. According to historian Krzysztof Pomian, collectors typically strive to improve their social status by removing certain objects from use and reinscribing them with personal meaning.[14] Theorist Jean Baudrillard agrees, explaining that human relationships with objects are motivated by passion and that 'once the object stops being defined by its function, its meaning is entirely up to the subject.'[15] At the Natural History Society, however, many specimens were acquired to be given away, not possessed, for a useful purpose – to increase the exploitation of mineral deposits within the province. Amateur New Brunswick geologists were passionate about discovering and classifying geological formations, and they identified themselves with particularly impressive or rare finds. All the same, their ambitions were imbricated in a culture of geology that emphasized practical concerns as much as personal and scholarly ones.

A fascination with geological formations flourished throughout the nineteenth century, leading members of the Natural History Society to believe that their gifts would be met with interest and reciprocity. Though the popularity of geology declined in Britain after 1860, it remained strong in Victorian Canada, where, according to historian Suzanne Zeller, geologists promoted industry by searching for vendable mineral deposits.[16] In 1841, the Geological Survey of Canada began by looking for coal in the southern parts of Ontario and Quebec. Economically driven surveys of the Maritimes occurred even earlier, with Abraham Gesner and John William Dawson undertaking research during the 1820s and 1840s respectively. Ambitious New Brunswick amateurs were inspired by these men, and in the 1860s they took Dawson's advice by founding the Natural History Society of New Brunswick.[17] All of these geologists also participated in the acts of collecting and exchange. Contributors to the Geological Survey of Canada during the 1850s amassed an impressive number of specimens, using them to represent Canada's mineral wealth at London's Crystal Palace in 1851 and at later world's fairs.[18] Early members of the Natural History Society similarly participated in local exhibitions, and addressed an international audience by means of their mineral 'gift-sets.' They did so to insist, however, on the unique regional identity of New Brunswick, rather than to convey messages about national interests. By circulating objects around the world, New Brunswickers created a range of meanings while both participating in and reshaping the broader culture of geology.

The Exchange System

The act of exchanging material from the Maritimes for international objects was not pioneered by members of the Natural History Society. When Nova Scotia–born Abraham Gesner (1797–1864) opened his public Museum of Natural History in downtown Saint John in 1842, he placed advertisements in several newspapers, proclaiming that his regional specimens would be traded for 'those of Foreign Countries.'[19] Gesner hoped to benefit from the wealth of international items brought into the active port city by ships' captains, sailors, missionaries, and visitors. Printed in 1842, the catalogue of Gesner's collections lists much non-native material, including 'insects of the savannah' provided by Captain Davys, a New Zealand bow and arrow donated by Mr C.E. Ratchford, and ova of the common conch delivered from the West Indies by a certain Dr Yates.[20] Some 1,130 entries, however, describe those minerals collected in large part by Gesner himself during the 1830s when he worked as a physician in the fossil-rich region of Parrsboro, Nova Scotia, and after he was appointed provincial geologist of New Brunswick in 1838.[21] Once government funding for his geological work ended, Gesner established the Saint John museum as a money-making venture. He planned to capitalize on both entry fees and the sale of 'complete sets of minerals of Nova Scotia, of sixty specimens each, (arranged,) ... [and] price[d] £6 per set.'[22] Gesner's entrepreneurial scheme was ultimately unsuccessful, and in 1846 his collections were seized as payment by creditors. The specimens were then accepted – somewhat reluctantly it seems – by the directors of Saint John's Mechanics' Institute, and subsequently acquired by the Natural History Society in 1890.[23] Gesner's mineral and fossil specimens finally entered the New Brunswick Museum in 1929, and can be examined there today. Many of them were clearly meant to be sold or traded, as they have 'for exchange' written in his hand on their underside.[24]

Gesner understood the display, sale, and exchange of his objects in monetary terms. His approach was not uncommon, and a market for natural history specimens grew throughout the nineteenth century. In 1893, an advertisement sent by A.J. Pineo of Berwick, Nova Scotia, to the Natural History Society, for example, urged teachers to purchase mineral collections for $5.00 because of their 'large practical value' in educating school children.[25] Members of the Society were apparently not tempted by this offer, but they did market their own specimens and also drew from the eight thousand fossils collected at the Fern Ledges by Charles Frederick Hartt (1840–76), a founding member of the Natural History Society who in 1868 would become the first professor of geology at Cornell University. In 1867, the Society agreed to use 'less valuable duplicates of common specimens of Devonian plants' to assemble some thirty or fifty sets for sale.[26] The members were also interested in trading other objects, and the minutes of an early meeting record their decision to order a large display case with drawers to store 'minerals for exchange.'[27] Though no description of these duplicate materials has survived, a list of the forty-eight minerals and crystals sent to the Buffalo Society of Natural History in 1865 includes quartz and albertite.[28] The 'Devonian' fossils were also sent far and wide, including to such prestigious recipients as the Smithsonian Institution in 1868.[29] When the corresponding secretary of the Natural History Society, Samuel F. Kain – an employee at the Customs House in Saint John and an amateur meteorologist – broached the topic of exchange with other societies and museums, his letters sounded like advertisements. A missive dispatched in 1895 to the Public Museum in Milwaukee boasted that 'we also have some specimens of fossil plants of Devonian age from the celebrated Fern Ledges of Lancaster near this city. The fossils are very rare and would be of value and interest to the palaeontologists of your city.'[30]

The sheer number of exchanges engaged in by the Natural History Society of New Brunswick indicates that the practice was both commonplace and international in scope during the nineteenth century. The society sent letters of inquiry to fellow societies in Russia, New Zealand, Tasmania, Germany, France, and throughout North America. Recipients of items from New Brunswick included the United States National Museum of Natural History (created as part of the Smithsonian Institution in 1858), the Free Museum of Science and Art in Philadelphia, and organizations in Berlin, Bremen, and Toronto. Sometimes the corresponding secretary of the Natural History Society asked for specific items in return. The letter sent to Milwaukee explained, for example, that 'our collections in archaeology and ethnology are small and we are anxious to increase them.'[31] The Society nevertheless often received geological gifts in kind, including the fossil plants sent by a society in Richmond, Virginia.[32] Among the more exotic specimens received in exchange for New Brunswick fossils were the Japanese bird skins acquired from Alfred Morrissey in 1899. Yet the bird skins were subsequently forwarded to the Field Columbian Museum to broker a second exchange; in that case, jewellery from Paraguay was received by the Natural History Society.[33]

These exchanges might appear to have been entirely practical, as a way for societies with little funding or government support to increase their collections in lieu of purchasing acquisitions. This interpretation is partly correct, for the letters sent around the world by the Natural History Society specified objects desired because they would fill a gap in the collections. At the same time, international exchanges served another pragmatic goal, namely, that of increasing the amount of reference material needed by those scholars studying local natural history. George F. Matthew (1837–1923) was an amateur geologist and paleontologist who sought to acquire a wide array of trilobites and other fossils for comparative purposes as he classified newly discovered fossils in New Brunswick.[34] Despite being employed full-time as chief clerk of the Customs House in Saint John, Matthew was internationally recognized as an expert in Cambrian geology, publishing his research in journals around the world.[35] As a founding member of the Natural History Society, he used the influx of geological material primarily for scientific purposes. This kind of 'specimen swapping' between scientists continues to this day.

Nineteenth-century object exchanges between collectors and museums nevertheless had many layers of meaning, and are not fully explained with reference to practicality. The well-documented exchanges of material from the Natural History Society of New Brunswick to the Field Columbian Museum and back shed light on the intricacies of these transactions. Correspondence and accession records from both institutions indicate that in January of 1893, Kain sent a letter to Chicago offering fossils for exchange, and almost immediately received a response from the director of the Field Columbian Museum, F.J.V. Skiff, indicating that 'the Curator of the Department of Anthropology has pottery to the value at least of $25 which he would be willing to exchange through the Department of Geology for the Devonian plants offered by you for that purpose. If it meets with your approval, therefore, please send specimens on approval in value not to exceed $25, and in weight not to exceed fifty pounds, and the Curator of Geology will undertake to procure for you in exchange an ample equivalent.'[36] The Natural History Society then forwarded to Chicago 'a box of Devonian fossils (24 specs., 19 species),' and by May were in possession of twenty-three pieces of pottery sent from the Field Columbian Museum. The specimens, 'obtained in nearly all cases from mounds and graves,' receive only terse descriptions in the New Brunswick accession records: from Peru a 'black bottle with arched handle, spout and bird decoration'; from Nicaragua a 'red cup with white finish and red designs'; and from Costa Rica a 'tripod cup, with handles and decorations in relief.'[37]

This exchange was pointedly monetary in tone, using the sum of

$25 as a measure for determining both the quantity and quality of the goods traded. Yet when Skiff informed the corresponding secretary of the Natural History Society that a selection of Indian pottery had been forwarded, he characterized the event in terms of courtesy rather than material gain. Nonetheless, in the same letter Skiff told the New Brunswickers that the fossils his institution had received were not of equal value to the pottery that had been sent by it. According to him: 'As near as can be estimated, this collection more than compensates for the 24 specimens of Devonian Fossil Plants received from you, but the balance may remain in favor of this Museum, and if at some future time you happen upon other Geological specimens that you may think of value to the Museum, they will be appreciated, and absolve any indebtedness that may remain.'[38] These representations of the exchange are ambivalent, simultaneously characterizing it as an economic and a social activity. On one hand, the fossils were accepted as a form of gift, in which the objects returned were based more on the magnanimous recognition of a social relationship than anything monetary. On the other hand, Skiff noted that a debt was still owing from the Natural History Society, indicating that the polite exchange remained firmly within the realm of economic considerations.

The interaction between the Natural History Society of New Brunswick and the Field Columbian Museum combined forms of exchange often analysed separately by anthropologists. In his well-known study, Marcel Mauss argues that in 'archaic' societies gift giving is a complex ritual that helps to constitute social relationships rather than merely signify them. Participation in such exchanges is obligatory, and the initial recipient of a gift must offer a 'return gift' in keeping with kinship, legal, economic, religious, and other social structures.[39] In his analysis of Mauss's ideas, anthropologist Maurice Godelier argues that gift giving in modern capitalist societies tends to be simpler, consisting of commodities that change hands.[40] Christopher Gregory argues that commonplace commercial transactions bring partners together only temporarily: '... whereas before the exchange, each partner was dependent on others to satisfy his needs, afterwards each party is once more independent and free of obligations to others.'[41] The objects traded in capitalist societies are thus wholly alienated from those providing them. Mauss argues that in contrast to this system, archaic objects retain the *hau* or soul of the original gift-giver, which ultimately compels the objects to return to their original owners. Although Mauss's theory of the *hau* is contested, it nevertheless highlights a point that is more generally accepted: in traditional forms of gift exchange, objects retain a strong connection with their origins, and are not fully commodified.[42]

Like the gift exchanges occurring in non-Western societies, those initiated by the Natural History Society were meant to establish rather than confirm relationships. Very few of the selected recipients were personal friends or acquaintances of the members of the Society. Aside from the singular mention of the 'exchange catalogue' circulated by the Field Columbian Museum, there is no evidence to indicate exactly how New Brunswick administrators selected the destinations for their gifts. They may have consulted the 'International Scientific Directory' to discover the names, locations, and specializations of like-minded natural history enthusiasts. This source included information about members of the Natural History Society, and was referred to by other collectors in the letters they sent to New Brunswick requesting exchanges during the late 1890s.[43] In any case, numerous records indicate that when members of the Natural History Society sent duplicate fossil, mineral, and archaeological material to museums and natural history societies around the world, they often approached prestigious organizations, such as the Smithsonian Institution, hoping to form beneficial connections with them.

The gift exchanges cultivated by members of the Natural History Society involved expressions of obligation. Recipients of fossils from New Brunswick were sometimes hesitant to accept them when they had nothing suitable to offer in return. In 1896, Kain sent a 'Devonian fossil collection and some pottery fragments' to the son of Sir John William Dawson, George M. Dawson (1849–1901), then the director of the Geological Survey of Canada in Ottawa. Dawson acknowledged receiving 'a little box of archaeological specimens' from Kain but responded with some anxiety, writing: 'I fear that we are not in a position to exchange in kind for these specimens and I therefore hesitate to accept your sendings.'[44] Dawson understood that the initial gift was not free of social expectations, and considered declining it when he could not reciprocate appropriately. In another case, the gifts sent by the Natural History Society were not entirely satisfying to their recipient. In June of 1896, G. Brown Goode, assistant secretary of the United States National Museum of Natural History, thanked the Society for sending fossils, noting: 'I take pleasure in sending you a collection of (tinted) casts of prehistoric implements for the Museum of your Natural History Society. This collection is sent in exchange for the specimens received from your Society in May, and constituting accession No.30.651. I may add that, although these specimens are of interest to us, we are still desirous of obtaining as many implements as possible representing the various forms found in your region.'[45] While noting the reciprocal basis of his 'gifts,' Goode implied that he would prefer to receive archaeological specimens from New Brunswick in subsequent interactions.

This courteous communication alludes to the power dynamics involved in such gift exchanges. According to Godelier, 'The gift decreases the distance between protagonists because it is a form of sharing, and it increases the social distance between them because one is now indebted to the other.'[46] Mauss argues that each gift is part of a system of reciprocity involving the honour of both the giver and the recipient. If the value of the exchanged gifts was uneven, a competitive pursuit of honour could result. In 1893, Skiff drew attention to such an imbalance, suggesting that members of the Natural History Society had overrated their local fossils, which were in his opinion not worth the set amount of $25. This situation highlighted the social distance between the local New Brunswick Society – not recognized as a provincial institution until it became part of the New Brunswick Museum in 1929 – and the more prestigious museum in Chicago. The Natural History Society attempted to pay off its debt by sending a second box of specimens to the Field Columbian Museum in 1896. Skiff claimed not to recognize the gesture, writing: 'I am in receipt of a small package, containing fragments of pottery, pieces of flint, etc. bearing the label of your Society which I suppose was sent by you, but as I have no correspondence regarding the specimens I am unable to determine why they were sent.'[47] The matter was ultimately resolved, and by 1899 another round of exchanges took place between Saint John and Chicago, exemplifying the continuous gift cycle described by Mauss.

The exchanges negotiated between museums were meant to increase, if not exactly the 'honour' of the participants, then at least their status as legitimate purveyors of natural history. During the nineteenth century, the Natural History Society of New Brunswick dispatched letters and gifts in two concentrated efforts, during the 1860s and the 1890s. These decades correspond with efforts to establish the Society and raise its profile. The first fossil sets were constructed shortly after the Society was founded in 1862 and primarily sent to established organizations in the United States, including the Natural History Society of Buffalo in 1865. The second push to initiate exchanges occurred in the 1890s, when members were trying to revive the group after a relative dearth of activity. The minutes of the meetings of the Natural History Society indicate that it was quite active into the early 1870s, with members planning to extend the opening hours of the museum and embark on regular field meetings as late as April of 1874.[48] Yet the next entry in the minute book dates from 1880, and it calls for the 'revival of the Society,' with efforts to contact old members and to attract new ones.[49] The surviving records provide little information about the initial reasons for the decreased level of activity, but it must have been exacerbated by the great fire of 1877, which devastated the city of Saint John, reducing much of it – though not the Museum of the Natural History Society, then housed in the Mechanics' Institute – to ashes.[50] Efforts to rebuild the city and its culture occurred throughout the 1880s, and included the establishment or re-establishment of a range of social clubs.[51] During the 1880s the continuing members of the Natural History Society focused on local events, holding regular meetings, public lectures, and fundraising events.[52] By the 1890s, however, they again emphasized international exchanges, mailing specimens throughout Canada, the United States, Europe, and beyond. No doubt encouraged by the influx of Gesner's material once the contents of the Mechanics' Institute Museum were acquired by the Natural History Society in 1890, these exchanges were designed to produce an institutional presence and identity for the Society. The next flurry of exchange activity took place after the founding of the New Brunswick Museum, when wealthy philanthropist Alice Lusk Webster orchestrated gift exchanges of art objects rather than natural history specimens to enhance the institution's international reputation, as discussed in chapter 3 of this book.

The trades were arranged not only to put the Natural History Society on the map, so to speak, but also to place samples of New Brunswick geology in important collections all over the world. Once accessioned, the specimens were officially deemed worthy by an external arbiter and preserved on a more or less permanent basis. The fossil plants sent to the Field Columbian Museum in 1896, for example, are currently stored in its Botany Department.[53] Like the archaic objects analysed by Mauss, these exchange items have never been entirely severed from their origins in New Brunswick. Both the accession records and museum labels at the Field indicate where the fossils came from. In his study of early nineteenth-century English geology, Knell argues that when individuals donated geological specimens to established collections, they received a 'linguistic payment' in the form of flattering written descriptions of the objects, and the labels that noted their donors.[54] The New Brunswick fossils also acted, however, as metonymic representations of the geology and geography of New Brunswick.

Nineteenth-century gift exchanges between museums conformed to

Mauss's characterization of archaic gift giving in multiple ways: they created social relationships, required reciprocation, participated in the negotiation of power, were meant to increase the status of donors, and involved objects never wholly separated from their origins. All the same, in other ways the exchanges were like straightforward commercial transactions. In keeping with the first trade negotiated between the Natural History Society and Field Columbian Museum in 1896, the second one was discussed in precise monetary terms. In 1899, Kain sent a gift of nineteen Japanese bird skins to the Museum in Chicago, requesting Indian pipes in return.[55] After learning that no pipes were available, he asked for a range of Mexican and European paleolithic implements, listed as duplicates in the 'exchange catalogue' circulated by the Field Columbian Museum.[56] In order to determine what should be sent to New Brunswick in exchange, the director of the Field wrote to Charles B. Cory (1857–1921), a founding member of the American Ornithologists' Union and collector of bird specimens living in Boston, entreating him to evaluate the skins. Skiff noted that 'this seems to me to be the only way to discriminate as to how much of the material [Kain] has selected should be sent. I might add that his list is quite formidable.'[57] The director implied that Kain had suggested material worth more than the proffered bird skins. Kain was aware of this possibility, for he had concluded his letter by saying: 'In case these articles exceed in value the 19 Japanese Bird Skins we will endeavour to equalize matters on a future occasion.'[58] Once the skins were evaluated at $35, Skiff asked his curator of anthropology to supply Kain with items of equivalent value.[59] In the end, the Natural History Society accepted from Chicago a return gift of thirty-two Paraguayan objects, including an 'ear ornament of feathers, Chamaccoco Brabo,' an 'ear ornament of snake rattles and feathers, Tupi,' and a 'necklace of colored beads and monkey bones, Guato.'[60]

This complex exchange, involving multiple international communications, internal memos, and the services of an ornithology expert, took ten months to conclude. Though it both created and reinforced a web of connections between museums and natural history enthusiasts, the trade was prominently framed as a commercial enterprise. The Japanese bird skins were valued in terms of an abstract monetary amount, and the anthropological items were selected to match that amount, rather than simply reciprocating for the skins themselves. In that sense, the objects traded were like commodities that were bought and sold in a rather impersonal manner. In its narrowest definition, a commodity is something useful that can be turned to commercial or other advantage; it is an article of commerce that is processed and resold according to the laws of supply and demand.[61] Though emphasizing equivalence rather than profit, both parties exchanged natural history objects for their personal benefit, engaging in a calculated, self-centred market transaction rather than a strict gift exchange. The nineteenth-century museum marketplace provides further evidence for the arguments of sociologist Pierre Bourdieu, who argues that gift exchange 'never ceases to conform to economic calculation even when it gives every appearance of distinterestedness by departing from the logic of interested calculation (in the narrow sense) and playing for stakes that are non-material and not easily quantified.'[62] Of course, the exchange between the Natural History Society and the Field Columbian Museum indicates that economic calculation could be prominent in the museum marketplace even when polite disinterestedness remained part of the negotiations.

Yet the 'gift-sets' circulated by the Natural History Society were not initially considered valuable, even by the Society itself. When first constructing the sets in 1867, members decided to use 'less valuable duplicates of common specimens of Devonian plants,' indicating that the samples were neither treasured nor rare, despite claims made to the contrary in letters sent to potential gift recipients.[63] The fossil plants that constituted the greatest number of gifts given by the Natural History Society were not inherently useful, and there was no real demand for them before they were put into circulation through gift exchange. International collectors and museums only began requesting geological samples from the Natural History Society years after the fossil plants had been sent out as gifts.[64] Nor were the specimens received in exchange for the fossils described as unique or exceptional. Several of them were, after all, listed as duplicate material in the exchange catalogue of the Field Columbian Museum. Until placed in the marketplace, this material was relatively useless and usually stored out of sight. The museum marketplace was fuelled by surplus items that selected institutions did not need, and perhaps did not even want.

It is therefore difficult to consider the fossil gift-sets as commodities, according to the narrow definition offered above. They were not useful, initially desired by others, or subject to the laws of supply and demand. It seems clear that the fossil 'gift-sets' had to be acquired by others before they could be considered valuable. Perhaps more importantly, the fossils and minerals sent by the Natural History Society had to be acknowledged with a return gift that also served to measure their value, in material and monetary terms. Yet even the materials received in exchange cannot strictly be considered commodities, for their precise nature remained relatively unimportant. Although members of the Natural History Society made specific requests for objects, such as 'Indian stone pipes,' they would gratefully accept just about anything proffered by the targeted museum, as long as it was in some way different from the things they already had. The accession records provide only cursory descriptions of these items, and the minutes of the Society's meetings barely mention them. The Japanese bird skins gained by the Natural History Society through a fossil exchange were later sent out to broker another trade, indicating that acquiring the skins was not the purpose of the initial enterprise. Indeed, one begins to suspect that exchange itself was the primary goal of such trades, rather than the collection or display of specific items.

According to anthropologist Arjun Appadurai, '... exchange is not a by-product of the mutual evaluation of objects, but its source.'[65] Inspired by the writings of both George Simmel and Friedrich Engels, Appadurai's approach shifts attention away from the commodity as a product – evident in the more narrow definition above – and toward the process of commodity exchange, or what he calls the 'commodity situation' of particular objects. Appadurai argues that 'the commodity situation in the social life of any "thing" [can] be defined as the situation in which its exchangeability (past, present, or future) for some other things is its socially relevant feature.'[66] Thinking in these terms reveals the nineteenth-century museum marketplace as providing a context in which practically any object could temporarily become a commodity. Once inside the museum, an object was apparently removed from this commodity trade, though it could be re-exchanged and thus re-enter a commodity situation. Anthropologist James Clifford has already discussed the political implications of the ways in which collected objects shift between cultural categories, from inauthentic artifacts to authentic masterpieces, depending on historical and institutional factors.[67] This discussion shows, however, that objects could also move in and out of a commodity situation, and that this situation was created by means of negotiation rather than by individual collectors imposing personal meanings on the objects.

Within the museum marketplace, the New Brunswick fossils and minerals were simultaneously equated with and differentiated from objects such as Peruvian pots and Paraguayan ear ornaments. The items traded between museums were substituted for one another, and considered comparable, but were ultimately valued for their difference from one another. This setting is similar to what linguist Ferdinand de Saussure has called the paradigmatic relationship between words within the codified language system. According to theorist Jonathan Culler, 'Paradigmatic relations are the oppositions between elements which can replace one another.'[68] In this arbitrary system, signs are chosen from a range of other signs, and take on meaning in relation to each other according to a set of socially constructed conventions. When New Brunswick fossils and minerals entered the museum marketplace, they did so primarily in relation to non-Western objects, whose meanings – at least to the members of the Natural History Society – were generalized in terms of exoticism, foreignness, and diverseness. The fossils did not possess intrinsic value, and their significance arguably remained unstable within the museum marketplace. Efforts to fix a price of $25 initially failed because the specimens were evaluated differently by the Society and the Field Columbian Museum. The set of fossils sent to Chicago had to be supplemented with archaeological pottery and flints from New Brunswick. During the second exchange, fossils were traded for bird skins later valued at $35 and equated with a shifting group of objects: Indian pipes, paleolithic instruments, Paraguayan ornaments. Many of these 'exotic' objects were already recognized as desirable because they had been displayed at the World's Fair of 1893, but clearly their values remained negotiable and dependent on what else was circulating at the time.

Given the unstable nature of the museum marketplace, it is difficult to adhere to a structuralist approach by reconstructing the system of connotations on which the meanings of these objects were based. This particular case study indicates that the significance of the New Brunswick objects was not predetermined, and could vary according to their evaluator. Certain rules are nevertheless clear. Recognition of another, more established institution or collector was required in order for value to be awarded to the fossils. The Columbian Field Museum was the more powerful institution, and it decided the worth of the New Brunswick objects by referring to specialists in paleontology and ornithology to assess them, and using its own surplus material as the benchmark of value. Demanding more or other items was the initiative of staff at the museum in Chicago, and there is no evidence that members of the Natural History Society ever complained, requested more materials, or assigned monetary amounts to objects during any of the exchanges in which they participated. This situation changed once the

New Brunswick Museum became an established provincial institution, and Alice Lusk Webster assertively negotiated trades with international institutions.

Though the meanings of objects were relational within the museum marketplace, they became more fixed when exhibited within museums. The significance of the objects was still in large degree based on paradigmatic relationships, for it continued to be identified in terms of the differences between the objects. At the same time, once exhibited, the objects acquired meaning within a sequence of display, in keeping with what Saussure would characterize as a syntagmatic relationship. Like museums such as the Louvre – deemed a 'universal survey museum' – the Natural History Society strove to represent different countries and disciplines, noting, for example, the dearth of archaeological and ethnological objects.[69] Unlike a large survey museum, however, sustained coverage of non-local material was never a goal at the much smaller Museum of the Natural History Society, and 'foreign' objects were presented in terms of wonder, in keeping with an early modern cabinet of curiosities.[70] Even in 1908, when curator William MacIntosh embarked on a reorganization of the collections after the Society moved into a more spacious building, cases of what he called 'foreign material' were placed in the hallway outside of the archaeological rooms exclusively devoted to New Brunswick relics.[71] For the most part, only local specimens, including mammals, minerals, and shells, were carefully classified. The 'other' objects were grouped together and displayed outside of the central narrative, offering a visually stimulating contrast to the exhibitions in the official galleries. Instead of providing the standard against which local materials were measured and became desirable, the international objects acquired through trade and by donation became a foil or framework for them. In that sense, they acted like what philosopher Immanuel Kant has called the *parergon*, those adjuncts, like the frames around paintings or drapery on statues, that separate what properly belongs to a work of art from what remains outside of it. In his critique of Kant, philosopher Jacques Derrida argues that these margins function as more than ornamental additions because they crucially differentiate between the intrinsic and extrinsic aspects of a work.[72] Within the Museum of the Natural History Society, local specimens became visible and took on meaning in contrast to the marginalized 'foreign' material. Within the museum marketplace, however, those same foreign objects had overtly determined the value of what were at that point 'marginal' local specimens.

Advancing Local Geology

The Natural History Society exchanged more than the mineral, fossil, and archaeological items collected within New Brunswick. It also traded copies of its journal, the *Bulletin of the Natural History Society of New Brunswick*, published on a nearly annual basis between 1882 and 1914. In this case, however, there was no negotiation. The *Bulletin* was simply traded in kind for the publications of other natural history societies. Records show that the Society typically printed 500 copies of its *Bulletin* to disseminate, and that during the 1890s its 'exchange list' included societies in Chile, France, Belgium, Britain, Norway, Brazil, Australia, the United States, and Canada.[73] The first volume of 1882 urged other 'Societies and Public Bodies' receiving the *Bulletin* to send their own publications in return.[74] This expectation was apparently met, for the Society's annual report of 1886 affirmed: 'The past year has been one in which much valuable work has been done. Our publications are sought for by kindred societies – not only in Canada and the United States, but also in Europe – and thus our Province, with its natural resources, has been brought under the notice of many who otherwise would have remained in ignorance of its advantages.'[75] According to this statement, the ultimate goal of the *Bulletin of the Natural History Society of New Brunswick* was in keeping with the original mandate of the Society to promote the natural resources of New Brunswick.

The contents of the *Bulletin* nevertheless addressed a range of topics instead of emphasizing geological and mineral resources, areas highlighted by the Society's founders in 1862. The publication included, for instance, brief descriptions of the field-day outings held by members of the Society, their monthly meetings, and the annual reports of the various committees. The bulk of the *Bulletin* was made up of original articles on local mammals, botany, insect pests, and weather patterns written by the amateur and professional researchers belonging to the Society. These reports often took the form of lists identifying the various plant and animal species found in New Brunswick, particularly newly discovered species. The *Bulletin* of 1885 proudly noted that 'the knowledge of our birds, plants, minerals, fish, etc., has been greatly increased and made readily available by means of Catalogues and the Bulletin published by the Society.'[76] Dr W.F. Ganong, professor of botany at Smith College in Massachusetts and a native of Charlotte County, New Brunswick, was a regular contributor to the *Bulletin*, and in 1889 he published an extensive and well-illustrated account of the economic mollusca in

Acadia.[77] Geological material was certainly included in the publication – particularly in the form of original articles written by George F. Matthew – but it by no means dominated the *Bulletin*'s representation of the Society and its work.

Why, then, did the Natural History Society almost always select local fossils and minerals to give as gifts throughout the nineteenth century, when other specimens could have been offered? The most obvious answer is that the Society had many surplus geological specimens, and that it was convenient to send them around the world because such samples were small, portable, and durable. While this explanation is sensible, members of the Natural History Society could easily have sent other items as gifts, including the numerous duplicate plant or insect specimens in their collections. The Society was clearly interested in the scientific knowledge and uses of plants, noting the desire to publish a list of the economic plants of New Brunswick in the *Bulletin* of 1887.[78] Yet geological samples were preferred as gifts for multiple reasons that can shed additional light on the exchange system described above. The fossil and mineral specimens sent from New Brunswick became valuable to those outside of the province after being positioned within the museum marketplace, but they were initially selected for exchange because of their ability to convey desirable images of both the Natural History Society and the province of New Brunswick.

When members of the Society highlighted geological samples, they reinforced existing government policies aimed at industrializing New Brunswick and exploiting its mineral resources. Signalling their support for these policies, the members courted recognition from both the provincial and local governments –bodies they continually lobbied for increased funding.[79] Several members of the Society worked directly for the government by participating in the Geological Survey of Canada, an organization that obtained permanent status in 1877 and became a separate department, reporting to the minister of the interior, in 1890.[80] Like the early nineteenth-century geological studies done in Britain, the reports written by New Brunswick surveyors focused on the economic potential of the land, and promoted its ability to contribute to the industrial economy.[81] Loring Woart Bailey, a graduate of Harvard and Brown Universities who became a professor of natural science and geology at the University of New Brunswick in 1860, was an honorary member of the Natural History Society and regularly presented special lectures in Saint John. After working for the Survey during the summer of 1863, he published a 'Report on the Mines and Minerals of New Brunswick,' noting that 'the main object of this exploration should be the collecting of such facts and materials as would best advance the knowledge and development of the mineral resources of New Brunswick.'[82] According to him, even the mere description of geological formations could contribute to this goal because 'every observation which tends to increase our knowledge of the position and relations of the rocks which bear them, tends also to their direct development.'[83] Sending out geological samples was in keeping with these bluntly stated industrial goals.

The international promotion of mineral specimens was a long-standing strategy used by the federal government. According to historian Morris Zaslow, the Geological Survey of Canada publicized 'Canada's natural resources at home and abroad,' in part by creating displays for numerous world's fairs.[84] When Sir William E. Logan (1798–1875) headed the Survey, he organized a mineral display for the 1851 World's Fair in London, categorizing Canada's minerals according to their economic uses as 'metals requiring peculiar chemical treatment, mineral or stone paints, minerals applicable to the fine arts, materials applicable to jewelry, minerals applicable to glass making, building materials and miscellaneous materials.'[85] The next director of the Survey, Alfred Selwyn (1824–1902), produced Canadian mineral displays for the exhibitions in Philadelphia in 1876, Paris in 1878, London in 1886, and Chicago in 1893.[86] Such mineral displays were featured at the World's Columbian Exhibition in Chicago, placing them within the same context as the 'Indian pottery' later exchanged for New Brunswick fossils. Members of the Natural History Society were clearly aware of this method of display, for they participated in the provincial exhibitions that had many of the same economic and patriotic goals as international exhibitions, despite being aimed at a smaller, more local audience. In 1880, George F. Matthew removed the geological collections from the Museum of the Natural History Society and arranged them at the Provincial Exhibition held in Saint John that year. The display was awarded a prize of twenty dollars for being the 'best collection of the useful minerals of New Brunswick.'[87] In 1898, an even larger mineral display organized by the Society was positioned directly beside the exhibit of the provincial government, and said to 'constitute an important feature of the Fair.'[88] When members of the Society sent similar specimens around the world, they both engaged in an established mode of promoting the utility of geology and extended their localized efforts to an international audience.

Yet the geological 'gift-sets' sent out by the Natural History Society could also convey more subtle messages about New Brunswick and its inhabitants, particularly when they featured fossils instead of minerals. Historian Martin Rudwick argues that fossils had to be collected *in situ* by locals, unlike the specimens examined by zoologists and botanists. According to him, 'While the study of animals and plants was certainly dependent on locality, the study of fossils was and is even more so. Most animal and plant species can be found in appropriate habitats over fairly wide areas, but even the commonest fossils generally have to be collected from extremely limited localities ... which may not be known or accessible to any but those living close by.'[89]

Arguably more than other forms of natural history, geological research was informed by those who lived in the region under investigation. During the nineteenth century, geological knowledge was founded on extensive and thorough periods of fieldwork, and those who had an intimate knowledge of the landscape could comment authoritatively on local fossils, compensating for inadequate manpower by directing professionals to their locations. Various directors of the Geological Survey of Canada recognized this aspect of geological research, and Logan in particular liked to hire resident amateurs who 'were well versed in local situations' as surveyors.[90] Though himself a trained scientist, Bailey urged the government to employ 'woodsmen,' or 'men living in the vicinity and acquainted with every hill and every brook,' to perform a more thorough geological survey of New Brunswick.[91] When members of the Natural History Society selected mineral and fossil samples for exchange, they thus promoted both local expertise and knowledge, important issues to a group composed mainly of amateur natural history enthusiasts.

The knowledge of amateurs, or what Rudwick calls 'savants,' was not always respected. In his analysis of the 'Great Devonian Controversy' – a nineteenth-century debate about the stratigraphical composition of certain parts of Wales – Rudwick contends that amateurs 'might have impressively accurate local knowledge, particularly of good localities for fossils, but the elite and accomplished geologists [of the Geological Society of London] would only rely on that knowledge at a strictly "factual" level.'[92] In some ways, the fossil samples sent by the Natural History Society reinforced the hierarchical system wherein local amateurs would collect fossils for other, more professional, scientists to interpret. Yet several of the most prominent geological researchers in New Brunswick took more than a fashionable interest in natural history.[93] Charles Frederick Hartt, the man who collected many of the 'Devonian' fossils sent around the world by the Natural History Society, was an esteemed professor of geology who gained international recognition for his extensive surveys in Brazil before his untimely death in 1876.[94] George F. Matthew was, however, even more closely associated with the geological work of the Society. Matthew laboured extensively with the Geological Survey, publishing a 'Report on the Superficial Geology of New Brunswick' in 1878, among many others.[95] His Survey work was motivated by his primary interest, namely, the study of Cambrian fossils. Though officially an amateur who never pursued geology full-time, Matthew made substantial and internationally acclaimed contributions to paleontology, which included describing and photographing the first authentic Precambrian fossil as well as discovering more than three hundred new species of fossils. He was especially prolific in the study of Cambrian trilobites and, because of this important work, became president of the Geological and Biological Science Department of the Royal Society, and was awarded the prestigious Murchinson Medal by the Royal Geographical Society of London.[96] It is often assumed that Matthew's position in the Customs House interfered with his geological research, and yet the two occupations sometimes reinforced each other. In 1884, Matthew received a letter from the Smithsonian Institution requesting his assistance with the international dispersal of natural history specimens through the Customs House in Saint John.[97] No doubt Matthew's reputation as a collector, scientist, and expert in the art of exchange influenced the Society's decision to have geological specimens sent as gifts to more prestigious institutions. The fossils were associated with him and other well respected members of the Society who were, like the specimens, native to the province.

During the nineteenth century, the pursuit of geology was more generally linked with a certain kind of person, namely, the middle-class gentleman. Historian Roy Porter describes the 'gentlemanly amateur geologists' of nineteenth-century Britain who considered themselves too affluent, liberal, and open-minded to apply for professorships.[98] As Knell points out, however, geology was a relatively accessible practice because it did not require expensive equipment. It was pursued by a wide array of people, including those working-class men and women who collected specimens for sale.[99] According to Knell, working-class collectors who sold specimens to museums were not respected, with acquisition records failing to record their names in contrast to the written recognition awarded to those who donated objects.[100] Prestige was given only to those 'generous' collectors who supposedly pursued geology in order to increase knowledge of the natural world. This context sheds more light on why members of the Natural History Society engaged in gift exchanges of 'civilized' geological specimens, avoiding the pursuit of 'filthy lucre' even as they increased the standing of the Society and its collections. Though members had initially spoken about selling some of their duplicate fossils, there is no evidence that they ever did so. Fossil specimens were particularly able to bridge the social distinctions made between utilitarian and 'pure' science. They were considered 'hard facts' that provided geologists with evidence for the comparative dating of rocks and strata, but were also linked with the less practical and thus more gentlemanly pursuit of knowledge of the earth's history.[101]

Most members of the Natural History Society were not from the elite classes, but they were concerned to create a middle-class image in both their self-representations and public events. The Society hosted, for example, Sir John William Dawson at a carefully planned reception in Saint John in 1888.[102] The minutes of the Society's meetings portray the group in an entirely positive light: listening attentively to invited speakers, engaging in animated but always genteel discussions, and enjoying the refreshments dutifully provided by the Ladies' Auxiliary.[103] Although female geologists were active in Europe, in New Brunswick the Geological Committee was exclusively composed of male members. Members of the Ladies' Auxiliary participated in other committees, including the botanical and entomological groups, a gendered aspect of the Natural History Society discussed more fully in chapter 3.[104] Imbued with connotations of gender and class, the geological 'gift-sets' sent around the world by the Natural History Society potentially portrayed the group as both masculine and civilized.

In addition to creating a desirable image for the Natural History Society, the geological material encouraged a particular understanding of the province. It is already clear that such specimens were meant to represent New Brunswick as a land rich in mineral resources and ripe for increasing industrialization. In terms of their materiality, the fossils carried, however, other meanings. As hard facts, fossils had positive connotations and conveyed a sense of solidity and 'place' in a way that samples of insect pests (or even common minerals) could not have. Fossils were also valued as intriguing aesthetic objects. Rudwick argues that fossils were judged according to their rarity, state of preservation, and location, being considered more valuable if they originated in a remote part of the world.[105] In his letters, the corresponding secretary of the Natural History Society had described the New Brunswick fossils as rare, an exaggeration also made by early nineteenth-century English geologists hoping to trade their own fossils with the French.[106] It is now difficult to consider New Brunswick a remote or exotic locale, but during the nineteenth century it could have been perceived that way by many living elsewhere, including the American tourists and sportsmen who increasingly flocked to the area.[107]

Even as geology was conflated with industrialization during the nineteenth century, the practice retained some of its earlier, more romantic associations. Literary critic Noah Heringman argues that 'the experience of nature as landscape and the resulting, all pervasive images – of magnitude, formlessness, inscrutable antiquity – are mainly responsible for the growing interest in geology in the later eighteenth century ... and for its formation as a full-fledged discipline by the early Victorian period.'[108] Once researchers agreed that the geological strata of England and the Continent had been reliably mapped, the practice lost its aura of adventure. Yet North American accounts of geological fieldwork remained filled with images of intrepid men who took their bearings by compass, battled the natural elements, and hunted for their own food.[109] The notion that geology was pursued by leaving urban life and engaging with nature continued to inform late nineteenth-century discussions of New Brunswick geology. In their Survey reports, both Bailey and Matthew drew attention to the rugged landscape of the province, noting their struggles to travel through it on foot and by canoe.[110] Although apparently at odds with the desired representation of New Brunswick as a cradle of civilization populated by gentlemen, these reports typically asserted that the province could support prosperous towns and villages.[111] Instead of a romantically unruly landscape, Survey reports depicted New Brunswick as eminently controllable and 'colonizable' by inevitable industrialization and development. The sheer vastness and materiality of the landscape nevertheless remained, linking the later reports with eighteenth-century accounts of the sublime expansiveness of nature. Despite their diminutive size, the fossil samples sent as gifts by the Natural History Society conveyed irrefutably solid evidence of the province's rich, unique, and even exotic heritage, something that more common insect and plant specimens could not accomplish.

In many ways, both fossil and mineral samples were ideally suited for the 'civilized' gift exchanges initiated by members of the Natural History Society of New Brunswick. The specimens had many possible meanings, representing economic development, local expertise, scholarly pursuit, class, gender, history, and a solid sense of place. Given the long-standing display of mineral specimens at international exhibitions, such material was relatively familiar, and easily acceptable to societies with established collections. With their multiple layers of significance, the gifts sent by the Natural History Society could suit almost any group of recipients. Yet even as members of the Society had important reasons for selecting geological materials for exchange, it remains unclear exactly how the gifts were perceived by those who accepted them, and then sent something else in return. Recipients may simply have accessioned the mineral or fossil samples as interesting curios, or used them to fill gaps in the collections; they might also have placed them back into the museum marketplace, trading them with another institution for something altogether different.

Conclusions

Exchanges between museums were neither straightforward gifts without social expectations, nor capitalist endeavours aimed to produce profit. Though objects were acquired by means of these negotiations, expanding the collections was not their ultimate aim. This case study has indicated that to a large degree exchange itself was the goal, especially for fledgling organizations such as the Natural History Society of New Brunswick. Sending out mineral gift-sets positioned the Natural History Society in relation to a host of other societies, establishing its identity and legitimacy. The conventions of gift giving conveniently associated the Society with middle-class values and the generous effort to share knowledge, rather than pecuniary interests. The materiality of the specimens was nevertheless important, and geological samples were able to convey desirable messages about the Society and its home province. At the bluntest level, members of the Natural History Society sought to increase the value of their specimens by placing them within the museum marketplace. Once the Society's mineral and fossil samples entered prestigious collections around the world, they were officially recognized as authentic items worthy of display and preservation. It was first necessary for those specimens to be placed in relation to a range of other objects, and to be considered interchangeable with them.

This chapter has offered, however, more than a fuller understanding of the exchanges made between museums and other institutions. It has revealed information about the modern museum concept. Those who study museums have often approached them as sites of collecting and display. Yet the administrators of these institutions also expended a great deal of effort on giving things away. Emphasizing this aspect of museums makes them appear more as interim storage houses than as monuments dedicated to preserving valuable objects. It also directs attention away from those who collected and curated the objects, for these figures did not determine the meanings of the items destined for exchange. They placed them within an existing web of objects, in the hope that other organizations would recognize them as worthy. Studying exchanges between museums brings out the relational character of their collections, while revealing that the identities of these institutions were also relationally determined. Though only one case study was examined in this chapter, attending to the commonplace strategies of exchange between an array of museums would continue to expand the definition of the modern museum, a process that would also indicate how institutional identity was substantially formed outside of official exhibition spaces.

Considering the importance of the exchanges between museums can also illuminate current debates within critical museum theory. It has now become a truism that contemporary museums are newly commodified, and that this commodification has had a negative impact on almost every facet of the institutions: undermining the expert knowledge of their staff; increasing superficial exhibitions designed merely to entertain rather than challenge visitors; and allowing corporate interests to trump educational goals.[112] This chapter has shown, however, that economic and industrial ambitions were the backbone of such early museums as the Museum of the Natural History Society of New Brunswick. Critics of contemporary museums might claim that the corporate agenda has now more fully entered these institutions, controlling their content. As indicated in the next two chapters, business interests were present even in nineteenth-century museums, albeit arguably to a lesser degree than today. It is therefore important to consider the varying degrees and kinds of commodification in the history of museums, rather than assuming, as some critics currently do, that a 'pristine' museum past was subsequently ruined by commercial interests.

Yet I contend that the extent of commodification is not the primary issue in this debate. Instead, it is the place of commodification. In the past, economic exchanges occurred primarily within the museum marketplace located 'between' museums (and, of course, when administrators purchased items outright from sellers, a realm not discussed here).

Following Appadurai, I have argued that the museum marketplace created a commodity situation in which objects were understood in terms of their exchangeability for other things. Nineteenth-century participants nevertheless carefully avoided discussing this situation exclusively in terms of material gain, and framed it as a courteous realm of gift giving. This representation of the exchanges was accurate insofar as the 'gifts' functioned like the 'archaic' gifts described by Mauss, forging connections between the different societies, participating in power relations, and promoting particular donors. Various forms of this kind of gift giving and donor activity continue to build the collections of contemporary museums and seldom receive negative commentary.

In contrast, the commodification of objects within exhibition spaces provokes cries of outrage. A prime example of this occurred when advertising mogul Charles Saatchi increased the value of his contemporary artworks by having them displayed at the Brooklyn Museum of Art in 1997.[113] This economic activity took place inside of the museum 'proper' and was clearly visible rather than veiled in a cloak of civility. Saatchi acted more like a working-class fossil collector pursing pecuniary goals than a wealthy donor displaying his generosity. Connotations of class informed the responses to the exhibition in Brooklyn, as critics perhaps unconsciously strove to protect the elevated image of the museum as a realm outside of such 'crass' ambition. Yet unlike the nineteenth-century fossil traders, who seldom received respect from museums, Saatchi was a wealthy man, albeit one equipped with far more economic than cultural capital. I suggest that the negative response to Saatchi's exhibition from some art experts and museum professionals was primarily encouraged by his failure to recognize the traditional middle-class decorum of the museum, rather than by ethical concerns. In the end, I think this case shows how thinking about the different historical modes of commodification that have been supported by museums can lead to a fuller understanding of the current operations of these institutions. Instead of imagining that early museums were not involved in economic manoeuvring, critics can be more reflective about the particular kinds of economic pursuit taking place within museums in both the past and present.

Chapter Two

Learning to See: Vision, Visuality, and Material Culture, 1862–1929

Visual perception might seem to be a strictly natural process, and yet it has a history. Scholars from a range of disciplines now study visuality, moving beyond biological understandings of vision to examine historically and culturally specific ways of seeing the world. Art historian Hal Foster encourages the investigation of 'how we see, how we are able, allowed or made to see, and how we see this seeing or the unseen therein.'[1] Diverse research has revealed complex scopic regimes or ways of seeing in ancient, medieval, and early modern times, but many recent publications feature modern visuality. Art historian Jonathan Crary, for example, argues that during the nineteenth century vision was radically reconceived. Previously, seeing had been explained in terms of the camera obscura, a detached mechanism excluding the corporeal subjectivity of the viewer. In the 1820s, however, sight began to be located within an unstable human body, making vision seem both less reliable and more amenable to correction.[2] Crary's narrative has received various critiques, particularly for its simplification of early modern ways of seeing. His account has also been productive, inspiring scholars to refine it by analysing both localized visual practices and forms of resistance to dominant modes of looking.[3]

Examinations of visuality regularly interrogate the imbrication of looking and power. In a well-known study, cultural critic Tony Bennett considers how modern museums have acted as vehicles 'for inscribing and broadcasting the messages of power … throughout society.'[4] Like Crary, Bennett emphasizes changes occurring during the nineteenth century, when museums helped to produce an 'exhibitionary complex' by placing both objects and spectators on display. Bennett pays, however, greater attention than Crary to the effects visual practices had on viewers. Drawing on the work of historian and philosopher Michel Foucault, he claims that early museums were designed as disciplinary mechanisms capable of altering the habits, morals, and beliefs of the public. Nineteenth-century British reformers hoped that by undertaking spectacular educational activities in museums, the working classes would spend less time in ale houses.[5] Bennett's study usefully highlights the politics of looking, encouraging more careful analyses of the ways in which institutions have promoted particular modes of seeing. Some critics nevertheless find that he underestimates the potential for museums to act as 'arenas for complex negotiations of social constructions' rather than strictly as instruments of social control.[6]

This chapter continues both to expand on and challenge the arguments of Crary and Bennett by studying visuality in late nineteenth- and early twentieth-century New Brunswick. In order to avoid overarching narratives, it focuses on one institution in particular, the Natural History Society of New Brunswick, founded in Saint John in 1862. Its members, described in both the Introduction and chapter 1, strove to shape the observational abilities of New Brunswickers of all ages. The Natural History Society promoted a public museum exhibiting insect and plant specimens, programs of object-based learning in schools, and even a train filled with displays that travelled throughout the province. A range of visual experiences was meant to give residents a newfound appreciation of their region, equipping them simultaneously with a love of nature and an eye for economic opportunity. According to pedagogues at the Natural History Society, learning to see properly could have a positive moral effect on society, and produce what might be called geographical citizenship, an identification both of and with the visual aspects of the landscape. Though primarily drawing on European models of seeing, members of the Natural History Society adapted them to local circumstances, emphasizing the flora and fauna of New Brunswick. They held that once trained in the visual discrimination of their immediate surroundings, New Brunswickers would reveal the abundant, unique, and valuable natural history of the area to the rest of the world.

In addition to considering regional practices of looking, this chapter offers a broader picture of the social role of early museums in Canada. During the 1920s, members of the Natural History Society instigated the foundation of the New Brunswick Museum, donating to it a wide range of ethnographic, historical, and natural objects, especially geological specimens, stuffed birds and mammals, mounted insects and plants. Though virtually defunct by the 1930s, the Natural History Society continues to have a strong presence in the New Brunswick Museum, shaping its identity.[7] All the same, like other early Canadian institutions, the museum of the Society has received little scholarly attention. A few accounts of the New Brunswick Museum and its precursors revolve around individual patrons and the objects they collected.[8] Nonetheless, members of the Natural History Society did far more than amass an important natural history collection. They contributed to the curriculum in New Brunswick schools, organized camping trips meant to teach youth to observe nature, and engaged in campaigns instructing children and farmers to identify insect pests. Reaching beyond the walls of their official buildings, members of the Natural History Society wanted to shape the everyday lives and sensations of New Brunswickers. Studying this institution reveals how it both interacted with and reconfigured historical beliefs about learning, nature, and the economy.

A more expansive knowledge of early museums sheds light on the characteristics of contemporary institutions, contributing to debates about their legitimate function. As indicated below, members of the Natural History Society did not separate museums from pleasure. They accentuated the value of amusement, linking the pursuit of diversion with both knowledge and the advancement of economic goals. In recent years, critics have decried the prominence of entertainment in contemporary museums, particularly those expanding museum shops and blockbuster exhibitions designed to attract an ample public.[9] According to them, the educational role of contemporary museums is experiencing a significant decline. A careful examination of the Natural History Society shows, however, that beliefs in a golden age of museums, when education trumped both amusement and commodification, may be based in fantasy.

Techniques of Vision

Crary examines how an observing subject is 'both the historical product *and* the site of certain practices, techniques, institutions, and procedures of subjectification.'[10] Like others exploring visuality, he is particularly interested in the impact of visual technologies such as the stereoscope, a nineteenth-century viewing machine enabling spectators to see pairs of photographic cards merge into three-dimensional scenes. Members of the Natural History Society certainly used visual technologies, including the magic lantern, an early form of the slide projector.[11] The most fundamental visual technique they promoted, however, was the collection and presentation of natural history specimens, predominantly those found in their region. During the first meeting of the Natural History Society in 1862, the forty-three male founders, including George F. Matthew, a customs clerk and amateur geologist, affirmed that residents as well as visitors needed to see and study the natural objects of New Brunswick in order to understand them.[12] Constructing a public museum in a room rented from the Mechanics' Institute, the early members filled it with mineral and fossil specimens, stuffed birds, and dried plants and insects.[13]

Members of the Society organized the rapidly expanding collections very slowly, for even in 1899 they called for volunteers to identify the geological specimens, which were almost entirely unlabelled.[14] By 1874 the objects had been moved to larger quarters in the downtown Market Building, and for the most part arranged by species or geographical origin. Nevertheless, a report of 1896 recommended that the foreign birds scattered throughout the shell, mammal, and geological rooms be more appropriately displayed with the domestic birds in the lecture room, alongside a stuffed caribou too large to fit elsewhere.[15] It was only when the Natural History Society was able to purchase a spacious two-storey building of its own in 1907 that the minutes reflected a desire to install the collection in what members called 'the manner of modern museums.' The curator, William MacIntosh, first employed in 1898, was especially proud of the fossil collection, mounted on wooden blocks against a beige wall that sloped so that every specimen could be seen.[16]

A primary goal of these museum displays was to focus the spectator's visual interest on individual specimens. Like other nineteenth-century natural history museums, such as the Redpath Museum of Montreal, which opened in 1882, in Saint John objects were primarily presented in a series of glass cases or on shelves. Spectacular dioramas, showing groups of stuffed animals within carefully crafted simulacra of their natural habitat, were installed at the American Museum of Natural History in New York during the 1920s, and the Museum of the Academy of Natural Sciences in Philadelphia in the 1920s and 1930s.[17] Such expensive exhibits were beyond the means of the Natural History Society in New Brunswick, which furthermore adopted a more Baconian approach to ordering the products of nature, emphasizing the inventory, description, and methodical observation of natural history, rather than the creation of immersive environments.[18] The methods of the New Brunswick collectors are perhaps most comparable to those of Irish-born teacher John Macoun. Despite his lack of formal education, Macoun excelled in the study of botany, working for the Geological Survey of Canada for thirty years, and becoming Dominion botanist in 1881. A voracious collector, more than a hundred thousand of his plant specimens remain in the Natural History Museum of Canada. Yet Macoun was not overly concerned with making careful field notes or labelling his specimens. Asserting that 'a good collector ... must have a trained eye,' he argued that a thorough collection would transmit knowledge, making textbooks and by extension most written text unnecessary.[19] Almost all of the active members of the Natural History Society of New Brunswick were similarly self-trained, focusing on the practical methods of collection rather than on the creation of abstract theories. They insisted that objects could educate the eye of the average person, and that natural history was not the exclusive domain of specialists.

Many nineteenth-century American museums were likewise fuelled by what historian Steven Conn calls 'naked eye science,' which affirmed that the study of natural history rested on the close observation of specimens.[20] This approach was hardly an American invention, however, as its best-known practitioner was the Swiss-born scientist Louis Agassiz, founder in 1859 of Harvard's Museum of Comparative Zoology. One of Agassiz's students reported being given a small pickled fish and being instructed to learn directly from it, without resorting to books. For a full week, the young student scrutinized the fish, noting both its minute details and basic physical features, such as bilateral symmetry.[21] This assignment was regularly used by Agassiz to teach the method of close observation, rather than the structure of a particular fish. The ability to recognize and distinguish between visual elements could then be applied to diverse specimens, leading to an extensive knowledge of the natural world. Agassiz's students did not simply see what was already there; they needed to learn how to observe, a process that took time, concentration, and, ultimately, a myriad of specimens. When members of the Natural History Society promoted this kind of productive looking, they were perhaps inspired by the theories of Agassiz himself, as he was an active corresponding member of the Society.[22] Agassiz's methods may also have been introduced by Charles Frederick Hartt, who began working as an assistant and student in the Museum of Comparative Zoology during the 1860s. Though specializing in geology rather than zoology, Hartt resembled his teacher in his voluminous collecting; eight thousand of the Devonian fossils he gathered at the Fern Ledges in Lancaster, New Brunswick, were purchased by the Society for its museum in 1863.[23] As indicated in the previous chapter, duplicates of these fossils were often given away by the Natural History Society, an act of gift giving which created relationships with similar organizations while promoting the New Brunswick society.

Yet what sets the Natural History Society of New Brunswick apart from other North American institutions is its prescient attempts to promote the skills of close observation outside its museum's walls. During the late nineteenth century, the Society began distributing to selected public schools pieces of bamboo as well as local ores, fossils, and stuffed birds 'not considered valuable to [the] collection.'[24] These casual loans gradually became more formalized until by 1907 small collections of native insects and fossils were prepared for the use of public schools throughout the province.[25] According to MacIntosh, in 1909 some 98 loans were made to schools, but in 1915 a total of 274 specimens were loaned, with a further 57 objects or collections of objects given to schools outright.[26] These numbers escalated on an annual basis until the curator was overwhelmed by orders from teachers throughout the province. The loan program, clearly both established and appreciated, was continued into the twentieth century. When the New Brunswick Museum officially opened to the public in 1934, it was equipped with a School Service Department, which, at its height, employed three women exclusively devoted to handling the extensive loan program.[27]

The techniques of display related to the loan collections differed from those of the museum installations, but no teachers' kits survive to enable a detailed analysis of them. Photographs were taken, however, inside the School Service Department in the 1940s, providing some indication of how the specimens were presented to students. Commissioned from Saint John photographer Louis Merritt Harrison, the images were used in a celebratory history of the New Brunswick Museum written by W. A. Squires, the curator of what was then called the Natural Sciences Department.[28] The photographs were designed to promote the museum as an educational resource staffed by diligent employees. One image shows three women working in a crowded room, with posters lining its walls (figure 2.1). These placards feature the shapes of animals common to New Brunswick, and one delineates the life history of a frog, in keeping with MacIntosh's descriptions of the original loan materials. The second, slightly later photograph displays bird specimens in wooden Reiker mounts on top of the shelves in the background (figure 2.2). This presentation format was used by MacIntosh to create specimens for the

2.1 L. Marie Hansen and R. Florence Harned in the School Service Department, New Brunswick Museum. Silver print, 19.7 × 24.9 cm., by Louis Merritt Harrison, 1940. 1989.83.1208. Courtesy of the New Brunswick Museum, Saint John, New Brunswick.

loan program as early as 1914.[29] The static arrangement of these stuffed birds would not allow for hands-on exploration, nor even for diverse views of the contents enclosed behind glass. Presenting birds as conquered trophies, the Reiker mounts imply nature is both knowable and containable, an historically specific understanding of nature discussed in more detail below.

Like the posters of frogs and other creatures, the emphasis of these mounted specimens is on the outline and overall shape of a typical example. Both types of loan object resemble diagrams, a format associated with the expression of scientific ideas. By distilling observations

2.2 Genevieve Thorne and Gloria Roulston in the School Service Department, New Brunswick Museum. Silver print, 20.3 × 24.9 cm., by Louis Merritt Harrison, 1940. 1989.83.1207. Courtesy of the New Brunswick Museum, Saint John, New Brunswick.

into a simple formula, they provide a principle that can be tested and developed in subsequent research.[30] The loan objects offered principles of observation, or ways of seeing the world. Rather than simply commit to memory the appearance of these objects, students could compare and contrast their shapes both within and outside of the classroom. By using the posters and mounts to categorize animals, students were encouraged to understand the natural world as an ordered realm of calculable variety.

Even as these loan specimens were potentially less amenable to careful scrutiny than the museum displays, both techniques of vision were meant to teach observational skills. Around 1908, MacIntosh began devising notes to accompany each specimen or hand-drawn poster, explaining how it should be presented to students. Addressing overburdened teachers, the notes implied that at least some written text was necessary to ensure the proper education of the eyes. MacIntosh's annual report of 1916 indicates that 1,824 typed nature study lessons were mailed to teachers in 1915, with an additional 52 prepared in response to their specific demands. By the early 1930s, a grant designated for educational work from the Carnegie Corporation – an entity discussed in chapter 5 of this book – enabled more than 22,000 notes to be printed for teachers each year.[31] Lists from the 1930s itemize the subjects covered, including regional birds, mammals, corals, minerals, crustacea, fish, insects, fossils, economic products, and 'the Indians of New Brunswick.'[32] The few notes that survive typically identify and classify a particular animal, or offer the 'life history' of an insect from egg, larva, and pupa to adult.[33] They primarily highlight, however, the direct observation of specimens. In 1912, MacIntosh sent his lesson on clovers to 42 different teachers before publishing it in the provincial *Report on Agriculture*. Approaching the history of clover in North America as an exciting story, MacIntosh praised the role of helpful bees and bacteria in propagating the clover that enabled farmers to fertilize their soil. In keeping with Agassiz's approach to close observation, MacIntosh further suggested each pupil bring a root of clover to school for observation, while studying 'the leaves and flowers in detail in the school room.'[34] The curator also wanted students to study the plants in the field, taking note of where they grew, and how deep their roots went into the ground.

A similar method of study was promoted by George Upham Hay, editor of New Brunswick material in the *Educational Review*, a monthly publication established in 1887 to provide teachers in the Maritimes with pedagogical information and resources. Hay became a teacher in 1873, ending his career over twenty-five years later as principal of the Victoria and Girls' High School in Saint John. Very active in the Natural History Society, he attended meetings, was a member of the botany committee, and was president of the Society for four years during the late 1890s. In addition to writing numerous articles for the Society's *Bulletin* – often based on research done in his own garden in Ingleside, New Brunswick – Hay gave lectures on botany, regularly focusing on how to teach it to children in primary as well as high school.[35] Unlike

MacIntosh, Hay did not favour teaching students the technical names of plants or animals. Instead, in close agreement with Macoun as well as Agassiz, he argued students should be told as little as possible, using books only as a last resort. On a windy day in June when dandelion heads were flying about, Hay advised teachers to have 'some of them brought into school, [and then] ask for suggestions about the curious appendages attached to the seeds and their uses.'[36] The young scholars should collect and draw seeds for days on end without the teacher doling out information, for the primary goal of the lesson was not to amass knowledge about plants but to arouse 'the spirit of observation, of investigation, and [to secure] sound mental training.'[37]

From its inception, articles in the *Educational Review* urged teachers to add nature study to their classes, at all grade levels. The first issue explained that one purpose of the journal was to supplement deficient textbooks by outlining natural science lessons, illustrated with native objects. A recurring feature called 'Ferndale School' proposed the study of a particular insect, plant, or animal, using a question-and-answer format. One early entry, written by Alexander H. MacKay, the editor for Nova Scotia, presents a lesson on cocoons. The 'teacher' begins by asking 'Johnnie' where he found his specimen, and then questions the rest of the students about the cocoon's colour and texture, permitting them to touch it. The instructor then takes a sharp knife and proceeds to reveal the cocoon's interior, attending to every detail.[38] Though this particular class outline does not require students to draw the specimen, many lessons in the Ferndale series portray the teacher making a sketch on the blackboard and asking students to do the same. In one study of a particular moth, for example, the teacher allows students first to count and then to look at its eggs under a magnifying glass, before inviting them to draw on the board an outline of the shape seen.[39] According to these long-standing lessons, students would acquire the skill of close examination through the performance of independent looking, meticulous counting, exhaustive description, and careful representation.

MacIntosh did not emphasize proficiency in drawing, but other members of the Natural History Society praised its ability to increase knowledge. Hartt, for example, was known as an excellent draughtsman who taught drawing in addition to producing his own diagrams for teaching.[40] Hay was likewise an early advocate of drawing, especially as a means of encouraging students to appreciate the symmetry and beauty of nature.[41] Other contributors to the *Educational Review* more explicitly linked the ability to draw with the ability to see. Revered E. Thring, the headmaster of Uppingham School in England, argued in 1887 that drawing was a pleasurable practice able to teach students to think in terms of shape.[42] Ten years later, an anonymous author claimed that in nature studies 'the pupil who is required to make a representation of an object in his science study must observe very closely and learn much of it in his efforts to depict its essential features.'[43] In both cases, drawing itself was not the desired end. Instead, the manual activity was understood as a technique able to produce visual skills.

Drawing had long been considered important to the acquisition of artistic ability, technical skill, and a cultured persona. During the eighteenth and early nineteenth centuries, however, pedagogues such as Henri Rousseau and Heinrich Pestalozzi claimed that learning to draw was inextricably linked with learning to see.[44] The Swiss-born Pestalozzi was arguably the most influential educational thinker during the nineteenth century, favouring a first-hand observation of nature rather than traditional methods of rote learning. According to him, drawing stimulated 'the ability to apprehend the outline of all objects and the features contained within the outline through correct perception (*Anschauung*) of the object itself, by means of similar lines.'[45] As we have already seen, this emphasis on active learning, direct perception, and the primacy of an object's outline or shape was common to proponents of nature study both within and outside of New Brunswick. Widely known, Pestalozzi's ideas were potentially conveyed to the Natural History Society through members who were graduates of the Provincial Normal School, an institution influenced by Pestalozzian theories since its inception in 1848.[46] Pestalozzi's pedagogical methods were not simply transferred, however, to the Maritimes. Pestalozzi approached drawing as a measured exercise able to lead a child from vague to clear ideas, yielding habits of 'order, accuracy, completeness and perfection.'[47] His drawing lessons were extremely rigid, with children striving to produce perfectly straight lines and specific geometric shapes. This strict method is a far cry from the one recommended in the pages of the *Educational Review*, where teachers asked pupils to sketch moth eggs and delineate the wings of butterflies.

From the 1860s through the early twentieth century, members of the Natural History Society and New Brunswick teachers strove to furnish students with the immediate experience of a range of specimens, gradually teaching them the skill of keen observation. In keeping with Crary's findings, they believed vision was a malleable activity, amenable to training in museums, classrooms, or the open air. Despite favouring different methods – some educators stressed drawing or written text more than others – all agreed that honing visual skills, and not the accumulation of facts, was the central goal of their teaching. Members of the Natural History Society additionally approached vision as an embodied act, dependent on the other senses. Whether stemming from the Natural History Society or the *Educational Review*, nature lessons stressed an object's texture, inviting students to touch specimens, or to see them opened to view by the teacher's knife. Advocates of drawing claimed the motions of the hand could lead the eye to see better, and allow the mind to think visually. Overall, vision was not limited to the operation of the eyes, but was conceived of broadly as a physical as well as intellectual endeavour. It was furthermore approached as an activity capable of having powerful effects; New Brunswick educators insisted that the careful observation of nature would improve the economic and moral tenor of society.

Effects of Visual Training

The economic benefits of collecting and displaying specimens of natural history were underscored during the first meeting of the Natural History Society in 1862, and repeated well into the twentieth century. Founding members affirmed that their organization would both foster science in New Brunswick and develop its natural resources, its supposedly vast mineral deposits.[48] This utilitarian approach to nature study ultimately stemmed from Britain, where eighteenth- and nineteenth-century botanists adhered to a Baconian belief in the ability of science to improve everyday life.[49] Many Canadian institutions espoused such practical goals. According to historian Suzanne Zeller, geological research in Victorian Canada was designed to promote industry by searching for marketable mineral deposits.[50] Members of the Natural History Society similarly encouraged industrialization as one of the Society's primary ambitions, even as they praised the beautiful forests of New Brunswick, and lamented the destruction of birds hunted to provide the feathers ornamenting fashionable hats.[51]

In an apparent contradiction, participants in the Natural History Society simultaneously advanced the exploitation and protection of nature. Yet this combination of beliefs was not unusual at the time. Environmental historian Richard Judd argues that scholars have tended to adopt dualistic views of nature, separating a utilitarian approach from an aesthetic one.[52] His study of concepts of nature in nineteenth-century New England shows, however, that an aggressive urge to reshape nature coexisted with a perfectionist vision of the ideal balance between nature and culture. Members of the Natural History Society clearly adhered to this historical belief system, for in 1901 they lobbied government for the creation of a provincial park near the Tobique and Nepisiguit Lakes, specifying the park's usefulness in preserving the land for forestry research as well as the recreation of citizens; in 1896 these same officers had campaigned to have a creosoting timber plant built in Saint John.[53] Unlike debates surrounding the development of the Yosemite Valley in California during the early twentieth century in which Sierra Club member John Muir rejected the commercialization of nature, whereas his colleague Gifford Pinchot supported the efficient use of natural resources, there is no evidence of struggles within the Natural History Society of New Brunswick.[54] Its members apparently agreed that conservation efforts were not opposed to industrialization.

A few men even used the Natural History Society to promote their own business interests. During the 1920s, a nature lesson disseminated by the Natural History Society presented 'Facts on the History, Growth and Manufacture of Tea.'[55] The material was obviously provided by the Red Rose Tea Company, as the bottom of each page is stamped with the logo 'Red Rose Tea is good tea.' Notably, the founder of the Red Rose Tea Company in Saint John was Theodore Estabrooks, an active member of the Society. His pamphlet provides an example of what has been called educational advertising. Commonplace at the time, educational advertising was also adopted by American companies such as Du Pont, which created exhibitions championing the wonders of chemical products for the New York Museum of Science and Industry in the 1930s.[56]

Promoting the practical uses of nature not only was potentially self-serving, but it also provided a strategic defence of the Natural History Society and its activities. The mantra of 'usefulness' appealed to a broad public as well as politicians. In his annual report of 1909, MacIntosh noted that when he rearranged the mineral specimens into groups showing their economic uses, intrigued visitors examined the specimens more carefully.[57] Members of the Natural History Society made similar efforts to appeal to local and provincial government in their continual requests for funding, drawing attention to the potential economic contributions of their institution, and stressing the increasing accessibility of the museum, which was open to the public free of charge.[58] In addition to hiring attendants to extend opening hours throughout the week and on holidays, the Society provided guided tours for various clubs, teachers, and young students. While government funding always remained at minimal levels, their efforts to attract museum visitors were successful; annual attendance increased continually, from 150 visitors in 1895, to 1,100 in 1899, 6,000 in 1912, and 8,775 in 1916.[59]

Members of the Natural History Society had specific economic information to impart to their audience. The nature lessons sent to schools, for example, regularly taught students to distinguish between types of lumber, identify valuable minerals, and enumerate the processes required to produce commodities such as tea or linoleum.[60] The Natural History Society's campaign against the destructive brown tail moth provides another striking example of the conflation of economic interests and nature study. Around 1907, MacIntosh, largely self-trained in entomology, was contacted by the provincial Department of Agriculture about the threat of the brown tail moth, then moving into New Brunswick from the Eastern United States to decimate apple orchards. MacIntosh eventually visited almost all the schools in the province, informing children of the moth pests, and teaching them how to identify both the moths and their nests. With the support of the government, by 1911 he had also offered the children a monetary incentive of ten cents for every nest they found and mailed to him at the Natural History Society's museum. The archives include many letters sent to MacIntosh by children requesting payment for their conquests – letters smeared with moth guts, or with holes in the envelopes and a notation in MacIntosh's hand indicating 'specimen escaped.'[61] Most interesting about this anti-moth campaign is the unity of the museum curator's efforts to teach children the sheer pleasure of engaging with nature, a knowledge of the agriculture of New Brunswick, and entrepreneurial ambition.

MacIntosh's efforts to stimulate the rural economy were not exclusively directed at children. In his curatorial report of 1914, he noted that 'a fine series of insects for exhibition and educational work [were] prepared for the Educational Train ("Better Farming Special") sent throughout the Province by the Agricultural Department of the Province of New Brunswick.'[62] Largely because of his work on the brown tail moth campaign, the provincial Department of Agriculture paid MacIntosh to accompany the Better Farming Special, a CPR train equipped with visual displays as well as a dining and sleeping car for curators. During the month of June in both 1912 and 1914, the train travelled throughout New Brunswick, stopping at many small towns and villages to invite inhabitants aboard. The exhibits inside the train corresponded with governmental policy promoting what MacIntosh called scientific agricultural education, emphasizing how to recognize the economic woods of New Brunswick, and increase crop yields. One of the installations prepared by MacIntosh, for example, showed mounted specimens of weeds accompanied by coloured drawings of the complete plants, and labels explaining the best methods to use in their suppression.[63]

The Natural History Society and the government were united in their attempts to produce ideal farmers. They also explained how to recognize such farmers. In his nature lesson on clovers, MacIntosh noted that thrifty farmers would plant clover rather than pay for more expensive commercial fertilizers.[64] Other lessons drew attention to farmers with bad habits. These men ignored the presence of injurious insects, endangering their neighbours' crops as well as their own. The *Educational Review* of July 1887 included a Ferndale School lesson on the destructive potato beetle. After questioning the fictional students about the visual appearance and negative effects of the beetle, the teacher wonders, 'If one farmer in this community were not particular about combating the beetle, and all the others were, what would be the result do you think?' The students reply in a chorus that he would raise a crop of beetles, prompting his unhappy neighbours to 'look after him.' The pupils then pledge to repeat their nature lesson to 'every farmer and every person in the school section.'[65] In the end, the students are taught not only to identify injurious insects, but also to distinguish good from bad farmers, in the hope of convincing the latter to become responsible citizens.

Members of the Natural History Society participated in the reform efforts meant to ameliorate economic conditions in New Brunswick. During the 1880s, Canada, and particularly the Maritime provinces, experienced a general economic decline. The Natural History Society clearly endorsed those agricultural programs aimed at increasing productivity by 'modernizing' Maritime farming during this era, initiatives discussed in detail by historians such as Timothy Lewis.[66] Equally evident is the importance placed by members on the industrialization of New Brunswick, an emphasis in line with the efforts of local entrepreneurs, some of them active members of the Natural History Society, to increase industrial expansion during the late nineteenth century. Like the Maritime businessmen analysed by historian T.W. Acheson, participants in the Natural History Society insisted that the region would become the industrial hub of Canada, given its coal and iron deposits, textile factories, and steel production.[67] They not only supported specific projects like the creosoting plant in Saint John, but also trained New Brunswick students to recognize the opportunities available in the natural world surrounding them, thereby reinforcing the traditionally resource-based economy. This focus on youth was in some ways a standard educational strategy, but it was also informed by the increasing migration of young people from the region. Patricia A. Thornton argues that out-migration was potentially one of the causes of the economic decline in New Brunswick and the other Maritime provinces. From the 1860s to the 1920s, close to half a million people left the Maritimes to seek gainful employment elsewhere; during the 1870s, Saint John lost about 29 per cent of its total population, including 40 to 50 per cent of its youth.[68] Though not an official economic program, when the Natural History Society instructed students to seek and pursue natural resources in New Brunswick, it implicitly encouraged them to remain in the province.

Reinforcing this goal, the Natural History Society taught pupils to cherish their native province, and develop a bond with it. Learning to 'appreciate beautiful views in the district' was a part of the grade four curriculum after 1908, but members of the Society had encouraged children to admire the local landscape since at least the 1870s.[69] The Society regularly arranged outings to New Brunswick landmarks such as the Fern Ledges, explored by Hartt, and Rockwood Park in Saint John, so that students could study fossils, flora, and birds. At the same time, annual camps were instituted by George F. Matthew, featuring nature lessons offered by him as well as esteemed scientist William F. Ganong, professor of botany at Smith College in Massachusetts and a Charlotte County, New Brunswick, native.[70] These events were usually attended by mixed groups consisting of male members, the women allowed to become associate members in 1881, and the boys and girls who joined as junior members after 1883 and 1908 respectively.[71] The theme of an outing in October of 1909 at 'Camp Nature,' located above Nerepis Station, was explicit in its glorification of the province. The audience gathered at the camp co-owned by MacIntosh and A. Gordon Leavitt, treasurer of the Natural History Society for over thirty-five years, was treated to a lecture on the 'advantages of New Brunswick as a place of abode.'[72]

Such lessons endorsed interacting with nature, rather than particular rights, as the basis for a kind of 'geographical citizenship.' According to cultural geographer David Matless, geographical citizenship establishes the 'knowledge and appreciation of landscape's beauty, morphology and history' as the foundation for good citizenship.[73] His analysis of British culture during and immediately following the Second World War links the aesthetic enjoyment of landscape, movement for the creation of parks, and performance of coastal surveys with the struggle to reconstruct a unified sense of national identity. The study of the natural world took on an even more urgent role for residents of British colonies or former colonies attempting to forge self-awareness in relation to their unique terrain. Constructing a sense of nationalism required knowing the peculiarities of one's own soil, climate, forests, and mountains.[74]

New Brunswick pedagogues of the late nineteenth and early twentieth centuries specified regional and local identity, rather than any homogeneous or nationalist view of Canada. The information they taught to students was not primarily about Canada, but instead featured local specimens, landmarks, and natural resources. Though European models of looking were adopted by the Society, their application to the landscape, foliage, and birds of New Brunswick provided students with views different from those available outside of Canada, or even in the central and western parts of the country. Through their museum displays and nature lessons, members of the Natural History Society implied that becoming a good citizen of the province entailed scrutinizing one's immediate natural surroundings, and applying the knowledge thereby gained in a manner that would serve the local community. According to them, the ideal inhabitant of New Brunswick was disciplined, undertaking a continual surveillance of the land in order both to appreciate its beauty and to alter it in the name of prosperity.

In keeping with this regional production of model citizens, the Natural History Society affirmed that nature study would improve the character of the New Brunswick populace. This belief implies a romantic and perhaps even theological understanding of nature, commonplace at the time. During the Victorian era, nature induced a sense of wonder often linked with religious awareness and considered able to have a restorative effect on people.[75] Few Society members mentioned God directly, apart from Senator John V. Ellis, the long-time president of the Natural History Society who died in 1913, and Hay.[76] Many other members nevertheless endowed nature with spiritual or intangible qualities able to benefit devotees. Even the factual scientist Ganong claimed that the careful observation of nature enabled one to move 'nearer to that conception, grand and ennobling when fully grasped, the true basis of all scientific knowledge,– the fundamental unity of Nature.'[77] In 1909, the annual report of the ornithology committee of the Society claimed more concrete effects, confidently stating that its museum displays had 'no doubt prevent[ed] bird destruction for fun, or in order that their mangled remains or parts may be used as hat or other ornaments.'[78] This vaguely theological approach to nature was not at odds with economic efforts to control the natural world, for historian Keith Thomas argues that insisting on humans' rightful domination of nature was a long-standing part of Christian belief.[79]

Nature study's character-building ability informed the rationale for teaching it in schools. In 1908, R.P. Steeves, the director of elementary agricultural education in New Brunswick, wrote a textbook for teachers, outlining an official nature-study course for rural common schools in the province.[80] He, like other educators, believed that if children worked diligently in school gardens, they would learn about weeds and insects while incurring habits of thoroughness and self-reliance. Steeves recommended that pupils begin working in divided garden plots in grade one, and continue each year until grade eight. The careful regulation of bodies and spaces would, he affirmed, produce a disciplined citizenry.

School gardens were also meant, however, to create a good impression of the region. In the *Educational Review* of December 1890, an anonymous author described a pretty schoolhouse with well-kept grounds in the village of Westfield, near Saint John, as having a beneficial impact on the entire community. At the same time, the author claimed those visitors passing by the school could simply glance out their railway car windows to witness the refinement of the area.[81] In 1894, Chief Superintendent Inch of New Brunswick agreed that 'the school house and its surroundings may generally be taken as an index of the intelligence and public spirit of the people in any community.'[82] Given this association of visual presentation with identity, it is not surprising that educational textbooks began to provide lessons on how to care for both school grounds and personal property. In a textbook first published around 1911, John Brittain argued that nature itself would provide the best guide for beautifying home and school grounds, directing students to adorn the land tastefully with trees, shrubs, flowers, and grassy lawns.[83] Faith in the positive effects of landscaping was long-lived, for an agricultural textbook published in 1942 noted that improving the appearance of schoolhouses by transplanting trees from the forest would have a favourable impact on visitors to New Brunswick.[84] These lessons represent a simultaneous interaction with and alteration of nature; students first learned to appreciate the visual beauty of their regional landscape, and were then instructed to recreate that landscape in order to produce pleasing visions of the 'natural' beauty of the province.

Despite their regional focus, New Brunswick pedagogues were continually concerned about how the rest of Canada and the outside world perceived their province. Members of the Natural History Society argued that if inhabitants observed the land appropriately, they would not only contribute to the economy while engaging in self-improvement, but would produce a more positive image of New Brunswick and its people. Thornton argues that during the 1920s the Maritimes was increasingly considered a backward and economically stagnant part of Canada.[85] Fears of such opinions were already shaping the activities of the Natural History Society in the nineteenth century. In 1894, Hay, for example, asserted that residents should discover as well as catalogue all the plants and minerals in the province in order to avoid being deemed a 'non-progressive people.'[86] In 1888, Ganong encouraged amateurs to take up the practice of natural history, which could be self-taught; those living near the seashore could examine echinoderms because patient and accurate observers 'may at any time add to science a substantial contribution.'[87] Like Hay, Ganong believed the rugged and undiscovered land of New Brunswick offered ambitious dilettantes the opportunity to contribute to learned discourse while enhancing the authority of both themselves and the region.

Nature study was meant to have multiple effects, shaping the people of New Brunswick as well as the province's economy, landscape, and international reputation. But whose interests were actually served by lessons in the careful observation of natural history? The answer to this question is not obvious. Members of the Natural History Society clearly attempted to transform the province and its inhabitants in terms of their own beliefs about the proper structure of society. In that sense, they were like the moralizing reformers of nineteenth-century England described by Bennett. The museum of the Natural History Society was used to broadcast powerful messages, legitimating the 'scientific' possession and control of the land. As various scholars have shown, natural history collections had long functioned in this way, for even during the early modern period 'cabinets of curiosities' had demonstrated the power of the prince, his dominion over the natural world, and his social prestige. During the modern era, taxonomic natural history collections asserted the necessity of human control over nature, ordering the natural world in synchrony with efforts to construct social and political order.[88] Participants in the Natural History Society similarly gained social capital through their activities, while endorsing such bourgeois values as discipline, the pursuit of education, and material acquisition through collecting.

At the same time, the clerks, shop owners, teachers, and physicians who participated in the Natural History Society cannot easily be characterized as a homogeneous group promoting its own interests. The Society regularly invited the acting lieutenant-governor of the province, or senators such as Ellis, to serve as figureheads, thereby currying political favour while aspiring to an elevated social status.[89] Yet the active leaders of and participants in the group were for the most part neither wealthy nor from the privileged classes. They were not, for example, akin to the elite sportsmen described by historian Bill Parenteau, who during the nineteenth and early twentieth centuries lobbied for restrictions on hunting and fishing that placed the interests of sportsmen above those of local residents.[90] The Natural History Society was more inclusive, with members offering to waive the minimal annual fees for those unable to afford them.[91] Though not exactly democratic – its rigid structure marginalized women, a topic I discuss in chapter 3 – the Natural History Society was not an elitist force able to oppress the 'lower' classes.

In contrast to Bennett's discussion of nineteenth-century British museum founders, members of the Natural History Society did not strive to replace bodily entertainments with intellectual ones. The entertainment of both adults and children was a long-standing goal of the Society. According to New Brunswick pedagogues, pleasure was among the important results of nature study in school. Hay proclaimed visual training allowed access to 'joys otherwise denied to those who have not the "eyes to see,"' while the minutes of the Society noted that students visiting the museum had 'received instruction as well as pleasure.'[92] Other events were more physically oriented, with little direct connection to the study of natural history specimens. In 1914, the young Hildred Simonds wrote, for example, that during the winter months members of the junior associate branch had enjoyed snowshoeing, tobogganing, and social evenings at the museum.[93] Despite failing to mention nature, her comments are in keeping with the arguments of historian Carl Berger, who notes that natural history groups flourished during the nineteenth and early twentieth centuries because they provided leisure activities considered both socially appropriate and physically beneficial to participants.[94] All the same, numerous events sponsored by the Natural History Society were designed to attract an audience and appear to have had little to do with educational goals. In 1924, for instance, the Ladies' Auxiliary hosted an 'Oriental Exhibition' at the museum, featuring displays of Asian art and costumed women serving tea, an event analysed fully in chapter 3. Other female members gave talks on their trips to Europe, as well as on literary texts unrelated to natural history. These events were accompanied by culturally apposite singing, dancing, and food consumption. Such popular kinds of socializing included male members of the Society, particularly the annual *conversazioni*, when dignitaries as well as the general public were invited to hear speeches, examine specimens, but mostly to eat and drink – the topic receiving most of the attention in surviving notes and minutes. In keeping with Foucault's arguments about the productivity of power, the Natural History Society was designed to teach lessons of discipline, hard work, and the love of nature, but it also enabled potentially undisciplined opportunities for entertainment and bodily pleasure.[95]

Conclusions

Studying the Natural History Society reveals vision as an historically, culturally, and even regionally specific activity. It further exposes the important status of observation, a valuable skill requiring time and effort to develop. A range of educators expected positive results to emerge from visual training, including the development of mental capacities, the ability to perceive a beautiful landscape, and recognition of superior timber. Ultimately, looking was meant to alter New Brunswick as well as its people, transforming the land into consumable views or commodities, and its people into fulfilled, tenacious citizens. The construction of New Brunswick did not occur exclusively through representations of it – in stories, maps, paintings, or museum displays – but also in visual perceptions of the region: perceptions guided by advice about what should be noticed, and how best to regard it.

Museums fostered this visual training, contributing to school curricula, government programs, and leisure activities in New Brunswick. The impact of the Natural History Society extended far beyond the displays in its museum, to include school loan collections, the Special Farming Train, and camping trips. Contributors to these museums strove not merely to deliver information about natural history, but to affect everyday life in the province by shaping the economy as well as the surroundings of inhabitants. Amusement was crucial to this mission rather than opposed to it.

Today the social and economic influence of museums is less apparent. The decline of these institutions concerns some scholars, who claim the traditional mission of museums has recently been replaced by efforts to please visitors. According to historian Brian Young, Canadian museum workers must now devote their time to entertaining visitors rather than to preserving historically important objects. In his commentary on American institutions, political scientist Timothy Luke similarly argues that 'history displays are being redefined to complement, if not fit into, the larger orbits of the entertainment industry.'[96] He is alarmed by the Disneyfication of museums, a process that empties politics and historical depth from exhibitions, reducing them to diverting spectacles. These critics contend museums are no longer educational institutions, and can barely be distinguished from shopping malls or amusement parks.

The preceding analysis of visuality in New Brunswick casts doubt on such claims. Though some current museum displays may indeed be superficial, museums have not been subject to a sudden increase in entertaining activities. These institutions have long been devoted to amusing the public, and not exclusively concerned with the care and display of objects. They have, furthermore, promoted the production of commodities, and have even delivered the advertising messages of corporations. It is important to consider the historically specific forms of commodification and entertainment in today's museums. So what has changed? I contend that the status of vision itself, not the 'educational' content of museums, has declined. While museums remain committed to looking as an active, intellectual pursuit, the broader culture and school system no longer reinforce this belief. Since the middle of the twentieth century, vision has increasingly been construed as a strictly passive and sensual distraction, unable to have a positive impact on society. In fact, the visual perception of North American mass media is popularly portrayed as a negative act that increases violent tendencies or lulls viewers into a state of numbness. Museum critics reinforce this denigrated understanding of vision when they condemn as mere spectacle the displays currently offered in museums.

Of course, there are other reasons for the decreasing status of museums. Scientific practice is now largely devoted to the pursuit of invisible objects, such as atoms or cells.[97] Complex visualizing technologies have replaced the commitment to naked-eye science, making natural history displays seem both outdated and relatively useless. In contrast, art galleries have retained some authority because art professionals, critics, and historians continue to value a trained eye. They associate looking with knowing, a formulation no longer operative in other disciplines, including anthropology and history. Because museums are essentially visual, their importance will increase only when vision is re-evaluated as an historically specific, learned skill worthy of analysis. Museum professionals, art historians, educators, and those trained in cultural studies can work together to produce a new understanding of vision, one that does not return us to previous approaches, but instead reveals how seeing is inseparable from assumptions about status, land, and identity.

Chapter Three

Offering Orientalism: Women and the Gift Economy of the Museum, 1880–1940

A photograph from 1924 shows three unidentified members of the Ladies' Auxiliary of the Natural History Society of New Brunswick standing inside their Society's museum in Saint John (figure 3.1). Normally devoted to the display of local birds, insects, and geological specimens, the museum had been temporarily transformed into an 'Oriental bazaar,' a fundraising event at which the ladies served tea and cake while dressed in Japanese, Chinese, and Indian costume. Another photograph (figure 3.2), taken eleven years later in the new museum building that replaced the Museum of the Natural History Society when it became a provincial institution, shows museum cases filled with the Asian objects collected by Alice Lusk Webster, a wealthy patron who founded the Art Department of the New Brunswick Museum in Saint John during the 1930s. Her interest in Asian culture implies a continuity of women's work within the old and new museums. Lusk Webster nevertheless distinguished herself from the members of the Ladies' Auxiliary, arguing that they and their 'pink teas' should be laid 'away in lavender on an upper shelf.'[1]

In this chapter, I consider two generations of female participation in New Brunswick museums. Although Lusk Webster strategically denounced the entrepreneurial, cake-baking activities of her predecessors, she had much in common with them. Most women active in the Ladies' Auxiliary were the wives, sisters, or daughters of male members of the Natural History Society. As volunteers, the ladies raised money to furnish the rooms of the museum, and funded the female staff member who kept the doors open to the public. Along similar lines, Lusk Webster was involved in the New Brunswick Museum largely because of her familial relationship with one of its male administrators; her hus-

3.1 Unidentified members of the Ladies' Auxiliary of the Natural History Society of New Brunswick, Oriental Exhibition, January 1924. Silver print mounted on card. X16534. Courtesy of the New Brunswick Museum, Saint John, New Brunswick.

band, Dr John Clarence Webster, was a major benefactor of the institution and vice-president of its board until his death in 1950. She likewise worked in a volunteer capacity, struggling to increase the material possessions and fixtures of the New Brunswick Museum. Furthermore, the honorary curator of the Art Department had a comparable interest in Asian art. After inheriting some Asian objects from her family, she had expanded her personal collection with purchases, sometimes made with her husband while travelling throughout Europe and North America.[2]

Yet Lusk Webster differed significantly from the members of the

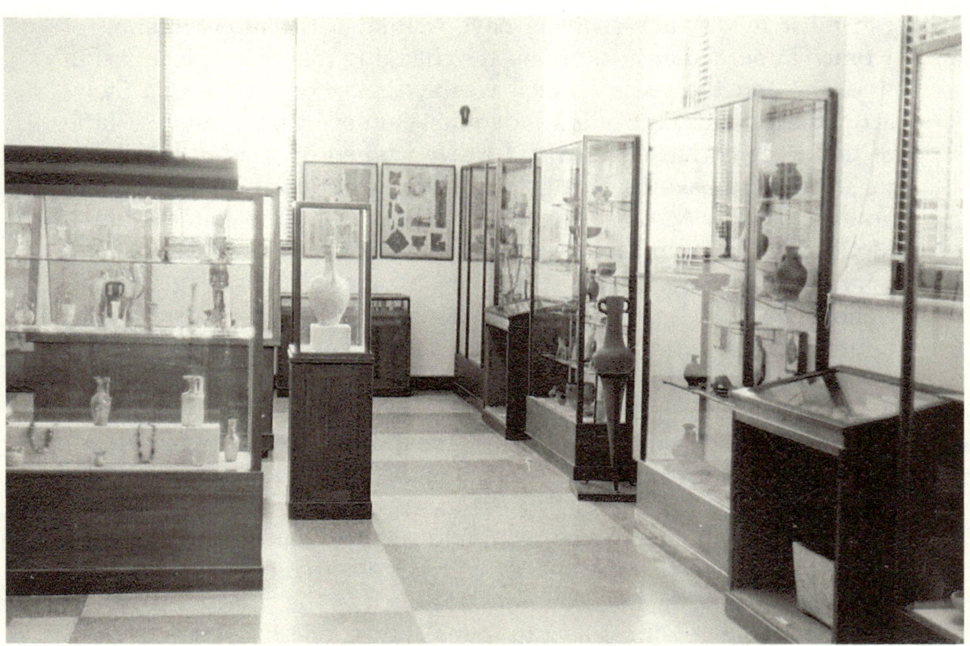

3.2 Overall view of display cases in the Art Department of the New Brunswick Museum, 1930s–1940s. NBM–F41–14. Courtesy of the New Brunswick Museum, Saint John, New Brunswick.

Ladies' Auxiliary. From a prominent New York family, she had been educated in France, specializing in both art-making and its history. As the wife of a wealthy doctor, she had greater social and cultural capital than most participants in the Auxiliary, and was eventually involved in the administration of the New Brunswick Museum, serving as the first vice-president of its executive board after her husband's death.[3] Lusk Webster aligned herself with male curators and connoisseurs, especially C.T. Currelly, director of the Royal Ontario Museum of Archaeology in Toronto. After studying the installation methods used in Toronto and at other major museums, she based her Art Department on the principles of coverage and classification, and rejected the costumed social events that had been hosted by her female predecessors.

Comparing the museum work performed by members of the Ladies' Auxiliary with that of Alice Lusk Webster both reconfirms and challenges previous accounts of women's marginal status in North American museums. A few scholars have examined the representation of women in particular institutions, the changing role of female museum workers, and the goals of such wealthy collectors as Isabella Stewart Gardner and Gertrude Vanderbilt Whitney.[4] Comparatively little of this research has emphasized either women or gender in relation to Canadian museums, though a notable exception is historian Brian Young's chapter on what he calls the women's culture fostered in the McCord Museum in Montreal from 1921 to 1975.[5] According to him, white, middle-class, conservative women were able to manage the collections with a degree of freedom because of McGill University's continuing ambivalence about the value of the museum. Analysing the position of women within the Natural History Society and the New Brunswick Museum provides another case study, one that highlights the opportunities women had to reshape those collections while recognizing distinctions between members of the middle and upper-middle classes.

To a certain extent, my research produces a familiar story of women's efforts to gain power and authority within male-dominated institutions. At the same time, the gift economy supported by the museum structure provided women with strategies to make their presence known, especially by donating objects to the collections. During the late nineteenth and early twentieth centuries, members of the Ladies' Auxiliary gave insect specimens, textiles, and stuffed mammals to the Museum of the Natural History Society, ensuring that their names would be recorded in the official accession records.[6] Alice Lusk Webster shifted direction in the 1930s and 1940s, exploiting her international connections to secure artworks for permanent display in the New Brunswick Museum. She continued, however, to engage with the museum's gift economy, reshaping the mechanisms of exchange that had been employed by the male members of the Natural History Society during the nineteenth century (analysed in chapter 1). Instead of increasing the value of local geological specimens, Lusk Webster traded sections of her family's art collections for Asian and European decorative objects. Her enterprising methods were in keeping with her upper-middle-class status, but Lusk Webster's focus on 'foreign' decorative art unsettled the traditional identity of the natural history museum and raised the ire of some of its male administrators, as indicated below.

Women's potentially transgressive contributions to museums in New Brunswick should be both acknowledged and celebrated, but they can also be examined critically for reinforcing dominant discourses of class, gender, and race. Members of the Ladies' Auxiliary participated, for example, in fashionable forms of Orientalism, masquerading as Asian women to enhance the colonial project of the museum. Though these women donated objects to the Museum of the Natural History Society, they often treated the institution as a site of consumption, staging the acquisition and appreciation of such personal possessions as Asian textiles within it. They primarily organized social events in relation to the museum, and did not collect, label, or arrange objects into pedagogical, permanent displays. In contrast, Lusk Webster argued that the ideal museum would offer lessons in good taste to the 'lower' classes, becoming a place of learning rather than a venue for entertainment. Deliberately rejecting the long-standing associations of femininity and desire with Asian material culture, Lusk Webster promoted a disembodied version of Orientalism. Instead of wearing Asian costumes, she hung lifeless garments within cases, displaying them according to chronology, national origin, and style. In short, Lusk Webster positioned herself as a learned connoisseur and teacher. Her performance of gender and class diverged from that of her predecessors, shedding light on the various ways women could use museums to produce their identities, even in relation to such a presumably common theme as Orientalism.

In his famous publication of 1979, literary theorist Edward Said defined Orientalism as both 'a style of thought based upon an ontological and epistemological distinction made between "the Orient" and … "the Occident"' and a long-standing academic practice which produces the Orient as an exotic other to the supposedly rational, civilized, and masculine West.[7] This influential study remains a touchstone for postcolonial theory, but has also been subject to debate. Recent responses complicate Said's binary division between East and West by studying the participation of white women in Orientalist practices, expanding his discussion of gender, and including considerations of consumer culture. Such scholars as Sarah Cheang, Mari Yoshihara, and Stacey Loughrey Sloboda contend that Orientalism is a heterogeneous and contradictory discourse that takes different forms in particular cultural and historical locations. They examine how women were key participants in diverse Orientalisms, reshaping them not simply to invent an other, but also to claim authority within male domains.[8] This chapter emphasizes Chinese visual culture to analyse the kinds of Orientalism produced in both the Museum of the Natural History Society and the New Brunswick Museum, reflecting on how they could be liberating as well as confining to women.

The Women of the Natural History Society, 1881–1932

The Ladies' Auxiliary was formed as a subsidiary branch of the Natural History Society of New Brunswick in 1881. The minutes of 9 May record that 'on motion it was resolved that a class of Associate members be instituted for ladies whose names shall be approved by the council, who shall be admitted to all the public business of the society upon payment of one dollar per annum.'[9] The formal admission of women into the group occurred during attempts to revive the Society, which was created in 1862 but had been dormant since 1874. In 1880 a number of the key founding members, including long-time president George F. Matthew – an amateur geologist and palaeontologist who gained international praise for his work on local fossils – began contacting previous participants while attempting to attract new members and raise the public profile of the organization.[10] For the most part, the first women to gain entry were related to male members, but other women eventually joined, including Miss Belle Nugent, a Saint John teacher admitted in 1886.[11] The associate members were primarily white, middle-class, adult women of varying ages from the Saint John region. During the 1880s, the number of women involved in the Ladies' Auxiliary was modest, with, for example, only forty-one female associates in 1886. Women continued to join the Natural History Society, however, and by the early twentieth century they outnumbered the male members.[12]

Women had likely been participating informally in the Natural History Society since its inception, preparing food for social occasions. In the minutes of 1865, male administrators thanked anonymous ladies for having provided refreshments at the annual *conversazione*, an event to which the general public as well as dignitaries were invited to the Museum of the Natural History Society to hear talks given by male members.[13] According to the archival records, even after becoming associate members women continued to perform this role, with the minutes of 28 February 1882 suggesting that 'the ladies who assisted in getting up the conversazione last year be requested to do so again.'[14] The members of the Ladies' Auxiliary also accomplished a range of other conventionally feminine tasks, decorating the Society's rooms for the various *conversazioni*, forming a committee to purchase a new curtain for the lecture room in 1892, and uniting with the female members of the Historical and Loyalist Societies to arrange a picnic lunch for the Royal Society of Canada, which held its annual meeting in Saint John in 1904.[15] The minutes indicate that associate members continually consulted with male administrators when undertaking these projects, asking permission to collect and spend money.

The women nevertheless failed in their efforts to become full participants in the Natural History Society. From its inception, the Ladies' Auxiliary was ancillary to the parent group, paying an entry fee of $1.00 whereas the men paid $2.00 for their memberships. When male administrators asked the Ladies' Auxiliary to host social events to raise money for the Natural History Society in 1925, the women suggested that they instead be allowed to become full members, providing funds with the increased dues they would pay.[16] The idea was promptly mooted. At an earlier meeting, Emma Fiske, a long-time participant in the Ladies' Auxiliary, had proposed full membership for the women. According to Secretary-Treasurer Harriet B. Holman, 'She had hardly finished reading when a man back of me in the hall jumped to his feet in great indignation, and said "When the Women come in, the Men go out."'[17] The women did not always capitulate, for when M.R. Rankine, periodically secretary-treasurer of the Ladies' Auxiliary, read her annual report to the male administrators of the Natural History Society in 1922, she defiantly noted that the women's fundraising efforts produced 'money which we spend as we choose, [and] no exception can be taken to our reckless generosity, or our business methods, should any criticism occur to the practical male "members in full standing."'[18] She implied that male administrators did not always approve of the purchases made by the Ladies' Auxiliary, which by then included various furnishings for the rooms of the Natural History Society as well as a piano. By 1927 the women had declared that they formed a 'separate organization within the society,' but they did not receive full status within the Natural History Society until 1943, when the group was virtually defunct.[19]

Despite their strategic refusal in 1925, members of the Ladies' Auxiliary were devoted to raising money for the Natural History Society. In 1900, for example, the Scientific Supper Committee of the Ladies' Auxiliary provided $30.00 to purchase a 'much needed geological case' for the museum. Later sales enabled the acquisition of more elaborate cases and a reflectoscope used to project images during the Society's lectures.[20] In 1906 the women held a successful loan exhibition and high tea in Saint John's York Theatre, charging an entry fee of 25 cents for the opportunity to see such items as Mrs A. L. Holman's Peruvian mummy sheet.[21] Linking the public display of their personal items with generosity rather than egotism, the members of the Ladies' Auxiliary made a point of giving the $323.62 they raised as a gift to the Natural History Society.[22]

Volunteer fundraising efforts were often organized by female societies during the nineteenth and early twentieth centuries. Historian Cecelia Morgan finds that Canadian Christian women hosted bazaars for charity, thereby attracting media attention to the value of women's work.[23] Along similar lines, historian Lynne Marks has shown how religious women in small towns in Ontario used profits to improve church interiors.[24] According to historian Kathleen D. McCarthy, American women likewise engaged in 'non-profit entrepreneurship,' finding a respectable outlet for their commercial ambitions by donating the monies raised to museums and social clubs.[25] Scholars who study the development of a consumer society in the United States argue that in relation to such charitable events, consumption was linked with gift giving to reframe it as a morally acceptable activity. Historian Alice Taylor, for example, claims that the organizers of the anti-slavery fairs in Boston between 1834 and 1858 promoted shopping as a form of political behaviour, asking women in particular to buy for the sake of the slave.[26] Held annually during the Christmas season, Taylor argues that abolitionist fairs created the concept of holiday shopping while portraying the purchase of material goods as an action performed to benefit another. During fundraising bazaars, members of the Ladies' Auxiliary similarly presented consumption as gift giving, while raising their status both within the Natural History Society and the wider public sphere.

Members of the Ladies' Auxiliary also donated personal possessions to the Museum of the Natural History Society, receiving the 'return gift' of having their names inscribed in the accession registers and occasionally in the minutes of the Society's regular meetings.[27] The records of 16 September 1898 indicate that 'the Secretary was requested to convey the Society's thanks to Miss Warner [a local botanist] for her valuable collection of New Brunswick plants.' In 1894 another member of the Ladies' Auxiliary, Mrs Mary Lawrence, a teacher in Saint John, was thanked for her donation of a caribou; considered a 'fine specimen' worth about $40.00, it was immediately installed in the Society's lecture hall.[28] The accession records show that the women continued to offer a wide range of objects during the early twentieth century, notably many of the Aboriginal items displayed in the museum, baskets and textiles that had initially been bought by the women as personal possessions.[29] Long-standing associate member Catharine Murdock arguably made the most substantial gift by leaving money to the Natural History Soci-

3.3 Façade of the Museum of the Natural History Society of New Brunswick, purchased in 1907, Saint John (now destroyed). Silver print on mounted card, by Arthur Gordon Leavitt, c. 1910. 13305 (1). Courtesy of the New Brunswick Museum, Saint John.

ety in her will of 1909, enabling the Society to pay off the mortgage on the building purchased to house the museum in 1907 (figure 3.3).[30] Repeated acts of gift giving allowed the members of the Ladies' Auxiliary to demand recognition and respect within the Natural History Society, while displaying feminine qualities expected at the time, such as selflessness and benevolence.

The Oriental Exhibition, held the second week of January 1924, is perhaps the most compelling example of the contributions made by women to the Museum of the Natural History Society. According to a newspaper report encouraging public attendance at the exhibition, 'the upper floor of the museum will be converted into an Oriental bazaar, and tea will be served by ladies in Oriental costumes.'[31] The photograph of three costumed women portrays their complex position within the museum during this event, showing them as simultaneously subordinate and significant (figure 3.1). In her analysis of nineteenth-century exhibitions in Canada, historian E.A. Heaman elaborates on the conflicted status of women, who were supposed to be both modestly retiring and easily available to the male gaze.[32] The three members of the Ladies' Auxiliary embody this contradiction, for they appear to be objects on display, akin to the banners and vases surrounding them. Yet the elegant women also assert themselves within the redecorated museum, claiming to be a crucial part of it. The impact of the latter strategy is suggested by the survival of this photograph, an important archival document that can shed light on the politics of female masquerade within the museum, as well as the regional response to and reinterpretation of the Orient.

The Oriental Exhibition was a success, apparently attracting both a large audience and the attention of local newspaper reporters. Another contemporary newspaper report described the 'curios' on display as well as the women who had given them to the Museum of the Natural History Society, including Dr Catherine Travis, Dr Mabel Hanington, and Loretta Shaw.[33] All were New Brunswick–born and either had worked, or were currently working, as foreign missionaries. After graduating from Johns Hopkins University in 1905, Dr Travis practised in Connecticut and Serbia before moving in 1918 to the Honan (or Henan) Province in China, where she worked at St Paul's Hospital in Kweitch until the late 1930s, eventually managing her own clinic. In 1923, Dr Travis sent gifts of clothing and other textiles directly from China to the Natural History Society, and these were displayed in the Oriental Exhibition, but she ultimately donated over two hundred Chinese objects to the institution, including silver finger-rings, ceramics, metalwork, lacquer ware, and dolls.[34] Dr Hanington was another physician who served as a medical missionary, in Fujian Province, South China from 1904 to 1918. When she returned to Canada, Dr Hanington joined the Ladies' Auxiliary and in 1919 offered twelve pieces of Chinese clothing and accessories to the Museum of the Natural History Society.[35] In contrast, Loretta Shaw, who was not a physician, served as a missionary in Japan, teaching at the Bishop Poole Girls' School in Osaka from 1905 to 1935. Altogether she provided the museum in Saint John with over four hundred Japanese artifacts, including costumes, ceramics, lacquer, books, and photographs. The newspaper article specifically noted that

3.4 Interior of the Museum of the Natural History Society of New Brunswick, Oriental Exhibition. Gelatin silver print mounted on card, January 1924. X16535. Courtesy of the New Brunswick Museum, Saint John, New Brunswick.

the bags donated by Shaw in 1924 were installed in the Oriental Exhibition, along with all of her previous gifts.[36] The temporary installation organized by the members of the Ladies' Auxiliary honoured these women, highlighting the diverse forms of Asian material culture that they had given to the Museum of the Natural History Society.

Not all of the objects displayed in the exhibition were gifts. A second photograph of the interior of the Museum of the Natural History Society shows the Oriental Exhibition without human inhabitants, portraying the same room adorned with wall hangings, and filled with Asian sculptures, vases, figurines, and an umbrella (figure 3.4). According to Andrea Kirkpatrick, former curator of Canadian and international art at the New Brunswick Museum, this image includes items that were never accessioned by the Natural History Society, and cannot be found in the current collections of the New Brunswick Museum. Similarly, most of the clothing worn by the three women who posed inside the exhibition cannot be identified with anything now in the museum.[37] Newspaper reports of the Oriental Exhibition in 1924 confirm that many of the objects surrounding the women were there temporarily, in keeping with the exhibition held at the York Theatre in 1906. Mrs Francis Ayscough, for example, lent a small collection of Chinese pottery and jade, which ranged from early mortuary figures to fifth-century Chun Yao pottery and a Ming Dynasty olive green bowl with floral decorations.[38] Born Florence Wheelock in Shanghai in 1875 to a Canadian father and American mother, Ayscough was a well-published sinologist and translator who gave academic talks around the world but spent most summers visiting family in the seaside village of St Andrews, New Brunswick, about 100 kilometres from Saint John.[39] Her possessions mingled with those owned by various members of the Ladies' Auxiliary, transforming the Museum of the Natural History Society into a simultaneously domestic, commercial, and exotic space.

This multi-layered event was informed by the international exhibitions which flourished primarily in North America and Western Europe from the 1840s through the middle of the twentieth century. A substantial scholarly literature examines how these displays participated in, among other things, the creation of modernity, national identity, and class distinctions.[40] The best-known example is the Great Exhibition, sometimes referred to as the Crystal Palace Exhibition, held in London in 1851, which promoted British industry alongside samples of both manufactures and culture from such countries as Australia, India, France, and China. Typically located in large metropolitan centres, these grand exhibitions often featured ethnographic installations of objects as well as living people, creating an exotic form of entertainment while confirming the 'superiority' and 'civilized' nature of the Western world.[41] Smaller exhibitions, primarily celebrating local manufactures and natural resources, were periodically held in such cities as Saint John.[42] In August of 1842, for example, the Mechanics' Institute – formed in 1838 to provide instruction by means of a museum, school, and lectures – hosted an exhibition of paintings, copies of the Elgin marbles, mechanical models, domestic manufactures, and 'a large collection of Indian dresses, war instruments, charms and a neatly finished wigwam, containing a little old fashioned Indian, who looked as wise as Solomon, but was as quiet as a mouse.'[43] This event notably included a 'Ladies' Bazaar,' though its contents remain unclear, with newspaper reports revealing only that it was beautifully decorated and featured the sale of slices of a sponge cake that measured thirteen feet six inches in circumference.[44] Many other substantial local and provincial exhibitions were held in either Saint John or Fredericton during the late nineteenth century, with members of the Natural History Society providing stuffed birds and samples of New Brunswick coals, albertite, bituminous shale, graphites, and gypsum to the exhibition of 1883, as well as to various world's fairs.[45] The Oriental Exhibition was thus one in a long line of similar spectacles in the city and the province, though it uniquely combined an ethnographic focus on Asian products with the decorating and food sales associated with a traditional ladies' bazaar.

Like the ladies' bazaar or women's pavilion included in many provincial, national, and international exhibitions, the Oriental Exhibition celebrated feminine accomplishments.[46] In the surviving photograph of the Museum of the Natural History Society, the wall hangings on the right side, luxurious Persian rug on the back wall, and tables laden with porcelain statuettes, ceramic vases, and dolls create a somewhat crowded interior. A single page of written text appears beside one of the banners, but the installation is generally lacking in labels, implying that visitors were meant to experience the overall effect of the transformed space, engaging with individual objects on their own terms. The women's work is nevertheless visible in the care taken with the display, its contents signified as precious by being placed in cases and under protective bell jars. By arranging these ceramics and textiles, the members of the Ladies' Auxiliary refashioned the museum into a domestic interior – a decidedly female space – demanding respect for their decorating skills. A similar demand was made explicitly in the annual report of the Ladies' Auxiliary in 1922, when the secretary-treasurer adopted a rather defensive tone to argue that 'our usual donation to the Society took the form of decorating the lecture room, a worthy undertaking.'[47] By staging the Oriental Exhibition, the ladies redecorated another space, reinforcing but also surpassing their previous activities. During the exhibition, the women curated the museum, displacing, however briefly, the minerals and stuffed mammals that had for the most part been acquired and arranged by men.

Even as the museum was recreated as a feminine space, it was also commercialized and literally called a bazaar in the newspaper report described above. Patrons paid an entry fee to view the installation and were then invited to disburse additional funds for the tea and cakes offered by the ladies. Unlike the earlier loan exhibitions in which the women participated, during the Oriental Exhibition the sale of food took place directly inside the museum building, celebrating food production and consumption as legitimate activities crucial to the social and financial existence of the Natural History Society. Commercial exchange was invoked less directly when members of the Ladies' Auxiliary installed their personal possessions within the museum, and wore the exotic clothing that they had purchased for just such costumed events. The women exhibited their consumption of commodities, in this case without donating them to the museum, while also displaying their taste and refinement in a public forum. This combination of cultural display with commercialism was equally central to the success of larger fairs, though scholar Tony Bennett has argued that bodily and intellectual activities, such as art appreciation, were gradually separated from one another, with the midway zone of amusement located at the edges of 'more serious' cultural displays.[48] At the vastly smaller Oriental Exhibition of 1924, cultural and physical consumption were barely distinguished from each other; on the contrary, their mutual dependence was revealed.

The careful installation of personal possessions alongside those loaned by Ayscough and donated by missionaries enhanced the public profile of members of the Ladies' Auxiliary, associating them with respected, educated women. More than avid collectors, Ayscough, Dr Travis, Dr Hannington, and Shaw regularly published accounts and gave public lectures about their experiences in Asia. Dr Travis, for example, described her work in such missionary bulletins as *The Living Message*, while Shaw delivered a talk entitled 'Japan and Its Problems' at a meeting of the Natural History Society in 1911.[49] Ayscough was the only figure to attain an international reputation, giving invited talks throughout North America. According to art historian Catherine Mackenzie, the esteemed sinologist lectured while dressed in Asian clothing. When Ayscough spoke in 1923 about Chinese poetry and culture before the Women's Canadian Club in Saint John, she wore a 'gown of scarlet silk with beautiful embroideries' that was 'such as those worn by the Japanese of today and exactly similar to the gowns worn by the women of China in 700 A.D.'[50] Ayscough's appearance was part of her scholarly performance, which veered toward the theatrical, much to the apparent delight of audiences. Lacking a formal university education, the translator and linguist displayed her embodied knowledge of Asian culture, gained from having lived half of her life in Shanghai, where she had received private instruction from Chinese masters.[51] Ayscough's informed wardrobe choices would have been among the most recent and memorable displays of Chinese costume in Saint John, addressing an audience similar to that at the Oriental Exhibition. Although taking up the role of hostesses instead of pedagogues, and wearing inventive rather than authentic wardrobes, the costumed members of the Ladies' Auxiliary could have reinforced such references to female learning.

These women certainly promoted female knowledge at other events, notably when they gave talks as part of their association with the Natural History Society. Lectures had been an important part of the Society from its inception. Members met every Tuesday evening to hear a presentation on botany, geology, or zoology, among other topics, usually given by a prominent male member of the group, such as George F. Matthew, but also by invited male guests. The only reference to a female speaker appears in a Saint John newspaper, the *Daily Sun*, on 7 March 1894. A brief column notes that a member of the Ladies' Auxiliary, Miss Eleanor Robinson, had presented at the regular meeting her article on Dr Silas T. Rand, a nineteenth-century missionary who had worked among the Micmac and documented their language.[52] Perhaps in response to their exclusion from speaking at the regular meetings, the members of the Ladies' Auxiliary initiated their own lecture series in 1899. Held on Thursday afternoons, it was eventually named the Kate M. Matthew Lecture Course, after the long-standing president of the Ladies' Auxiliary. In this series, female lecturers spoke on a range of topics, including birds, fossils, and specific objects in the museum's collections. Many women discussed their recent travels, describing the architecture and culture of Egypt, France, Spain, or Japan. In 1908, Mrs F.A. Foster's talk, entitled 'My Impressions of Paris,' for example, covered cathedrals and art galleries, while advising her listeners to visit Paris in May and stay for a month with a French family.[53]

The women of the Ladies' Auxiliary positioned these public lectures within the framework of charitable fundraising, charging entry fees, which were then donated to the Natural History Society. The afternoon talks were well attended, according to the minutes, and about nineteen were given each winter, with the last presentation of each month aimed at children. In October of 1915, President Katherine Matthew portrayed the lecture series as a gift to the public as well as an educational offering in keeping with the primary mandate of the Natural History Society.[54] These lectures were clearly social occasions, involving food consumption, musical interludes, and ethnically relevant costumes. The president and the other members of the Ladies' Auxiliary implied that socializing, eating, and listening to lectures were complementary educational activities. Yet the lecture series also provided members of the Ladies' Auxiliary with the chance to pursue self-promotion, both within and outside of the organization. The authors and titles of the lectures were listed in the annual report provided by the ladies, which began to be printed in 1903 along with other reports in the *Bulletin of the Natural History Society of New Brunswick*.[55] This journal, published on a nearly annual basis between 1882 and 1914, was disseminated to all members of the Society, as well as many international organizations. Several of the lectures given by women were either summarized briefly or published in full in one of the Saint John newspapers, particularly between 1904 and 1914.[56] Despite being framed in terms of benevolence, these talks potentially transgressed the hierarchical structure of the Natural History Society by positioning women as authority figures and making a public display of female autonomy.

In some ways the Oriental Exhibition continued to promote female agency, at least in terms of museum curating and food production. Yet the women did not actually give lectures in relation to the show. On the contrary, they served visitors while dressed in Asian costume. Like the Aboriginal man who in 1842 was compared to a mouse, the members of the Ladies' Auxiliary were part of the exhibition; they were specimens on display. Unlike the man seated in the wigwam, however, these women were white and middle-class, overtly playing the role of the exotic other. It is difficult to determine whether this Asian role-playing highlighted, reconfirmed, or undermined the women's historically marginalized status within the Natural History Society. It may have worked in tandem with the assertions of female agency discussed earlier, counteracting them with non-threatening images of supposedly docile women. According to Stacey Loughrey Sloboda, the eighteenth-century Chinese room created by literary critic and hostess Elizabeth Montagu in London was designed to forestall potential criticism of her 'intrusion into the masculine sphere of intellectual community.'[57] Perhaps the female autonomy staged in the Oriental Exhibition was tempered when the women adopted subservient poses, offering themselves up to the scrutiny of visitors.

At the same time, this kind of role-playing was highly fashionable during the early twentieth century, when white women engaged with various forms of Orientalism. Curator Juliet Kinchin describes how Victorian women used the same fabric for their clothes and the upholstery in their drawing rooms to express a unified character, while aristocratic bohemian hostesses of the 1920s greeted guests wearing Asian clothing, including Chinese sleeveless dragon coats, to convey their creativity.[58] Other scholars contend that during the nineteenth and early twentieth centuries, European women donned Asian costume in order to adopt masculine postures. Cheang, in particular, discusses how British women wore the oversized robes formerly owned by Chinese men during the 1920s, replacing the absent male body with a modern female body that remained feminine even as its boundaries were extended.[59] The looseness of the Chinese coats contrasted with form-fitting Victorian fashions, creating a sense of what Cheang calls the 'emancipation of the body.'[60] In North America, comfortable Chinese clothing caused a scandal as early as 1915, when the *San Francisco Chronicle* pictured young white women wearing long silk coats over pantaloons, worriedly asking, 'Will American Women Adopt the Chinese Costume?'[61] Contemporary literature associated Chinese textiles with both pleasure and non-conformity, enabling them to become 'a part of defiant modern femininities, focused on a new generation of increasingly independent women who smoked, wore make-up, bobbed their hair and sought access to higher education, professional training, and the vote.'[62]

The central woman in the New Brunswick photograph from 1924 is, however, sporting a coat and skirt resembling those worn by affluent Chinese women – not men – during the Qing Dynasty (1644–1911). The tapestry on the left of this image depicts a royal lady wearing a rather similar coat and skirt, reasserting the link between the New Brunswick woman and the material objects on display. The elaborate headdress of the costumed member of the Ladies' Auxiliary is easier to identify, for it looks like the phoenix crown worn only by the empress.[63] Listed in the accession records as a 'bridal crown' from South China made of brass, beads, and a kingfisher feather, it was one of the objects given to the Museum of the Natural History Society by Dr Hanington in 1919 (figure 3.5). According to Nicole Brouillet, formerly a curatorial assistant at the New Brunswick Museum, the crown is based on the coronet associated with empresses of the Ming Dynasty and Han rule, but is simpler than those worn by high-ranking women.[64] The unidentified member of the Ladies' Auxiliary had assembled an eclectic costume, combining female clothing of different ranks designed for various functions and from distinct eras in Chinese history. She played at being a

3.5 Bridal crown, South China, brass, beads, and Kingfisher feather, likely Qing Dynasty, 34 × 23 × 32 cm. Gift of Dr Mabel Louis Hanington, 1919. 1873 (42) [1]. Courtesy of the New Brunswick Museum, Saint John, New Brunswick.

Chinese lady/bride while serving tea at the Oriental Exhibition in a manner that would seem to have reinforced rather than undermined traditional female roles.

The theatrical nature of the 1924 photograph suggests that the female hostesses at the Oriental Exhibition drew attention to the artifice of their temporary Asian identities. This posture was standard during the early twentieth century, when historical and cultural authenticity was not central to the pleasures of racial masquerade. Instead of basing their appearances on specific Asian male or female figures, the members of the Ladies' Auxiliary mimicked other white women, drawing attention to what Yoshihara calls their 'race knowledge.'[65] In her study of early twentieth-century American Orientalisms, the American studies professor argues that when white women portrayed Asian roles on stage in, for example, the popular opera *Madame Butterfly* – first performed in New York City in 1900 – their whiteness was foregrounded rather than disguised or displaced. According to her, such 'performances and the debates around them demonstrate that these acts of racial-crossing were as much about performances of white American womanhood as they were about enactments of Asian femininity.'[66] With their Asian costume, the New Brunswick ladies recreated the Orientalist tea houses then popular at international exhibitions and in major cities.[67] Since 1898, Vantine's Tea Room in New York, for example, had featured white women who dressed in kimonos and provided information about the art of making tea while surrounded by Asian furnishings.[68] Wealthier socialites had private Oriental tea houses designed on their own properties, and were known to host Chinese costume balls.[69] In the end, by dressing in Asian costume the members of the Ladies' Auxiliary played at being urbane socialites, dramatizing the privileges awarded to them as white, middle-class women.

The Asian theme of the exhibition may furthermore have facilitated the women's entrepreneurship. During the late nineteenth and early twentieth centuries, Asian visual and material culture was increasingly used not only in the décor of shops and tea houses, but also in various advertisements in Europe as well as North America.[70] In many cases consumption was conflated with the image of the Asian woman. According to Cheang's research, during the late nineteenth century in Britain representations of the Oriental woman were used to eroticize commodities and equate consumption with pleasure.[71] Having little to do with actual Asian women, this imagery was a construction of the Orient conflating desire, gender, and the exotic with the expanding marketplace. Within this broader context, the costumes worn by members of the Ladies' Auxiliary carried yet another layer of meaning: they drew on this popular association between Asian women and consumerism in a way that could simultaneously enhance and elide the capitalist function of the exhibition. The ladies presented the Oriental Exhibition as a genteel social occasion hosted by middle-class white women who modelled consumption as both an entertaining and charitable form of role-playing.

Was the Oriental Exhibition nevertheless a (domestic) feminist space?[72] The previous discussion suggests that this description would not be entirely accurate, and yet feminist politics were present in the exhibition. As a missionary working in Japan from 1905 to 1935, Shaw was a passionate advocate of women's emancipation, as well as a supporter of suffrage for Canadian women.[73] The Asian objects she donated to the Museum of the Natural History Society could not have conveyed these politics, and yet some of those given by Dr Hanington were infused with feminist critique, though her personal political positions are not as well known. In 1919, Dr Hanington donated to the Museum of the Natural History Society various Chinese shoes meant to be worn by women with bound feet, and this apparel was displayed in the Oriental Exhibition (figure 3.6).[74] A newspaper report of 1923 noted that after Miss M.E. Travis of Hampton, New Brunswick, returned from visiting her sister Dr Catherine Travis in China, she too had donated valuable gifts to the Natural History Society, including a lady's shoe which 'by its tiny size gives some idea of the torture the women endure in conforming to the ideals of beauty of their country.'[75] At this time, the very appearance of bound-feet shoes was linked with a critique of female body modification. The international exhibitions held in Philadelphia in 1876 and St Louis in 1904 had featured comparable shoes as objects revealing the uncivilized nature of Chinese society. Even the Nanyang exhibition of 1910, which was both organized and hosted by the Chinese government, portrayed the shoes negatively, arguing that the practice of foot binding hampered women's ability to contribute to the economy and was a national disgrace.[76] The inclusion of the tiny shoes in the Oriental Exhibition in Saint John could easily have been understood as a form of either feminist or ethnic critique.

Many members of the Ladies' Auxiliary were politically active. Emma Fiske, the outspoken woman who had demanded full membership within the Natural History Society, was also involved in the Ladies' Auxiliary of the Temperance Union and the Women's Enfranchisement

3.6 Shoe for bound foot, China, Qing Dynasty (1644–1911), cotton, silk, dyes, leather, wood, and metallic paper, 9 × 4 × 8 cm. Gift of Dr Mabel Louis Hanington, 1919 (1871). 1871 (2) [1]. Courtesy of the New Brunswick Museum, Saint John, New Brunswick.

Association.[77] Other associate members participated in local charities that benefited women and children, and as a whole the Ladies' Auxiliary was affiliated with the Saint John chapter of the National Council of Women, an international organization promoting the protection of women workers and supporting the suffrage movement.[78] In 1920 the members of the Ladies' Auxiliary had voted to endorse 'such measures, which are of interest to women, as the "Minimum Wage Act," and "Mother's Pensions."'[79] Although committed to women's enfranchisement, for the most part the ladies acted in accord with their white, middle-class perspective, supporting women's maternal roles with their charity work. The Auxiliary members implied that other women should have access to the lifestyle that they already enjoyed, including the freedom to choose their own clothing.

The Orientalism espoused in the Oriental Exhibition of 1924 is difficult to pin down, conveying female submission as well as assertion. Members of the Ladies' Auxiliary mimicked 'exotic' Asian women to move beyond the limits of their given roles without appearing to do so. These women claimed the right to appropriate the culture of others, participating in the imperialism of the museum to enhance their position as privileged white women. Challenging gendered roles went hand-in-hand with assertions of racial superiority. Yet the ladies also redefined the museum's space, transforming it into a domestic interior in a way that made feminine decorating skills central to the institution. The eclectic nature of the Oriental Exhibition undermined any emphasis on classification and chronology within the museum, replacing it with offers of bodily consumption and a hint of feminist politics. Though this alteration might have been transgressive, it was also temporary and, in many ways, reinforced dominant hierarchies of gender, class, and race. In contrast, during the 1930s Alice Lusk Webster strove to install Asian art in the New Brunswick Museum according to conventional museum standards. Her interventions were permanent and, in the end, potentially more threatening to the status quo.

Alice Lusk Webster and the New Brunswick Museum, 1929–53

After the New Brunswick Museum was founded in 1929, members of the Ladies' Auxiliary of the Natural History Society renamed their group the Women's Auxiliary and planned to remain active.[80] Even so, the women so prominent in fundraising during the nineteenth and early twentieth centuries practically disappear from the records that survive from this transitional period. In contrast, many male administrators of the Natural History Society retained key positions at the new museum, and are present in the archival documents until the late 1940s. This continuity was carefully orchestrated by the men, who had always wanted to create a provincial museum in Saint John, having included this goal in their mission statement of 1862. It was not until the 1920s, when grandiose institutions were linked with the attainment of civility, and considered a necessity in any established city, that New

Brunswick bureaucrats recognized the value of a provincial museum. The City Corporation of Saint John then donated $100,000, and the provincial government $150,000, toward a new building, sums considered insufficient by members of the Natural History Society.[81] The New Brunswick Museum received its sanction in 1929 primarily because the Society promised to forward all of its possessions to the new institution, including the building purchased in 1907, the collections, and more than $28,000 in funds. The members nevertheless insisted on retaining control, asserting that 'the Council of the Natural History Society shall have a prominent part in the management of said [new] museum.'[82] A number of long-standing male administrators were placed on the board of the New Brunswick Museum, and William MacIntosh, an entomologist who had been curator of the Museum of the Natural History Society since 1898, was named its first director.

The new building, begun in 1930 and finished in 1933, was a large structure with an imposing neo-classical facade inspired by a wing of the Metropolitan Museum in New York City.[83] This purpose-built museum was distinctive from the modified family home in which the collections of the Natural History Society had been displayed since 1907. Despite providing funds for the impressive new edifice, the local and provincial governments offered little continuous financial support, forcing the New Brunswick Museum to rely on such wealthy patrons as Dr J.C. Webster and his wife, Alice Lusk Webster. The Websters brought many changes to the museum, dividing it into three separate departments – Canadian History, Natural History, and Art – instead of privileging natural history specimens. This modification alarmed MacIntosh and other members of the Natural History Society, leading them into conflict with the Websters. According to Dr Webster, the resulting battle pitted the old guard – namely, members of the Society – against progressives like him who were striving to reform the museum.[84] He depicted the female members of the Women's Auxiliary as part of the old guard, and in a letter written in 1934 to H.O. McCurry, assistant director of the National Gallery of Art in Ottawa, Webster argued that 'one of our jobs is to clean up the situation in Saint John inherited from the past. There has been a Women's Auxiliary which has gradually ceased to be important, but as it contains some of the social leaders there disbandonment [sic] has to be considered most carefully.'[85]

Lusk Webster was similarly unimpressed with the Women's Auxiliary, making it clear that she had no intention of joining it. As the honorary curator of the newly formed Art Department, she approached the museum quite differently, deciding to amass important historical examples of art and craft, representing as many cultures as possible. Lusk Webster studied large international museums, including the Metropolitan Museum in New York City, drawing on them to create carefully labelled permanent displays, professionally installed in museum-grade cases.[86] Her vision of the ideal museum was distinct from that of the members of the Ladies' Auxiliary, who in their Oriental Exhibition had combined historical periods and different cultural traditions in a manner designed primarily for aesthetic effect. Lusk Webster weeded through the objects that had been donated to the Museum of the Natural History Society, storing what she called the 'tawdry' examples while preserving the few items she judged of good quality.[87] Like her husband, the honorary curator strove to make a clean sweep of the New Brunswick Museum, clearing it of old-fashioned displays, acquisition methods, and museum women.

In lieu of fundraising or straightforward donations, for the most part Lusk Webster expanded the collections of the Art Department by means of strategic gift exchanges. In 1934, she offered Currelly 17 fine Japanese paintings and a few other pictures owned by her family in exchange for 16 boxes full of Egyptian, Greek, Roman, Palestinian, and Asian material, some of them weighing as much as 311 pounds, according to the shipping records.[88] The 450 objects accessioned into the New Brunswick Museum included a Predynastic earthenware vase, a Roman lamp from the second century A.D. adorned with a dolphin and a trident, a Honan Temmoku-ware bowl, and many examples of Chinese porcelain. Other items were more practical in nature, such as the sample of a grain of trilicum wheat from 4000 B.C., two bone dice from the third or fourth century A.D., and bronze hairpins from about the same time.

By focusing on exchange, Lusk Webster reshaped the methods employed by the male administrators of the Natural History Society during the nineteenth century. Whereas the men had sent gifts to established organizations in order to create social connections, she rarely approached strangers and instead exploited previously established social links. As the men did, she sometimes offered a gift before requesting something in kind. In a letter written in December of 1939 to Miss Greenaway, Currelly's assistant at the Royal Ontario Museum of Archaeology, Lusk Webster casually mentioned that a box of books would be sent out shortly after Christmas as 'a *present* and Mr. Currelly can dispose of them as he sees fit, but if he can get me a copy of Bishop White's book on the tomb tiles as a quid pro quo, I should be glad to have it for the Library.'[89] She framed the gift to Currelly within the context of the holidays, and then mentioned the potential reciprocal gift from him as if it was a casual afterthought. In contrast to the late nineteenth-century trades between the Natural History Society of New Brunswick and the Field Columbian Museum analysed in chapter 1, there were no open discussions of monetary amounts between Lusk Webster and Currelly. In her chatty letters to Currelly, the honorary curator typically asked about family matters, and reported on the latest activities at the New Brunswick Museum before requesting specific items from his museum. She ended one lengthy letter by mentioning that another curator in Toronto 'told me that you had an extra Roman watering pot which I should be glad to have.'[90]

In her appealing letters, Lusk Webster was careful to position herself as a novice in need of Currelly's guidance, rather than as his intellectual equal. In a letter written to Currelly in 1934, she confessed: 'I realize fully that the absence of training is a handicap, but I am an apt pupil, and with your help and moral support, I hope to accomplish something for this benighted Province.'[91] By describing her dependence on Currelly's expertise, Lusk Webster not only potentially flattered her friend, but also portrayed him as a fellow benefactor of New Brunswick. She encouraged the director of the Royal Ontario Museum of Archaeology to take a paternalistic attitude toward both herself and the New Brunswick Museum, adopting the role of a generous patron of the arts able to help a province poorer than his native Ontario. The few surviving letters written by Currelly do not condescend to Lusk Webster, but simply answer her questions in a straightforward manner. The honorary curator nevertheless continued to recognize the hierarchical context of her relationship with him, and regularly ended her letters with expressions of gratitude. After elaborating a 'wish list' of objects including Greek, Syrian, Palestinian, French, German, Spanish, and Italian material, she again deferred to Currelly, writing: 'Please do not think that I am clamouring for all these things – I am perfectly reasonable and shall take what you find it convenient to give me – and be thankful.'[92] During the nineteenth century, the male administrators of the Natural History Society of New Brunswick had also been happy to accept what was given to them in exchange for their geological specimens, as long as it was different from what was already in the museum. Although Lusk Webster adopted a similar position, she always made specific requests for items needed to complete her chronological survey of the history of art and craft.

By 1935, Lusk Webster had arranged her objects in fourteen cases that contained mostly Chinese, Korean, and Japanese pottery. She strove to represent systematically the major historical periods, styles, and nations with at least one visual example, creating logical connections between the objects displayed. Lusk Webster wanted the objects to tell a story of change and development through their careful selection and juxtaposition. In contrast to the installation methods used in the Oriental Exhibition, she rejected decoration and domesticity. According to art historian Craig Clunas, twentieth-century museums increasingly focused on taxonomy, particularly in relation to items of luxury consumption originally designed for the Chinese domestic market. He contends that by classifying Asian clothing, ceramics, wine jars, and personal religious items, museum curators strove to undermine their strong association with femininity and domestic use. Because the institutional status of museums was defined against what was done in the home, Clunas argues, curators erased the function of Chinese art and placed it in an art historical narrative.[93] Lusk Webster clearly participated in this re-evaluation of Asian material culture, committing herself to both the academic identity and professionalization of the New Brunswick Museum. Drawing on the latest scholarly publications and guided by Currelly, she wrote labels that were brief and factual, neglecting to mention her patronage.[94] The Mandarin coats and priests' robes that Lusk Webster had acquired hung lifeless in carefully arranged cases; they did not adorn her body as she welcomed visitors in the manner of a hostess at the Oriental Exhibition of 1924.

Lusk Webster modelled her collections on the elevated tastes of connoisseurs, embracing the earlier, exclusive periods of Chinese art instead of highlighting the more recent Qing period admired by her predecessors in the Ladies' Auxiliary. In 1935 one of the cases in the Art Department was filled with ceramics from the Han dynasty (206 B.C.–A.D. 220), and two displayed pottery and tomb figures dating from the Tang period (A.D. 618–906) (figures 3.7 and 3.8).[95] Only a small part of one case was devoted to Qing ceramics. According to Clunas, elite collectors were less interested in Qing porcelain after the First World War, though it had been the primary focus of an early generation of collectors.[96] Art historian Stacey Pierson argues that during the early twentieth century, Qing ceramics continued to be associated with wealth and good taste, but more historical objects began appealing to the specialized kind of collector.[97] In keeping with this trend, Lusk Webster distinguished her collection from popular tastes, promoting an elevated

3.7 Case in the Art Department of the New Brunswick Museum, c. 1930s–1940s, featuring Chinese ceramics from the Han Dynasty (206 BCE–220 CE), including an earthenware hill jar, 24.1 x 19.7 cm. NBM–F41–5. Courtesy of the New Brunswick Museum, Saint John, New Brunswick.

understanding of Chinese ceramics in the Art Department and refusing the items of Qing material offered to her by Currelly.

Yet Lusk Webster could not ignore the desires of museum visitors and simply impose her elite values on them. She sometimes recognized middle-brow tastes, writing to Currelly in 1937: 'You were right as usual – the average visitor gloats over this very inferior exhibit [of Qing ceramics]. I ask you very humbly, what you can *now* give me to strengthen this group.'[98] The honorary curator reluctantly included more material culture from the Qing period in the Art Department, bowing to the preferences of the uninformed despite voicing her disdain for them.

Nor could she erase the gendered connotations of the objects in the Art Department without undermining her own position within the museum. Even as Lusk Webster presented the collections in terms of

3.8 Case in the Art Department of the New Brunswick Museum, c. 1930s–1940s, featuring Chinese ceramics from the Tang Dynasty (618–907), including tomb figures. NBM–F41–1. Courtesy of the New Brunswick Museum, Saint John, New Brunswick.

periods and dates, her personal history suffused the gallery. In addition to trading family heirlooms to acquire numerous items, the honorary curator made occasional donations. In a letter likely dating from 1946, Lusk Webster revealed to Currelly that she had reconditioned her family's antique Hepplewhite china cupboard and installed it in the museum, using its shelves to display porcelain and its drawers to store textiles.[99] Surviving lecture notes furthermore reveal that she spoke about herself when describing the objects in the Art Department. Even as Lusk Webster avoided adopting a position of authority in relation to Currelly, she did not hesitate to do so while giving guided tours of her installations.[100] Lusk Webster personally identified with many of the objects in the Art Department, narrating to audiences the ingenious methods that she had used to acquire them. In a kind of return of the repressed, references to both domesticity and female embodiment resurfaced in these lectures.[101]

When Lusk Webster performed within the museum, her speeches rivalled those of Currelly, who finally published accounts of his extensive collecting activities in a 1956 book entitled *I Brought the Ages Home*. This autobiography features stories of Currelly travelling through Egypt, Palestine, and Syria, outwitting unscrupulous dealers and avaricious locals in order to obtain authentic international objects for museums.[102] Lusk Webster similarly portrayed herself as an intrepid collector who found opportunities in foreign lands, though she mentioned the relatively tame England and France rather than the exotic locales frequented by Currelly. In letters to the director of the Royal Ontario Museum of Archaeology, interviews with local newspaper reporters, and speeches given to museum visitors, Lusk Webster described how in 1935 she had managed to secure early British-Roman and English material from the Guildhall Museum in London, including a fifteenth-century child's shoe, Roman nails, and a small pottery lamp.[103] She repeatedly boasted about having 'wangled' a thirteenth-century ball-flower from the dean at the Chapter of Westminster Abbey for the collections of the New Brunswick Museum.[104] In these self-presentations, Lusk Webster appeared as an assertive and independent woman, apparently unlike the nineteenth-century ladies involved with the Museum of the Natural History Society, though they too had given public talks about their foreign travels.

Sending potentially contradictory messages, Lusk Webster highlighted the ways in which her traditionally feminine housekeeping skills had enabled her to build the Art Department. She described her physical labour in the museum, which in the 1930s had included unpacking the hundreds of items shipped from Toronto, carrying them upstairs, installing them, and then sweeping the floors afterwards.[105] Lusk Webster explained how she had also painstakingly repaired the cast-off items sent to her. She had written to friends and relations in New York and Washington asking them to forward to the museum old lace and chipped teacups if they were otherwise of high quality. Lusk Webster claimed to have acquired her most valuable objects by raiding the 'rag-bags and dust-bins of my friends.'[106] In an undated letter written before 1935, she elaborated: 'I am the rummage sale and thrift shop rolled into one – I can make use of the most unlikely things ... fragments of old brocade – too far gone for service ... could be cleaned and mended for my textile study collection ... Broken crockery is my specialty – 12 specimens of Hang Hsi and Chien Lung porcelain rose like a Phoenix from two shoe boxes containing the sweepings of the China cabinet of Mrs. Beeknan Hoppins, overturned by a careless maid.'[107] Emphasizing her thriftiness, the honorary curator described how she had stayed up until the early hours of the morning, meticulously pasting the broken porcelain back together. Lusk Webster's letters and public speeches were filled with similarly heroic tales that portray her simultaneously as a thrifty, hard-working housewife and an adventurous archaeologist, who, like Currelly, rescued objects from those who did not truly appreciate them.

In keeping with such references to domesticity, Lusk Webster continued to value interior decoration, arranging the Art Department according to aesthetics as well as category and chronology. Her detailed letters to Currelly conveyed frustration at her inability to achieve rational displays based on coverage and classification, mainly because of economic restraints. In March of 1935, Lusk Webster confessed to using a loan collection of Oriental rugs simply to cover the blank walls in the sparse 'European' section of the gallery, without knowing how to identify or label them.[108] In 1939, Lusk Webster worried that her efforts to 'establish a relationship' between the items in her French case had failed miserably, for it contained a rather haphazard collection, including a Merovingian buckle, medieval tiles, a page from a fourteenth-century manuscript, an illuminated letter of the fifteenth century, a sixteenth-century fire brick, and various samples of porcelain faience from the eighteenth and nineteenth centuries.[109] Although the honorary curator hoped that these installations were only temporary measures, she wanted her cases to be visually pleasing as well as historically accurate. When discussing her Ming case in July of 1938, Lusk Webster complained that 'the brown earthenware tea caddy and the small turquoise blue glaze jar do not balance.'[110] She noted that her single Tang amphora did not 'fit in comfortably' with the items placed beside it.[111] Sending photographs of each case to Currelly, she asked him for substitutes that would fill empty spaces in her chronological displays but would also harmonize with the other objects in terms of colour, pattern, and scale. In the end, Lusk Webster often arranged objects according to aesthetic rather than educational principles, in a manner recalling the installation methods used by members of the Ladies' Auxiliary.

Also as the Ladies' Auxiliary had done, Lusk Webster insisted that her labour was not for personal gain. Whereas the ladies had contributed to the Natural History Society, Lusk Webster claimed to work for the people of New Brunswick, particularly those 'men and women, boys and girls, who [were] groping blindly for the finer things in life' in the 'backwoods' of New Brunswick.[112] Instead of focusing on women's voting rights or maternal benefits, Lusk Webster hoped to improve the taste and increase the cultural knowledge of what she considered the average New Brunswicker. Though she was not literally a missionary like the female donors featured in the Oriental Exhibition, Lusk Webster portrayed herself as a cultural missionary, bringing civilization to the well-meaning but uneducated populace of New Brunswick. Her method was colonialist in nature, and she built her own empire in the Art Department, hoping that her mostly Asian objects would establish her values within the province.

Despite portraying her labour as a gift, the Art Department directly benefited Lusk Webster. She gave authoritative lectures both within the New Brunswick Museum and throughout the province, acts that were remembered after her death. A 1953 obituary in Saint John's *Evening Times-Globe* claimed that Lusk Webster's passing was a 'distinct loss to the cultural life of New Brunswick' because she had made a 'significant contribution to this province's historical heritage.'[113] Even today Lusk Webster is credited on the website of the New Brunswick Museum with amassing the decorative arts collections, whereas the contributions made by the members of the Ladies' Auxiliary are largely forgotten.[114]

Yet the elite form of Orientalism promoted by Lusk Webster was just as contradictory as the version promoted at the Oriental Exhibition in 1924, both enabling and limiting her goals. The professional displays constructed by Lusk Webster eventually earned her the begrudging respect of male administrators, including her own husband.[115] During the 1930s and 1940s, Lusk Webster's efforts had not been well received by these men, who considered the Art Department an ornamental and largely unimportant part of the New Brunswick Museum. In contrast to the Canadian History and Natural History Departments, the Art Department received no internal funding. Lusk Webster was personally responsible for financing all of its furnishings, cases, and collections; eventually she even paid staff salaries, a point discussed in chapter 5. When she began installing hundreds of Asian and some European art objects on the main floor of the New Brunswick Museum around 1935, the director of the museum became extremely upset. MacIntosh had planned to place his extensive collection of stuffed New Brunswick mammals in the same large gallery space. In a friendly but firm manner, Lusk Webster convinced him to move a smaller version of his collection into the basement.[116] MacIntosh and other former members of the Natural History Society nevertheless continued to resent the fact that international, decorative art objects had displaced references to the natural resources of New Brunswick. They viewed Lusk Webster as an outsider promoting an elite vision of New Brunswick that was at odds with their own. Lusk Webster and her Art Department survived largely because of her wealth, social position, and sheer determination. She continued to fight for increased recognition and respect within the New Brunswick Museum until her death in 1953.

Lusk Webster's letters to Currelly indicate that she deferred to the male administrators, attempting to flatter them – the same way she related to Currelly himself.[117] She adopted a conciliatory stance at meetings, in contrast to the more aggressive identity conveyed during her gallery tours and lectures. Lusk Webster's performance of gender within the New Brunswick Museum therefore shifted according to context. When organizing the Art Department, she identified with male experts, endorsing the stereotypically masculine values of rationality and classification while downplaying such traditionally feminine concerns as decoration and consumption. Yet when signs of Lusk Webster's physical and domestic contributions resurfaced temporarily during her lectures, she reinforced the gendered norms of her era, displaying the value of women's work. In the manner of the members of the Ladies' Auxiliary, the honorary curator often created her identities in relation to Asian art, confirming racial hierarchies and appropriating the material culture of others in order to participate in the museum structure. She asserted herself as an elite white woman in relation to her careful arrangements of historical Asian ceramics. Even as Lusk Webster may ultimately have fared better than the Ladies' Auxiliary in terms of historical memory, this recognition came at a cost. Consider the two photographs introduced in the first paragraph of his chapter: though the women at the Oriental Exhibition are now anonymous, the image of the Art Department features neatly arranged objects, excluding any reference to the physical presence of Lusk Webster. By rejecting female embodiment and consumption, Lusk Webster's Orientalist displays not only helped to erase the important contributions made by her female predecessors, but may also have eclipsed her own role in building the New Brunswick Museum.

Conclusions

In this chapter, I suggested various ways in which the established system of gift giving enabled women's participation. For members of the Ladies' Auxiliary, donating objects to the Museum of the Natural History Society gave them the opportunity to be recorded in the organization's official documents. The women also decorated the museum, staging their costumed bodies within it to claim space in an unthreatening manner. While Lusk Webster continued to perform feminine duties linked with decorating and good taste, she took on a role previously denied to women in the museum, selecting and arranging objects for the permanent collections. Her methods relied heavily on the rituals of gift giving, using her social connections to arrange exchanges that promoted her elite values in the museum. She, too, performed within the institution, sometimes adopting the role of male connoisseur and at other times acting as an ambitious housewife, especially during those lectures which highlighted what was excluded from the cases: her embodied knowledge of the objects and the labour she had undertaken to acquire them.

My historical analysis indicates that the professionalization of museums included the suppression of women's long-standing contributions as well as their 'feminine' identities. This dynamic may continue to inform both contemporary museums and debates within the field of critical museum theory. As discussed in previous chapters, it is now commonplace for theorists to denounce the commodification of the museum, decrying the staged entertainments and 'blockbuster' exhibitions that increasingly appear in institutions both large and small. The main targets are corporate officials who use the spaces to promote their values and their products, but naysayers also claim that museums are newly devoted to visual pleasure and entertainment rather than to education – a point undermined by the discussion of fundraising events in this chapter.[118] Though the contemporary situation is by no means the same as that of the late nineteenth and early twentieth century, an historical view can be useful. The Ladies' Auxiliary of the Natural History Society held what Lusk Webster called 'pink teas,' bake sales, and special exhibitions to fund the museum building, its furnishings, and educational technologies. These social occasions ensured the development of the museum. When critics bluntly dismiss 'blockbuster' exhibitions and flashy fundraisers, they may do more than resent the overt presence of capitalism within the supposedly sacrosanct museum space. They may also inadvertently neglect women's role in museum building and reinforce long-standing gendered hierarchies, dismissing consumption as a 'feminine,' bodily activity, while assuming that references to decoration and fashion must be removed from museums in order for them to retain their professional, educational (and, by implication, masculine) authority.

Chapter Four

Libraries and Museums: Shifting Relationships, 1830–1940

In 2004 the Parliament of Canada merged the National Archives of Canada with the National Library, creating an entity called Library and Archives Canada, located in Ottawa. According to Ian E. Wilson, former Librarian and Archivist of Canada, this integration was groundbreaking because it established a 'new kind of knowledge institution designed to preserve Canadian heritage by combining the functions of an archives, library, and museum.'[1] The staff at Library and Archives Canada collect, preserve, document and make available to a diverse public such items as government records, books, family papers, newspapers, music, film, maps, photographs, documentary art, and painted portraits. Wilson insists that Canada is the first country to integrate these objects and services, but this convergence of institutions is not entirely novel. Many natural history, art, and historical societies founded throughout Europe and North America during the late nineteenth and early twentieth centuries were committed to the creation of both museums and libraries. Collections of objects, books, and archival documents overlapped in terms of their economic and social functions; among other things, they were meant to promote the exploitation of natural resources, provide aesthetic training, and enhance knowledge of local heritage. Museums and libraries were regularly housed within the same buildings, in keeping with the belief that reading books and looking at specimens or art objects were complementary educational activities able to foster a productive and civilized population.

In his influential study of the birth of the museum, cultural theorist Tony Bennett argues that late eighteenth- and early nineteenth-century British reformers considered public museums and libraries, along with parks, lecture halls, and playgrounds, to be places of instructive amusement that would improve the moral and physical health of the 'lower' classes.[2] According to Sir Henry Cole, museums would divert working men from ale houses, a point reinforced by James Silk Buckingham, who argued that libraries and art galleries would elevate the common man from a state of depravity to one of civility. Placing such comments within a broader historical context, Bennett argues that high art and its institutions were increasingly designed to serve the processes of governing. He contends that, along with other cultural venues, museums and libraries encouraged the working classes to emulate their 'superiors,' especially when they looked at others and were themselves looked at in spectacular venues.[3] Within newly rationalized public spaces, visitors could reflect on their 'selves' or identities, ultimately improving their personal tastes, industrial knowledge, and manners. Even as such cultural institutions raised the host city's national and international profile, they contributed to managing the local population – at least in theory.

Inspired by Bennett's groundbreaking work, this chapter analyses the historical associations between museums and libraries during the nineteenth and early twentieth centuries. Like Bennett my primary focus is on museums, but unlike him I diverge from a generalized narrative to explore case studies of the specific and practical arrangements forged between museums and libraries. In the text that follows, the Natural History Society of New Brunswick, established in 1862, acts as a point of comparison for the examination of the museums and libraries created by other societies in Canada. Members of the Natural History Society in Saint John collected an array of specimens and books until the 1930s, when their museum became a significant part of the New Brunswick Museum. As previous chapters indicate, substantial archival sources document how the founders of this early Canadian institution understood what we would now call the transfer of knowledge, collecting and disseminating written as well as visual forms of information. To enrich this assessment, I selected other societies – the Natural History Society of Montreal, founded in 1827, the Historical and Scientific Society of Manitoba, formed in Winnipeg in 1879, and the Art, Historical and Scientific Association, established in Vancouver in 1894 – undertaking archival research in each city. All of these societies created libraries as well as museum collections, and their various articulations of the relationship between reading and looking are addressed in my discussion below.

I narrowed my focus to the groups founded in Montreal, Winnipeg, and Vancouver because they were among the earliest in Canada, spanning the breadth of the country. Their archival records are relatively rich, and they feature multiple references to libraries and written texts. Each society included an interest in natural history, but not all were natural history groups in the strictest sense. The organizations formed in Winnipeg and Vancouver were more expansive, addressing artistic and historical concerns as well as those related to natural history. This chapter thus highlights the diversity of such early organizations, drawing attention to the similarities and differences between them. By focusing on libraries and museums, but also considering such issues as female membership and target audience, my discussion provides multiple narratives that do not cohere into an overall account. It aims to provide a fuller understanding of the complexity of these early organizations, enhancing the scant literature produced about them.[4] At the same time, this discussion deliberately challenges my emphasis on the Natural History Society of New Brunswick in the other chapters, reinforcing the degree to which the Saint John group was idiosyncratic and informed by local conditions. The society created in New Brunswick cannot support grandiose statements about all early natural history museums, a point I strive to recognize throughout this book.

In keeping with my arguments about the relational museum – I claim that museums are articulated in terms of other organizations – my turn toward libraries encouraged me to explore library history, a fascinating field arguably more established than that of museum history. The experiences of various members of natural history and other societies with the collection and dissemination of printed materials varied widely, and were influenced by such issues as the presence or absence of support from the Carnegie Corporation, an American philanthropical organization which between 1886 and 1917 spent over $56 million to construct 2,509 libraries throughout the English-speaking world, including 156 in Canada.[5] Libraries had existed in North America before Carnegie's intervention, but had tended to be private, lending books only to those with paid subscriptions. In his survey of American libraries built before 1876, Haynes McMullen argues that the Harvard College Library, formed in 1638, was among the earliest organized collection of books on the East Coast.[6] Public libraries expanded in the eastern United States during the 1880s, but purpose-built library buildings were still a rarity in the West. The situation was similar in Canada, with uneven library development across the country. It was sometimes difficult for smaller towns to accept Carnegie's offer to finance a public library, for he required that recipient localities provide both a site for the building and continuing revenue to fund its maintenance and staffing.[7] All the same, it could be easier to convince local governments to fund libraries than to finance museums, and in at least one case object collections were 'tacked on' to a Carnegie library, with some debate. Considering museums in relation to libraries contributes to a more diverse historical understanding of the two institutions, and questions the distinctions made between them in the past as well as the present.

My study indicates that during the nineteenth and early twentieth centuries, libraries were more highly valued than museums by government funding bodies. The occasional convergence of libraries with museums did not always enhance the display of material objects, and in several cases even undermined it. This finding is at odds with the current literature analysing the links between libraries and museums, which now often occur on digital terrain. Juris Dilevko and Lisa Gottlieb's *The Evolution of Library and Museum Partnerships* (2004) voices disapproval of the ways in which libraries can play a secondary role in digital collaborations, with librarians relegated to providing software.[8] The authors fear that libraries will lose their autonomy as they struggle (and fail) to compete with museums by offering 'edutainment' in the form of popular lectures as well as opportunities to eat and shop, instead of solid support for lifelong learning. Dilevko and Gottlieb decry the loss of what they see as the library's traditional function of making information accessible, echoing Ray Lester's prediction that museums are more likely to eclipse libraries than to converge with them in productive ways.[9] This rhetoric of decline is similar to the narratives formulated by some contemporary practitioners of critical museum theory, who argue that when museums move from a primary emphasis on preserving and displaying objects toward goals that are more commercial and entertaining, they effectively cease to be useful.[10] In keeping with the rest of my book, the comparative study below complicates these rather nostalgic accounts of early institutions by reconfirming that like museums, libraries were processes of continual change and negotiation, not neutral mechanisms existing outside of political and economic concerns. By considering the diverse circumstances in which museums and libraries were joined and then separated, I also allude to the professionalization of these entities, a theme explored more fully in chapter 5.

Reading Early Institutions

Previous chapters have already indicated how members of the Natural History Society of New Brunswick advocated the close observation of specimens to shape visual perceptions of nature. Yet they did not disdain written texts; already in 1862 members of the Society had begun to create a library to complement the museum.[11] A range of historical and scientific books and pamphlets could be signed out by members of the Society, or used on site by the general public. These printed collections were acquired through purchase, donation, and exchange. The latter method proved especially effective once members began publishing the *Bulletin of the Natural History Society of New Brunswick*, a scholarly journal launched in 1882 and traded for the publications of similar organizations around the world, including many in Europe, the United States, Russia, and Australia.[12] In 1908 the museum's curator, William MacIntosh, started to include written notes with each specimen that he loaned to New Brunswick middle schools, outlining its history and significance.[13] Emphasis on the complementary nature of looking and reading also increased within the exhibition spaces. In 1907, MacIntosh reorganized the collections, mounting the shells on black tablets so that 'every specimen can be seen, and the label at the front of each tablet easily read.'[14]

The Natural History Society of Montreal

More has been written about the Natural History Society of Montreal than the other societies, largely because it is, according to historian Stanley Brice Frost, the oldest scientific organization in Canada.[15] In May of 1827, twenty-six prominent men, including six physicians, two colonels, and three reverends, felt no need to justify the formation of a natural history society, claiming that 'the advantages derived from the knowledge of the natural productions of any country are too obvious to require to be dwelled upon.'[16] Like the society later established in Saint John, the Montreal group organized itself around a museum consisting primarily of minerals, plants, shells, insects, birds, and animals 'of the country,' with some foreign material included for comparison.[17] Specimens were acquired through donation – early gifts included a live bat, stuffed birds, and a dried swordfish skin – and the exchange of duplicates, though the latter method makes relatively fewer appearances in the Montreal records than in those of the Saint John society.[18] In Montreal, the men planned to organize their collections into four departments (Zoology, Botany, Mineralogy, and Miscellanies), hiring a 'keeper' to arrange, number, and catalogue each specimen.[19] This goal was clearly never fully achieved, for it was repeated in subsequent minutes calling for committees to classify the collection, and in discussions of the duties of the various curators hired throughout the nineteenth century.[20] Members of the Natural History Society of Montreal nevertheless insisted that looking at museum collections – whether labelled or not – would promote substantial thought, a point reinforced by the Natural History Society of New Brunswick.

Yet in Montreal the joys of looking were regarded with a certain amount of suspicion, with members arguing that 'the object of the Society is not so much to gratify the eye, as to afford solid instruction in the mind.'[21] Administrators worried that 'without [books], specimens can be regarded as objects of curiosity.'[22] Though during the early modern period collections known as cabinets of curiosity were designed to invoke wonder in viewers, filling them with the desire to know, the Montreal men seem to have linked curiosity with a kind of superficial pleasure, distinguishing the gratification of the eye from the discipline of the mind. They implied that if left to their own devices, eyes could be led astray, a position at odds with the methods of Agassiz described in chapter 2. In 1828 the men began forming a library that included titles such as Linneas's *General System of Nature*, Van Rensalaer's *Geology*, Conybeare and Phillips's *Geology*, Cleveland's *Mineralogy*, and various publications from the United States considered necessary for understanding and arranging the museum.[23] All the same, the members of the Natural History Society did not devote all of their attention to books, dividing their limited funds rather evenly among specimens, meteorological instruments, and publications.[24] They argued that books were ultimately inadequate on their own: 'Although books may point out with tolerable accuracy the distinguishing marks of species and genera, there is always some degree of ambiguity till they are compared with authentic specimens.'[25] Looking and reading were complementary activities, with specimens and books 'mutually dependent on each other – One without the other leaves the work half-done.'[26]

This understanding of knowledge acquisition was not unique. In 1887, Luigi Palma di Cesnola, the first director of the Metropolitan Museum of Art in New York, argued that museums were in effect libraries of objects, offering 'what the books do not and cannot supply,' while during the early 1900s, Oliver C. Farrington, curator of geology at the Field Museum of Natural History in Chicago, reported that 'the museum illustrates the objects of which the library tells; the library describes the objects which the museum exhibits.'[27] A range of museum men were eager to associate museums with libraries, claiming that a full understanding of the natural world could be gleaned only by engaging in both the close visual observation of material specimens and attentive reading of more abstract written texts: the two activities were ideally carried out at approximately the same time and in the same place.

Extending this theory of knowledge acquisition beyond their private collections, members of natural history societies attempted to house their organizations within public library buildings. When in 1830 the council of the Natural History Society of Montreal declared its current room inadequate for its expanding collections, it hoped to rent the third floor of the proposed public library.[28] In 1897 members of the Natural History Society of New Brunswick similarly lobbied – unsuccessfully, primarily for financial reasons – to have their natural history collections included in a new library building planned for Saint John.[29] Despite several efforts, the Montreal society did not join forces with the public library and in 1831 instead entered into a housing agreement with the medical faculty of McGill College (later McGill University). By 1837 it had relocated to a nearby mansion, inviting the Montreal library to rent rooms there.[30] Unfortunately, little information is available about this coexistence, which lasted at least until 1843, framing the natural history museum as a site of public education.[31] By 1856 the Natural History Society of Montreal was operating within a purpose-built edifice, occupying it until 1906 when the property was sold and the collections of books and specimens put into storage in anticipation of constructing a larger building; the delays and financial difficulties of this project contributed to the decline and bankruptcy of the organization, which officially folded in 1925.[32]

In keeping with the desired association between objects and books, members of natural history societies conflated the management of their specimen and library collections, often hiring one person to be both curator and librarian. In 1853 the 'Librarian and Curator,' in his annual report to the council of the Natural History Society of Montreal, noted that he had rearranged the collections, moving the herbarium and library downstairs.[33] In 1864, when the society was no longer housed along with the public library, the members awarded Joseph Frederick Whiteaves, a British paleontologist, the title of 'scientific curator'; he was also made responsible for running the society's library.[34] William MacIntosh, the curator of the Museum of the Natural History Society of New Brunswick, undertook a range of tasks, caring for the museum building as well as the collections inside it, executing secretarial work and organizing archival records. He simultaneously acted as the librarian, acquiring, classifying, and lending books.[35] During the 1880s and 1890s, MacIntosh supervised several young women hired to assist with this task. They catalogued the book collections, but also cleaned the objects in the museum and showed visitors through the exhibitions.[36] The gender politics and 'unprofessional' nature of this labour are discussed in the following chapter; here this information is raised to suggest that the intellectual and practical activities of managing objects and books were often related, thought to require similar organizational and social skills. Staff members apparently moved easily from handling objects to shelving books, from thinking about specimens to interacting with published texts.

The records of the Natural History Society of Montreal make no mention of women working in its library or museum. Male administrators began proposing women as associate members around 1866, and in April of 1867, John William Dawson, principal of McGill and intermittent president of the Natural History Society of Montreal for twelve years between 1856 and 1881, moved to amend the bylaws to allow a committee of 'Lady Associates to aid in the arrangements for the Conversazione,' by decorating the society's rooms and providing tea, coffee, and cake in a manner similar to the members of the Ladies' Auxiliary of the Natural History Society of New Brunswick.[37] Women did not become more prominent in the Montreal society until the early twentieth century. They were listed as members of the library, museum, and lecture committees in 1909, and by 1915 Carrie M. Derick, MA, a lecturer at McGill who would eventually become the first woman appointed to a full professorship at a Canadian university, became vice-president.[38] It seems that women were finally active at every level within the Montreal society precisely when it was in a state of steep decline.

From its inception, the Natural History Society of Montreal had a more elite and scholarly membership than the later New Brunswick group. During the nineteenth century, members included John Samuel McCord (d. 1865), a Supreme Court judge and amateur meteorologist, John Bethune (d. 1872), the Anglican rector of Montreal and acting principal of McGill from 1835 to 1846, and Dawson (d. 1899), an internationally renowned author who would be knighted.[39] While the Saint John group certainly included some belonging to the social elite, such as the lieutenant-governor of the province and members of the wealthy Ganong family, for the most part its participants were decidedly middle-class, with less formal education and few, if any, ties to the University of New Brunswick in Fredericton. In contrast, the Natural History Society of Montreal was dominated by McGill administrators and professors, as well as by such medical men as Andrew Fernando Holmes (d. 1860), a founding member who became dean of the Faculty of Medicine in 1843.[40] Although most of these men were amateur naturalists, their professional identities led them to target a relatively upper-class intellectual audience. The Natural History Society of Montreal devoted most of its resources to publishing the *Canadian Naturalist and Geologist* between 1864 and 1883, while excluding the socially inclined type of amateur intent on field trips and fundraising, a category dominated by, though not exclusively comprised of, women. In his article on the socio-economic significance of the museum of the Natural History Society of Montreal, historian Hervé Gagnon draws on different evidence to reach a similar conclusion, arguing that 'one may infer that the transformation of the NHSM into a place of dialogue and mutual benefits between finance and science deprived ordinary amateurs of natural history of their traditional place of leisure.'[41]

Unlike the society in Saint John, the Montreal group never created loan collections to circulate to local schools; nor did it maintain year-round opening hours for the museum before 1899. For the most part, the museum was opened only temporarily, to groups deemed worthy, such as the temperance league, and on holidays.[42] This limited access seems to have defied the desired association of the museum with a public library as well as the conditions of the annual grant from the Legislature – increased from 200 pounds in 1829 to 1,000 dollars in 1860 – which specified that 'the Museum and Library shall be kept open for the public under the regulation of the Society.'[43] Members were clearly reluctant to allow access, noting the possibility for theft and unruly behaviour in 1866.[44] Most striking is a letter written to the mayor requesting that two policemen be stationed in the museum to keep order whenever it was opened.[45] This mistrust of the public recalls Bennett's discussion of how nineteenth-century British reformers feared the influx of uncivilized 'mobs' into their museums, even as they hoped that museums would encourage the emulation of improved, upper-class behaviour.[46] In the end, this organization marginalized both informally educated amateurs and the general public, a characteristic that distinguished the Natural History Society of Montreal from the more populist Natural History Society of New Brunswick. Furthermore, the Montreal group's movement away from a connection with the public library (and arguably with the public itself) contrasts starkly with the relationship forged between the Historical and Scientific Society of Manitoba and the public library in Winnipeg.

The Historical and Scientific Society of Manitoba

When the Historical and Scientific Society of Manitoba was founded in Winnipeg in 1879, its goals were 'to collect and maintain a general library of scientific and popular literature, also to embody, arrange and preserve a library of books, pamphlets, maps, manuscripts, prints, papers and paintings; a museum of minerals, archaeological curiosities, and objects ...; to rescue from oblivion the memories of the early missionaries, fur-traders, explorers and settlers ... and to obtain and preserve [their] narratives in print, manuscripts, or otherwise.'[47] As this ambitious mandate indicates, the Winnipeg society emphasized the preservation of archival documents, in addition to collecting natural history specimens and books, an activity undertaken more sporadically in other Canadian natural history societies. The encompassing nature of the Historical and Scientific Society of Manitoba differentiates it from the groups formed in Montreal and Saint John; and, in fact, a more focused natural history society was organized in Winnipeg in 1920, about ten years after the decline of the inclusive organization. Far more records document the early Natural History Society – it continues to function – with its familiar efforts to study and promote the natural history of the province.[48] The Historical and Scientific Society was nevertheless revived in 1926 and again in 1944, surviving today as the Manitoba Historical Society.[49] As the earliest society in Manitoba to promote natural history, it is particularly interesting for the purposes of this chapter because of its long-standing connection with the public library in Winnipeg, an association that both ensured the society's financial survival and ultimately undermined its ability to attract amateur naturalists more interested in field trips and specimens.

Like the Natural History Society of Montreal, the Historical and Scientific Society was founded by members of the social elite, including its first president, Edmund Burke Wood (d. 1882), a member of the House of Commons in the late 1860s and early 1870s and chief justice of the

Manitoba Court of Queen's Bench after 1874, and twenty-five other men, variously reverends, colonels, doctors, military officers, businessmen, and lawyers.[50] Despite this stellar membership, the society lacked funding and, like the groups in both Montreal and Saint John, sought to acquire government support. Instead of simply being awarded grants either annually or sporadically, in 1881 the Historical and Scientific Society agreed to manage a circulating library and public reading room in exchange for free accommodations in the City Hall building and an annual payment of $600.[51] By 1892 this library consisted of some 10,000 volumes devoted to literature, science, and history. The substantial fiction collection included works by Johann David Wyss, Charlotte Bronte, Charles Dickens, and Sir Walter Scott. Though natural history books by Darwin and Huxley were among the titles circulated, they by no means outnumbered the other genres.[52]

The Historical and Scientific Society hired a librarian who would 'have charge and superintendence of the library and museum of the Society, and the care and arrangement of the books, manuscripts, maps, paintings, &c.'[53] Like the earlier societies formed in Montreal and Saint John, the Winnipeg group combined the activities of librarian and curator, arguing that they were essentially similar. The tasks of this employee – assumed to be male, though some assistants were female and a woman identified as Miss Inkster became the head librarian in 1888 – were to arrange and order all of the collections, taking particular care to separate and treat as private property those items belonging to the society rather than to the public library.[54] Various meeting minutes indicate that the museum housed at City Hall included marine invertebrates, a collection of archaeological objects prepared by Henry Ward, a mineralogist and paleontologist from Rochester, New York, and a number of muskets and bayonets supposedly used by Lord Selkirk and soldiers in their attack on Fort William from 1816 to 1817.[55] Although the original arrangement of these items is now unclear, they were necessarily displayed in close proximity to the written records, manuscripts, and reference books also contained within the small rooms that had been allotted to the society.

Even after accepting the responsibility of running a public library, the members of the Historical and Scientific Society undertook research, including a fossil-collecting trip arranged in 1882 by the Science Committee to the Selkirk quarries and Stony Mountain escarpment.[56] Yet the public library quickly became burdensome. The society's annual report of 1887 noted that it was difficult to maintain a large and popular library while simultaneously exploring the region and caring for material objects.[57] Subsequent reports complained about the lack of both adequate attention to and space for the specimens collected by members. Material objects were increasingly pushed to one side, housed in dimly lit hallways and stairwells, as the demands for library resources increased.[58] The mandate of the society, to perform research and collect quite broadly, was ultimately ignored as the majority of resources, energy, and time was poured into the successful public library.

By the turn of the century, the Historical and Scientific Society's dedication to managing the library services was no longer required, for a new public library, funded by American industrialist and philanthropist Andrew Carnegie, had opened in 1905, and it did not include spaces for either museum displays or the storage of archival records. One prominent member of the Historical and Scientific Society, George Jackson Laird (d. 1940), a professor of physics, chemistry, and German at Wesley College (now the University of Winnipeg), hoped that 'quarters may be assigned to the Society in the new Carnegie Library, where ample room may be afforded for rendering useful the valuable collection of books, maps, original documents and Indian curios possessed by the Society.'[59] Yet the affiliation between the Historical and Scientific Society and Winnipeg's public library did not continue. Although the society allowed the Carnegie library to retain around 2,000 of its reference books, it was effectively excluded from the space as well as from City Hall, using rooms in the basement of the Manitoba College to store some of its other books and removing its museum to the house of a certain Mrs A.C. Hutton.[60] Once the Carnegie library was established, the collections of the Historical and Scientific Society were scattered throughout Winnipeg, and what had long been the group's primary *raison d'être* as well as revenue source – managing a large circulating library – was gone.

Unlike the later Natural History Society of Manitoba, the earlier Historical and Scientific Society organized fundraising events, and strove to expand its membership, in part to finance a future free-standing museum. In 1884 the members arranged their first *conversazione*, which uniquely included an art exhibition – declared the first ever attempted in northwestern Canada – in the hope that 'the exhibition might lead to the undertaking of a permanent museum – an educative influence of the highest importance.'[61] The $450 profit was ultimately spent on books to enhance the library. Though the records are vague, the female members invited to join in 1883 were probably part of the organizing committee for this and subsequent social events. At the annual meeting that year, the Executive Council of the Historical and Scientific Society declared that women had been admitted, not simply to swell numbers, but because 'there are ladies of education, literary habits and good powers of observation who might be of much service in producing papers on the manners and customs of the native tribes, on matters of North Western history, or in the scientific department of the Society; as in botany or Indian remains.'[62] This emphasis on women as scholars rather than fundraisers or decorators stands in marked contrast to most of the official discussions of the members of the Ladies' Auxiliary of the Natural History Society of New Brunswick, as well as to the lack of any substantial discussion of women in the Montreal society before the early twentieth century. Many women did indeed join the Winnipeg society during the late nineteenth century, mostly teachers who desired access to the library, but also some who acquired a more intellectual status, such as Marion Samuel Bryce (d. 1920), a teacher, philanthropist, and lecturer who represented the Historical and Scientific Society at the meeting of the Royal Society of Canada in 1898.[63] In the end, the Winnipeg organization was more welcoming than that in Montreal, though this openness should not be overstated; it was still primarily populated by Winnipeg citizens from the middle and upper classes.

This brief account of the Historical and Scientific Society of Manitoba, and its association with the public library in Winnipeg, alludes to why some societies may have promoted libraries and written publications at the expense of other activities. City and provincial administrators recognized book collections as essential to public education and libraries as signifiers of civility more than they supported the display of material specimens; though museums were readily linked with learning and culture, they were often considered secondary to libraries. The less dramatic shift away from objects to books and written texts happened differently in Montreal, fuelled by that group's focus on a scholarly and elite audience rather than a popular one. Although the collections of the Natural History Society of Montreal increased steadily over time, they were ultimately placed in storage, as were those in Winnipeg, before being allotted to other institutions. In the Montreal case, they were divided between the McCord and Redpath Museums.

Art, Historical and Scientific Association of Vancouver

Though officially created in 1894, the Art, Historical and Scientific

Association was a more expansive version of the Art Association of Vancouver, founded in 1887. The renewed society maintained its focus on collecting and exhibiting artworks, but the constitution of 1894 also prioritized the formation of 'a Museum of Antiquities, especially of the remains of Indian life in B.C. and America.'[64] Stressing the urgency of preserving 'the rapidly disappearing relics of the early history of our Province,' members of the Art, Historical and Scientific Association feared that American and European relic hunters were depleting the historical and cultural property that in their opinion rightly belonged to the residents of British Columbia and should be displayed in 'our own Civic Museum.'[65] By invoking a narrative of loss and local property rights, members of the association both made a strategic demand for increased government funding and reconfirmed a patronizing view of Aboriginal culture: even as a romanticized Aboriginal past was embraced as a crucial aspect of provincial identity, the Anglo Saxon society members assumed that these 'primitive' cultures would inevitably become extinct in the face of modernity.[66] This representation of museums as safeguards of an inert past informed many other anthropological as well as natural history museums, but was especially pointed in western Canada.[67]

Members of the Art, Historical and Scientific Association of Vancouver used borrowed artifacts, including paintings and native 'curios,' to open what it claimed was Vancouver's first museum exhibition on the top floor of a prominent downtown building.[68] During this early period, the Art, Historical and Scientific Association purchased such exotic items as Japanese sword hilts, but mostly received donated international items and a small number of natural history specimens.[69] According to the group's president, Reverend L. Norman Tucker, in 1894, 'the object of our Association is to cultivate a taste for the beauties and refinements of life. We have the opportunity of making the hard and unlovely lot of our toiling and struggling fellow citizens a little less hard and unlovely.'[70] By focusing on the uplifting aesthetic benefits of these early installations, Tucker continued to promote artistic experience and taste within Vancouver, an interest begun in the earlier Art Association. He also positioned the members of his society as patrons who benefited the working classes, reiterating the goals of those eighteenth-century reformers described by Bennett.[71]

The upper- and middle-class members of the Vancouver society insisted that written material could have a similarly beneficial effect on the deprived labouring classes. Along with material collections, the constitution of 1894 vowed 'to establish a library of books, pamphlets, and periodicals bearing on the subjects of Art, Science, Mineralogy, & c. & on the Early History of Canada & of America.'[72] Yet these complementary collections remained sporadically unavailable to the public because, even after seven years of existence, the association lacked a home in which to install them permanently. In 1900, Secretary H.J. De Forest lamented that 'various schemes have been mooted whereby the possessions of the Society may be located in a place that will be more accessible to the public, but so far no definite conclusion has been arrived at.'[73]

Despite this complaint, archival records related to the early activities of the Vancouver society portray a group primarily devoted to high culture and entertainment. Local newspaper reports of the group's first *conversazione* in 1894 highlight musical interludes, cake, and ice cream rather than the scientific instruments that accompanied these activities in New Brunswick.[74] Some members of the Vancouver group undertook archaeological work – Charles Hill-Tout, a teacher, excavated local sites, including the Great Fraser Midden, publishing *Later Prehistoric Man in British Columbia* in 1895 – but a lack of funding was cited for the intermittent nature of such research.[75] For the most part, early meetings of the Art, Historical and Scientific Association featured literary discussions followed by musical performances, and often an 'impromptu dance.'[76] The civilized and social aspect of these events may have been encouraged by the prominent role of women in the group, in keeping with the influence and interests of the Ladies' Auxiliary of the Natural History Society of New Brunswick. Yet unlike the Saint John group, in Vancouver women were included as full members from the foundation of the association and quickly assumed leadership roles; in 1897, Sara McLagan, editor and co-founder of the newspaper *Vancouver Daily World* in 1888, for example, became the first vice-president of the association, which remained devoted to music, singing, dancing, eating, and discussing literature until the turn of the century.[77] Later chroniclers of the society drew attention to the contributions made by its female members, arguing that the earlier Art Association had failed precisely because it had excluded women.[78]

Between 1902 and 1903 the trajectory and image of the Art, Historical and Scientific Association changed. The group, headed by McLagan as president in 1903, negotiated with city officials for permanent accommodations on the top floor of the new library building then under construction.[79] Funded by the Carnegie Corporation, this would be the first purpose-built library in Vancouver, for the reading room established in 1869 was located in the New London Mechanics' Institute (and was accessible by subscription only) and the Vancouver Free Reading Room created by private citizens in 1886 was first installed in rented rooms and then transferred to a large space in the YMCA on Hastings Street.[80] In 1901, Andrew Carnegie had agreed to donate $50,000 toward more spacious library accommodations with his usual conditions: the city council of Vancouver was required to provide a building site and continuing support in the amount of $5,000 annually.[81] Members of the Art, Historical and Scientific Association engaged directly with city officials, agreeing to hand over its collections if the city would 'provide all proper means to preserve and keep preserved and in good order and condition the said collection.'[82] The two groups eventually confirmed that the association would continue to manage the collections, which would be installed on the top floor of the library building. All the same, the museum was an afterthought for the city officials, receiving an annual grant of only $100 from the city, an insignificant sum in contrast to the $5,000 dedicated to operating the library. Even as this level of financial support gradually increased – by 1912 it was $2,500 – the museum always played second fiddle to the library.[83]

In keeping with its inferior status, the museum opened its doors to the public long after the library was already functioning. Various delays prevented the timely construction of a long, winding staircase enabling access to the top floor of the Carnegie library.[84] The City Museum, as it was then called, was officially opened on 15 April 1905. Newspaper reports described the exhibitions, including a pair of stuffed sea lions, an Indian canoe covered with walrus skin, Chinese 'curios,' painted scenes of Hawaii and New Zealand, and a portrait of Captain Cook.[85] The original constitution of the Art, Historical and Scientific Association had vowed to 'form and preserve a collection of specimens of the ores and natural products of British Columbia and of Canada generally.'[86] This aspect of the group's broad mandate, however, finally came to fruition in the somewhat eclectic mixture at the City Museum, which attracted such gifts as samples of bark produced from a giant fir tree, a collection of birds and butterflies, ores, insects, garnets, minerals, shells, a deer horn, a tiger skin and tiger skull, along with Egyptian antiquities, two books about the Western Dene Indians, three pairs of Chinese footwear, two Chinese hand-painted silkscreen pictures, and nails of various sizes produced by women and children in pre-industrial England.[87]

The first curator was long-time secretary of the Art, Historical and Scientific Association, H.J. De Forest, a landscape painter born in Rothesay, New Brunswick, and educated in London, Paris, and Edinburgh. He was appointed with little fanfare; the minutes simply noted that 'it was obviously necessary that some responsible person should have a constant care of the properties, with ability to properly label, classify and arrange the collections.'[88] Though this definition of curatorship stressed the management of material objects, it highlighted the ability to care responsibly for them, rather than any kind of specialized knowledge. The next curator was another local artist, William Ferris, who made paintings and drawings, including some featuring scenes of the city of Vancouver. In his annual report of 1916, Ferris explained how he had attempted to rationalize the diverse items in the collections, installing glass shelves in the bird cases, placing images of ferns on the east-end wall, and mounting 150 specimens of British Columbian flora on the wall of the board room. He removed what he called 'much useless matter' from the City Museum and attempted to reorganize the remaining material.[89] Ferris also completed a catalogue of the collections, providing an inventory of the 86 flat glass-topped cases filled with minerals, fossils, ethnological specimens, exotic 'curios,' shells, reptiles, birds, and old books, and listing the sculptures, objects, and paintings that filled the remaining spaces.[90] This publication features photographs of the installations, revealing crowded rooms at odds with the curator's attempts to classify the collections. In one image, for example, a small stuffed brown bear is posed beside an ancient suit of Japanese armour (figure 4.1). In another photograph, a plaster copy of the Venus de Milo is surrounded by a perimeter of glass cases, while framed oil paintings and labelled photographs adorn the walls behind it (figure 4.2).

Both curators regularly complained about an inadequate amount of space within and funding for the City Museum. Made in letters, annual reports, and even in the foreword to the 1915 catalogue, pleas for more support and an independent building were linked with statistical accounts of the numbers of visitors, attesting to the value of the institution. According to De Forrest, the City Museum had immediately attracted an audience, with some 6,369 people touring the collections in February of 1905, the month after its official opening.[91] In his annual report of 1908, the curator noted an attendance of 23,500 during the previous year, drawn primarily from the Vancouver area.[92] In 1911 these numbers continued to increase, largely because the City Museum had become more accessible, opening for seven hours per day instead

4.1 Installation view 1, City Museum and Art Gallery, top floor of the Carnegie Library, Vancouver, before 1940. 547–E–1, File 3, Temp #10. Courtesy of the City of Vancouver Archives, Vancouver, British Columbia.

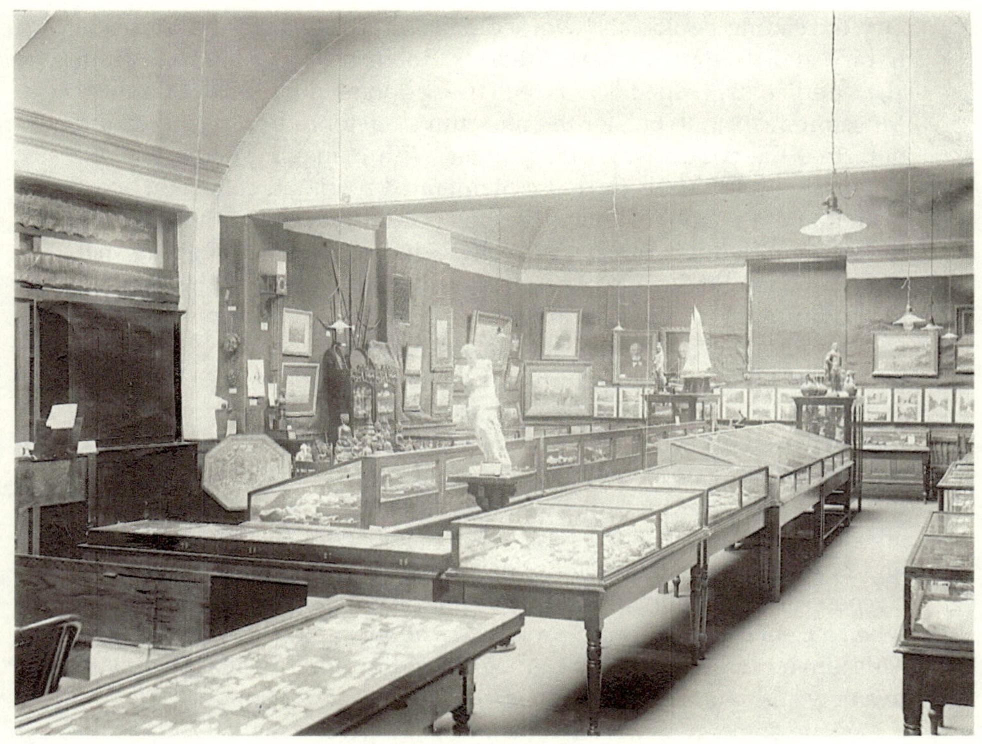

4.2 Installation view 2, City Museum and Art Gallery, top floor of the Carnegie Library, Vancouver, before 1940. 547–E–1, File 3, Temp #6. Courtesy of the City of Vancouver Archives, Vancouver, British Columbia.

of only three.[93] Unlike the museum of the Natural History Society of Montreal, the public was welcomed by the curators and directors of the City Museum in Vancouver, with little mention made of disturbances and regulations, despite earlier assertions about providing a civilizing and uplifting force for the downtrodden. Members of the Art, Historical and Scientific Association of Vancouver requested funds to improve public education, strove to extend access to the museum, and regretted the rather forbidding stairs that patrons had to climb in order to reach the exhibition spaces.

The Art, Historical and Scientific Association furthermore continued to view material objects as a form of visual learning complementary to reading books, and worked collaboratively with the Carnegie library and its staff. In 1928, Edgar S. Robinson, chief librarian from 1924 until 1957, helped T.P.O. Menzies, appointed curator of the City Museum in 1924, to bolster the museum's reference library, indicating both that the curator was still charged with managing books as well as objects, and that the museum maintained a printed collection apart from that of the public library.[94] An historical overview of the Art, Historical and Scientific Association written during the 1940s suggests that more fundamental forms of cooperation were fostered by the location of the museum and the library within the same building. According to the author, journalist and association member Noel Robinson, wartime efforts to escape current realities were encouraging the public to explore the past by reading historical books in the library, an activity that increased the number of visitors to the museum wishing to observe 'the artifects [sic] and other mementoes of preceding generations.'[95] By the 1940s, the City Museum welcomed more than 100,000 people annually, and the curator, along with other members of the Art, Historical and Scientific Association, amplified the long-standing demand for a purpose-built museum building; this plea was not answered until 1967, when a Centennial museum project was announced, although the City Museum occupied the entire Carnegie building after the library moved to a new and improved location in 1958.[96]

Despite some evidence of collaboration between the City Museum and the Carnegie library, the two institutions competed with each other. As indicated by the City Council's preferential support of library rather than museum buildings, the public library remained a primary concern and the museum an afterthought, recalling the situation in Winnipeg, where supporters of the museum were overwhelmed by a popular public library. Even when the City Museum was confined to the third floor of the Carnegie building, the expanding library threatened to encroach on its space, while consistently receiving more government funding and services. One minor issue that sheds light on the relative status of the library and the museum occurred in 1915, when the finance committee of Vancouver's City Council cut the janitor's salary from the grant given to the Art, Historical and Scientific Association, insisting that the man who cleaned the Carnegie library could also attend to the top floor, ultimately ensuring it would be largely overlooked and dirty.[97] By the 1920s the combination of museum and library functions within the Carnegie building became more controversial, with letters of inquiry being sent to the Carnegie Corporation of New York asking for confirmation that Andrew Carnegie had approved of the presence of the museum.[98] No such documentation was forthcoming. An article published in a local newspaper in 1924 declared, 'Museum to be Ousted,' referring to the negative response to the suggestion by some members of the Art, Historical and Scientific Association that a fee be charged for entry to the City Museum.[99] Menzies, the curator during these years of controversy, was not in favour when this suggestion was again made in 1940, asking Edgar Robinson to write to the secretary of the Carnegie Corporation to inquire 'whether or not the charging of a fee would be consistent with the policy of Mr. Carnegie in making a grant.'[100] The response from New York was unequivocal: 'We find, as in all instances in which Mr. Carnegie gave funds for a library building, that he was interested only in making possible a *free public library*, accessible to all who sought to use books and especially to those of poor estate. We have no record as to his being consulted as to the housing of a museum in the same building.'[101]

The issue of charging entry fees was eventually abandoned, but the debate points to the increasing conceptual and physical separation of libraries from museums, in theory if not immediately in practice. The movement toward a more rigid distinction between the two institutions was not unique to Vancouver. In 1924, Judson Jennings, then president of the American Library Association, complained that libraries were cluttered with objects extrinsic to library work. He asserted that 'in going about my own library, I have at different times found exhibits of dolls, or embroidery, or bird houses or even a collection of dead birds.'[102] Jennings argued that these 'foreign' exhibitions should be removed from libraries, though members of natural history and other societies had long considered the objects he mentions to be complementary to the act of reading books, rather than a distraction from it.

Conclusions

During the late nineteenth and early twentieth centuries, it was difficult if not impossible to maintain the ideal balance between looking and reading promoted by many early museum administrators and educators. The societies in Saint John, Montreal, Winnipeg, and Vancouver fostered collections of both objects and written materials, but none of them managed to place visual and literary modes of learning on an equal footing. The precise nature of the relationships forged between libraries and museums nevertheless differed in each case. The Natural History Society of New Brunswick produced its own library, without formally converging with the public library in Saint John, in spite of several attempts to do so. The Montreal group likewise fostered its own specialized natural history book and pamphlet collection, renting space to the public library for a few poorly documented years. In Winnipeg the public library initially enabled the existence of the museum installations created by the Historical and Scientific Society of Manitoba, but the demand for written materials ultimately overwhelmed the object collections. The situation in Vancouver was distinctive, for there the museum was hosted within and to a certain degree supported by the Carnegie library, even as the library remained dominant. In contrast, the Carnegie libraries built later in Saint John and Winnipeg pointedly excluded museum functions, despite similar proposals for a combined existence with the objects that had been collected by local societies. The Museum of the Natural History Society of Montreal was apparently never discussed in relation to a Carnegie library because the funds offered by the Corporation were ultimately refused by the city. Although in 1902 Mayor Raymond Préfontaine had requested monies from Carnegie to build a public library in Montreal, his plan was rejected by the powerful Catholic clergy, who wished to retain control over the reading materials made available to the public.[103] Although Bennett argues that museums and libraries were lumped together in the minds of British reformers, these case studies indicate that the institutions were in fact understood and produced in diverse ways according to specific local contexts.

All the same, some general principles informed each society discussed in this chapter. (1) They tended to be founded by social elites. The members of the Natural History Society of Montreal were, however, more academically minded and attached to the local university than those participating in the other groups. I have suggested that the Montreal society's particularly elite membership may have contributed to a greater emphasis on writing and a more negative understanding of the museum-going public. (2) Each group created diverse object collections, mixing natural history specimens with ethnographic objects, archival documents, and old books and coins, among other things. In keeping with other museums in western Canada, the Vancouver collection was formed to retain Aboriginal objects, an issue of less concern to those Canadian institutions located where the international 'scramble' for Aboriginal items was not as intense. The primary focus of collecting nevertheless varied throughout the country, with the early members of the Natural History Society of New Brunswick devoted to geological specimens, and those in Winnipeg foregrounding archival material associated with the history of the province. In addition to highlighting ethnological specimens, the City Museum in Vancouver featured artworks, hiring two early curators who were artists, in keeping with the group's roots in an art association. (3) All four societies employed curators or keepers who were non-specialists mostly tasked with caring for objects in a responsible way, while also acquiring and organizing libraries. Their education and hands-on experience were valued according to the priorities of each institution: the New Brunswick group favoured a self-trained entomologist; the society in Montreal hired a range of men, from a taxidermist-custodian to a self-educated paleontologist; in Vancouver, practising artists were initially considered most capable of managing the collections and presenting the public face of the association. (4) All of the groups, furthermore, strove to obtain larger, purpose-built edifices for their museums, and continually complained about a lack of adequate space and funding. In the end, the societies in Saint John and Vancouver achieved the most success with such efforts, for their collections are currently housed in independent museum buildings in their respective cities, whereas the museums created by the Natural History Society of Montreal and the Historical and Scientific Society of Manitoba were dispersed decades ago amongst other institutions.

It is now difficult to pinpoint why some societies established long-standing museum collections that remain open to the public, whereas others underwent amalgamation. The relationships forged between written texts and objects may have played a role. The groups formed in Montreal and Winnipeg were more committed to writing: the former in terms of scholarly publications and academic discourse, which may have undermined popular support, and the latter to the popular public library that ultimately pushed aside the collecting and display of objects. All four groups organized *conversazioni* and other events, but those in Saint John and Vancouver appear to have been especially concerned with socializing, maintaining a consistent focus on inviting the public into their museums. These groups furthermore experienced a high degree of female participation, although women remained marginalized in the Natural History Society of New Brunswick, as discussed in the previous chapter, whereas they quickly attained powerful positions within the Art, Historical and Scientific Association of Vancouver. The Montreal society did not encourage female participation until its later years of decline, but any attempt to establish a gendered pattern of success or failure is thwarted by the high degree of female participation in the Historical and Scientific Society of Manitoba, which encouraged women to become members and pursue scholarship, though precise accounts of what women actually did are sadly lacking from the records. All the same, one could conclude that a viable museum-building society was one that attempted to entertain as well as inform a diverse public, involved women in its organization, and remained committed to the collection of material objects while valuing literacy.

During the late nineteenth and early twentieth centuries, museums and libraries were clearly defined in relation to each other, even as museums were considered less crucial to promoting and demonstrating civility. Although some scholars now decry the secondary status of libraries, and fear that they will be overwhelmed by the popularity of entertaining museums, in the past the opposite could be true. Objects were ultimately considered ornamental additions to the more important circulation of books in both Winnipeg and Vancouver, and pushed out of other library spaces. The next chapter will show how a more strict separation of libraries from museums was fuelled by the Carnegie Corporation's policies during the 1930s and 1940s, when the emphasis shifted from spatial arrangements to the training of specialist curators and librarians.

Chapter Five

Gendered Professionals: Debating the Ideal Museum Worker during the 1930s and 1940s

Since the 1960s scholars have studied the ways in which museums have welcomed certain kinds of visitors while excluding others. After undertaking extensive visitor surveys at European museums, sociologists Pierre Bourdieu and Alain Darbel argued that the institutions reinforced class distinctions: working-class and rural people felt uncomfortable in the opulent surroundings of art galleries, opting to avoid them.[1] Much less has been written, however, about the selection of museum staff, a topic similarly informed by issues of class, gender, and education. During the early twentieth century, various museum directors discussed the ideal qualities of museum workers, considering their training and demeanour. John Cotton Dana, founder of the Newark Museum, for example, affirmed that staff members should possess the practical skills required to serve a diverse public, and he launched an apprenticeship program in 1925 to produce them.[2] Not everyone, however, agreed with Dana's service-oriented training; some preferred to emphasize the expertise required to manage museum collections. In 1936 members of the Canadian Museums Committee of the Carnegie Corporation – an American philanthropical association – declared that 'the urgent need in Canada is for the creation of an adequately trained Art Gallery and Museum personnel to replace, as opportunity permits, the casual, amateur and volunteer assistance with which most museum work in the Dominion is carried out.'[3] This chapter examines efforts to produce staff with an authoritative understanding of the objects in museums while driving supposedly unskilled workers out of the institutions.

According to sociological research, professional work typically features specialized knowledge, systematic training that leads to credentials, distinctive hierarchies that delegate power to those at the upper levels, and organizations that control who is allowed to work, usually by evaluating training programs and assessing performance.[4] North American museums were undergoing professionalization during the early twentieth century, with groups such as the American Association of Museums founded in 1906, and the Canadian Museums Association established much later, in 1947.[5] Members of these bodies considered training programs for museum workers, but professionalizing the museum world was a lengthy process, one scarcely begun during the 1930s and 1940s, especially in Canada. These decades were characterized by disagreement about who should work in museums, what kinds of work staff should perform, and the public function of the institutions. Studying early efforts toward professionalization highlights tensions related to class, gender, and educational capital, while revealing how the so-called amateurs and volunteers who had long contributed to museums resisted their demotion within and ejection from them.

To avoid generalizing, this chapter explores how the debates unfolded at the New Brunswick Museum, highlighting the ways in which the wealthy benefactors John Clarence [J.C.] Webster and Alice Lusk Webster endeavoured to hire professional staff. In many ways the couple agreed about how to raise the profile of the museum, striving to diminish the influence of members of the Natural History Society, which they referred to as the 'old guard.'[6] Yet they parted ways on precisely what type of museum worker should replace those supposed amateurs, and about how the new staff should be trained. J.C. Webster focused on dislodging William MacIntosh, the director of the New Brunswick Museum, who had learned museum work while serving as the curator of the Museum of the Natural History Society from 1907 until 1932. In 1935, Webster arranged to have a Carnegie fellowship awarded to Alfred Bailey, a recent PhD in history, who he hoped would succeed MacIntosh as director of the New Brunswick Museum. MacIntosh was not without resources, however, and a protracted battle ensued. A different kind of struggle occurred only a few years later in the Art Department of the New Brunswick Museum, then entirely financed by Lusk Webster, as discussed in chapter 3. Lusk Webster wished to hire a skilled curator to replace herself as the honorary curator. In 1941 she employed Edith Hudson, a young woman with a master's degree in art history, sending her for further training to Dana's apprenticeship program at the Newark Museum. This decision irked Lusk Webster's friend and adviser C.T. Currelly, who claimed that his own institution, the Royal Ontario Museum, could collaborate with the Canadian Museums Committee to offer a superior education in museum work. Yet by 1945 both

Bailey and Hudson had resigned from their respective positions in New Brunswick, casting doubt on the success of early efforts to professionalize Canadian museums.

The controversial situations involving Bailey and Hudson can be illuminated with reference to the understandings of legitimate labour developed at other museums and art galleries, but also in relation to the professionalization of libraries, institutions that were often associated with museums, as indicated in chapter 4. Though for the most part libraries were professionalized earlier than museums, the increasing specialization of library work accords with what occurred later in many museums: labour considered rote or manual in nature was delegated to women with college certificates, while aspects deemed more intellectual – acquiring, cataloguing, and managing collections – were awarded to men with university degrees. Engaging however briefly with the extensive literature on the development of libraries in North America provides needed support for my discussion of early efforts to professionalize Canadian museums because relatively little scholarly literature has been devoted to them.

Thinking about the history of museum professionalization enriches the current discussion of the appropriate role of curators within contemporary institutions. Cultural theorist James Clifford, for example, suggests that curators should no longer function as authoritative interpreters of objects, but instead be willing to collaborate with various audiences, facilitating their use of collections.[7] Other scholars like James Cuno are less enthusiastic about an apparent demotion of curatorial expertise, arguing that the intellectual contributions of curators are marginalized when museums aspire to please the public.[8] This chapter sheds light on these concerns, noting where they overlap with and depart from earlier controversies about the training and function of museum staff. The historical role of the curator has been analysed by such scholars as Barbara Maria Stafford and Tony Bennett, who explain that the status of curators improved when the spectacular displays of the Renaissance were replaced by more rational exhibitions during the Enlightenment.[9] Increasingly specialized curators attempted to direct visitors' experiences, writing detailed labels to show the unlearned how to see the objects and to reveal the evolutionary relationships between them. While inspired by such research, my chapter focuses on discussions of the identity of the curator and other staff, not exclusively on the management of museum objects. Given the relative dearth of publications on this topic, it is primarily based on archival research undertaken at natural history museums across Canada as well as at the National Gallery of Canada in Ottawa and the Newark Museum in Newark, New Jersey. In many ways, the final chapter of this book is designed both to lay the groundwork for and encourage further research on the status and training of museum workers in a range of institutions.

The Ideal Museum Man

There was no single kind of museum man during the nineteenth century, when the term 'curator' could be used in a broad and ambiguous manner. Members of the Natural History Society of Montreal referred to William Hunter, the man employed in their museum between 1859 and 1871, variously as caretaker, janitor, cabinet keeper, and curator.[10] His tasks were correspondingly diverse and included taxidermy, mopping the floor, cleaning the exhibition cases, and staffing the museum when it was open to the public. Yet when Joseph Frederick Whiteaves, a British paleontologist and fellow of the Royal Society of Canada, was hired to work in the museum in 1863, he was awarded the title 'Scientific Curator,' presumably to distinguish him from Hunter.[11] The minutes report that Whiteaves undertook more limited duties, primarily ordering and classifying geological specimens, while occasionally teaching classes on site. Such specialized curators were rarely hired to manage natural history collections during the nineteenth century, in part because most institutions had inadequate monetary resources.

William MacIntosh, consistently identified as the curator of the Museum of the Natural History Society of New Brunswick, received a rather modest salary.[12] As did Hunter, MacIntosh lacked formal training in natural history or museum work and lived on site, caring for the museum building as well as the collections inside it. He met with fund-raising committees, operated the magic lantern during lectures, greeted museum visitors, executed secretarial work, purchased coal to heat the museum, repaired the roof of its storage shed, and ordered supplies for the annual camping trips.[13] As an amateur entomologist equipped with honorary degrees from the University of New Brunswick – a master of science in 1921 and a doctorate in 1934 – MacIntosh also shared qualities with Whiteaves, a man who, although educated at private schools, had as his only degree an honorary LLD, awarded by McGill University in 1900.[14] In keeping with the esteemed Whiteaves, MacIntosh delivered educational lessons inside the museum and periodically worked for the government.

Despite such differences, most curators of natural history museums were expected to have an expansive, hands-on knowledge of the natural world rather than specialized training. This preference was in keeping with the nineteenth-century understanding of nature as an organic unity of all living things, available for study by generalists equipped with a keen eye and an enterprising spirit.[15] The Natural History Society of New Brunswick followed the Baconian approach adopted by many other societies, focusing on the inventory and description of nature in the belief that the observation of a wide range of specimens could educate the average person, rendering university training unnecessary.[16] Other Canadian institutions similarly embraced enthusiastic amateurs. Although lacking formal education, the Irish-born teacher John Macoun, for example, became Dominion botanist in 1881, and left more than 100,000 plant specimens to the Natural History Museum of Canada.[17] Norman Criddle (1875–1933) of Aweme, Manitoba, apparently never went to school but was able to become a nationally recognized expert in grasshoppers and their control, donating specimens to collections around the world, including the Canadian National Collection in Ottawa.[18]

Respect for knowledge gained exclusively by fieldwork had declined by the late 1890s. According to historian Robert E. Kohler, most nineteenth-century curators of American natural history museums were amateur collectors without formal credentials.[19] He calculates that only two of the eleven men hired by the American Museum between 1871 and 1892 had college degrees. That same institution, however, hired nineteen curators between 1895 and 1915: ten of them had doctorates, and only one was without academic certification. Kohler attributes this rather sudden change – evident at a range of other American institutions – partially to the increasing number of trained biologists produced by universities, but mostly to the growing social status of academic credentials and their ability to define modern, elite occupations while excluding the 'lower' orders as well as women from them.[20] Literary critic Lynn Merrill points out that science was only gradually separated from more popular forms of natural history. Yet she confirms that by the early twentieth century most scientists with degrees worked in laboratories, using expensive equipment to analyse the theoretical relationships between natural things, while amateur naturalists studied the appearance of nature in the field, a passionate endeavour linked as much with literature as with science.[21]

The anomaly of having an amateur adherent of natural history such as MacIntosh named director of the newly founded New Brunswick

Museum in 1934 is explained by local circumstances. The Natural History Society of New Brunswick played a crucial role in the creation of the New Brunswick Museum, donating its building, finances, and collections to the new venture, as discussed in chapter 3. Its members nevertheless wished to retain control of the collections, and MacIntosh was named as first director ostensibly to protect their interests. In many ways the long-time curator was well equipped to assume this position, given his knowledge of the latest developments in museums. From 1907 to 1910, MacIntosh had tried to modernize the Museum of the Natural History Society by focusing on coverage, classification, and the visual pleasure of visitors.[22] He had furthermore researched museums throughout North America, taking a one-month leave of absence from his curatorial position in 1924 to study various museums in the eastern United States. When plans for the New Brunswick Museum were confirmed in 1929, MacIntosh visited an additional sixty-five North American museums in twenty-one different cities, claiming that 'much information was gained which may be utilized in the building and arrangement of the new Provincial Museum.'[23]

All the same, MacIntosh found his authority challenged by wealthy newcomers to the New Brunswick Museum. The local and provincial governments had provided funds to construct the impressive new museum building, but support for its upkeep was lacking. In January of 1934, MacIntosh noted that the building remained closed, with the telephones removed, heat cut off, and one female staff member discharged.[24] Although MacIntosh called for increased government financing, the necessary monies ultimately came from Dr J.C. Webster and his wife, Alice Lusk Webster, figures discussed in the introduction to this book as well as in chapter 3. In addition to funding the everyday activities of the New Brunswick Museum, the Websters brought many innovations to the institution. Unlike the Museum of the Natural History Society, the New Brunswick Museum embraced Canadian history and international art in addition to natural history specimens. The new museum was furthermore to be divided into separate departments run by individual curators, a development which alarmed MacIntosh, likely because it undermined both the centrality of natural history and his former control of all the collections. The director's unhappiness only increased when Lusk Webster began installing Egyptian, Asian, and European art objects on the main floor of the museum, requiring him to move his prized assembly of stuffed New Brunswick mammals to the basement.[25] The spatial arrangement of the museum was based on more than practicality;

it inscribed the changing order of things, with natural history situated underground, fine art on the first floor, Canadian history on the second, and a library eventually installed on the uppermost level, not yet completed during the 1930s.[26] Scholarly literature and archival documents were positioned above material objects and specimens.

Webster was openly critical of the Museum of the Natural History Society and its supporters, referring to the latter as pitted against 'progressives' such as him and his wife who were striving to reform the New Brunswick Museum.[27] In 1935 he argued that MacIntosh 'was a good curator of a Natural History Museum [but] he is scarcely of the calibre to direct a Modern Museum ... due to his lack of a good education and of general culture.'[28] Webster's statement was informed not only by the declining status of natural history and growing importance of university credentials, but also by his views about what constituted 'general culture.' In 1926 he published *The Distressed Maritimes*, a study of the educational and cultural conditions in Canada, proclaiming that 'throughout the civilized world, there are certain well recognized standards by which the culture of a community may be determined ... These are an appreciation for good literature, fine architecture, painting, sculpture, music and the theatre; and, outwardly, there are evidences of these in the shape of private and public libraries and art collections, theatres, lectures, concerts and loan exhibitions of works of art.'[29]

Sounding like the eighteenth-century British reformers discussed in chapter 4, Webster argued that such evidence was 'almost entirely lacking' in the Maritimes. He strove to produce visible signs of culture by supplying the New Brunswick Museum with artworks and historical documents, while erecting markers across the Maritimes as part of his service on the Historic Sites and Monuments Board of Canada, which he chaired from 1943 to 1950.[30] Webster's understanding of culture explains how he could consider himself fit to work as an honorary curator, despite wanting education in museum theory and historical practice: he was possessed of both university degrees and a cultivated disposition. In contrast to Webster's worldly knowledge of all things civilized, MacIntosh was locally renowned for collecting moth specimens and performing handstands in his canoe during the annual camping trips sponsored by the Natural History Society.[31]

Webster's separation of culture into elite and lowly forms reinforces historian Lawrence Levine's arguments about the ways in which upper-class Americans strove to create rigid cultural hierarchies during the early twentieth century, distinguishing themselves from the influx of immigrants populating New York and other major cities.[32] The former obstetrician clearly differentiated himself from what he considered the uneducated population of New Brunswick, hoping to remove its members from administrative positions in the New Brunswick Museum, while using the altered museum displays to improve taste and civility throughout the province. His approach to museum reform adds weight to historian Eileen Mak's contention that despite diverse regional circumstances, Canadian museums were founded by and for the middle classes, designed to legitimate and promote their professionalizing ambitions.[33] These ends were no different from those of Europeans museums, according to such scholars as Tony Bennett and Eilean Hooper-Greenhill, for they similarly functioned as disciplinary mechanisms used by elites to transform the behaviour and tastes of the working classes.[34] Other cultural theorists have questioned, however, whether or not nineteenth- and early twentieth-century museums actually produced such results, noting that the 'lower' classes could resist hierarchical messages and use museums for their own purposes.[35] It will become clear below that MacIntosh and his supporters did not simply submit to the will of the Websters, but instead added their voices to those who called for museums to serve the common people.

Webster was nevertheless a powerful figure who left an indelible mark on the New Brunswick Museum, in large part because he chaired the Carnegie Corporation's Canadian Museums Committee, from its inauguration in 1933 until its demise in 1938. According to historian Jeffrey Brison, the American philanthropic organization launched this Canadian campaign 'to help transfer cultural authority and guardianship from individual patrons and entrepreneurs to a new, incorporated, national network of cultural professionals.'[36] Responding to the 1932 survey of Canadian museums commissioned from Sir Henry Miers and S.F. Markham – it ranked Canadian museums among the worst in North America because of inadequate financial support and poorly trained personnel – Carnegie Corporation president Frederick Keppel formed the Canadian Museums Committee to provide advice about the disbursement of funds for gallery development and museum training.[37] The members of this committee were almost exclusively powerful white businessmen who endorsed the Carnegie Corporation's dedication to traditional forms of elite culture.[38] Webster certainly conformed to this profile, publishing *The Distressed Maritimes* in support of the Carnegie report of 1922, which had offered to fund the consolidation of Maritime universities, then consisting of what it called five 'lower grade' institutions.[39] Deploring those who had refused to cooperate with this scheme, Webster was tenaciously committed both to Carnegie principles and to maintaining the homogenous nature of the Canadian Museums Committee. In 1933 he contested the addition of E.L. Judah to the group, arguing that the 'uneducated' museum technician at McGill University had misrepresented himself as a specialist, and threatening to resign 'if this man is to have a voice.'[40] Judah was precisely the kind of self-trained worker that Webster and other members of the Committee were trying to remove from positions of authority in museums.

Webster's primary ambition on the Committee was, however, to acquire Carnegie funds for the New Brunswick Museum, using its programs to replace MacIntosh with a more suitable museum director. He handpicked Dr Alfred Bailey to fulfill this role, a young man who had completed a doctoral thesis entitled 'The Conflict of European and Eastern Algonkian Cultures, 1504–1700: A Study in Canadian Civilization.' Webster and other members of the Canadian Museums Committee considered Bailey the perfect candidate, for not only was he equipped with university degrees, but – to use Pierre Bourdieu's terms – he additionally had legitimate cultural capital, some of it enhanced by the Committee itself.[41] Bailey was from a 'good New Brunswick family,' having been raised in Fredericton, the son of Loring Woart Bailey, a professor of chemistry and natural sciences at the University of New Brunswick.[42] In 1935 he used a $500 travel grant awarded by the Committee to visit museums in Wales and England before attending the annual conference of the British Museums Association in Brussels.[43] The Canadian Museums Committee promoted the firsthand experience of original artworks and documents, a principle endorsed by other institutions, including the American Association of Museums, which in 1917 recognized that for museum workers 'extensive European travel is very necessary,' and Paul J. Sachs, who at Harvard University's Fogg Museum from 1921 until 1948 taught hundreds of future museum professionals how to acquire quality artworks, compile useful bibliographies, cultivate relationships with dealers, and travel widely in order to become more marketable as museum professionals.[44]

Bailey also received a special Carnegie fellowship grant that allowed the New Brunswick Museum to hire him at a modest annual salary of $1,200 from 1935 to 1937. His official titles were assistant director and curator of both the John Clarence Webster Collection and European and Oriental Industrial Arts, otherwise known as Alice Lusk Webster's Art Department.[45] In 1934, J.C. Webster had donated his collection of historically significant maps, photographs, medals, paintings, sculptures, and original documents to the New Brunswick Museum; at the time, it was proclaimed the most valuable gift ever given to a Canadian museum.[46] Bailey's employment thus directly benefited Webster, for the young man was primarily occupied with the extensive Canadian history collection, cataloguing and installing it, in addition to giving public lectures, showing people around the museum, and responding to various requests for information.[47] Though Bailey's curatorial work focused on intellectual activities and historical research, it was broadly defined in keeping with the duties of nineteenth-century curators, and often involved interaction with the public.

In some ways, Bailey was like the other aspiring museum professionals funded by the Canadian Museums Committee. They were primarily young, with completed university degrees (though few had PhDs), and recommended by various members of the cultural elite. In 1934 letters of support for twenty-four-year-old candidate Donald A. Taylor, with a master's degree in geology, were written by the president of the University of Alberta, Robert C. Wallace, and Professor J.A. Allan in the university's Department of Geology and Mineralogy.[48] Taylor's application to pursue museum work in geology and paleontology was successful, and he was awarded a fellowship for ten months' study, which he primarily undertook at the Royal Ontario Museum, discussed below. He also used a separate travel grant to visit such American museums as the Pennsylvania Museum of Fine Arts and the Field Museum of Natural History before taking charge of the Museum of the University of Alberta in 1935. Many successful applicants were similarly trained in museum work at major central Canadian institutions.[49] Bailey's fellowship was considered 'special' because it was closer to the old-fashioned apprenticeship model. He received his award in the form of a salary that allowed him to learn on the job.

While Webster was pleased with Bailey's conduct at the New Brunswick Museum, MacIntosh deployed various strategies designed to drive the assistant director out of the institution. MacIntosh endeavoured, for example, to displace Bailey by selecting his own successor. In his late sixties and contemplating retirement, MacIntosh chose Gerald Sansom, a Moncton high-school teacher largely self-trained in natural history, to replace him as director of the New Brunswick Museum.[50] Sansom was clearly meant to replicate MacIntosh in important ways, for he was an older man who championed fieldwork in natural history and had devoted his life to educating school children. Although Mac-

Intosh promised to donate $500 annually toward Sansom's salary, the director could not compete with Webster's funding, and his proposal was rejected by key members of the Management Committee.[51] The Websters insisted that a man with university credentials in natural science would eventually be hired as a curator, not as director.[52] In a letter written in 1937 to H.O. McCurry, assistant director of the National Gallery of Canada and de-facto leader of the Canadian Museums Committee, Webster also claimed that MacIntosh 'now speaks of the domination of an outside body, and proclaims he can select and train a curator much better than the C. Committee. So much for his gratitude.'[53] According to Webster, MacIntosh viewed the Canadian Museums Committee as both meddlesome and foreign – perhaps alluding to its American funding – and did not feel sufficiently grateful for its interest in the New Brunswick Museum.

Webster was likely referring to the $9,000 awarded by the American office of the Carnegie Corporation to the New Brunswick Museum in three instalments between 1934 and 1937. Earmarked for educational purposes, it recognized the praise given by Miers and Markham to the innovative educational programs pioneered by MacIntosh, particularly the school services department, which sent specimens and study notes to teachers throughout the province, as described in chapter 2.[54] MacIntosh's annual reports to McCurry in Ottawa indicate that the monies were spent creating, repairing, and circulating this material.[55] Because the Carnegie Corporation was committed to disseminating morally uplifting knowledge to the 'lower' orders in addition to professionalizing museums, MacIntosh's work fell within its parameters. His goal was not, however, to civilize the working classes; instead, he wished to cultivate a love for and knowledge of how to exploit the natural world in young people, while providing their hard-working teachers with the necessary educational material. MacIntosh's commitment to the public nevertheless justified the large Carnegie grant, and the 'amateur' museum director managed to retain a degree of authority within the New Brunswick Museum – ultimately enough to force Bailey's departure from the institution.

Bailey left the New Brunswick Museum in 1938, noting 'I should rather starve than be under or connected with the Old Fiend in any way.'[56] MacIntosh consistently tried to make Bailey's working life difficult, but the last straw for Bailey was the director's attack on his dissertation, which was published as a book in 1938. Wanting the New Brunswick Museum to be associated with scholarly publications, Webster had used his personal funds along with Carnegie monies to release Bailey's book on behalf of the institution. Though permission to print the name of the New Brunswick Museum on the title page was granted by the chair of the Management Committee, he had neglected to inform the other members. According to archival sources, which exclusively reflect Webster's point of view, MacIntosh took advantage of this oversight and wrote letters to various libraries and institutions stating that the New Brunswick Museum had not authorized Bailey's book, implying that the young man had used the name improperly in an effort to increase sales.[57] When MacIntosh's actions were discovered by administrators at the museum, a second batch of letters was written to exonerate Bailey. This incident probably had little impact on the reception of Bailey's publication, which was ignored during the 1930s and 1940s primarily because its innovative combination of anthropology and history was too advanced for the field. When the book was republished by University of Toronto Press in 1969, it was praised as the first work of Canadian ethnohistory, and is now considered a foundational text.[58] The event did affect MacIntosh's standing, forcing him to announce his intention to resign by 1940. In a letter written to McCurry shortly after MacIntosh's actions had come to light, Webster triumphantly declared that the reformers at the New Brunswick Museum had scored 'a complete victory' because the director had been discredited.[59] In the end, however, Webster did not attain his goal of installing Bailey as the next director of the museum.

Webster framed MacIntosh's attack on Bailey's book in terms of simple pettiness, but it was consistent with the director's disdain for intellectual scholarship, which he felt should not be the primary occupation of a curator. MacIntosh wrote few reports and resisted Webster's suggestion that he produce a catalogue to document the natural history collections at the New Brunswick Museum. Instead, the director conveyed his knowledge orally by recounting Aboriginal legends and stories of his own adventures trekking through the New Brunswick woods to collect specimens.[60] In a remark aimed at Bailey, MacIntosh argued that a PhD was of no use to museum staff because 'a person holding that degree would not roll up his sleeves and get down on his hands and knees and perform [the] manual labour required of the position.'[61] Disputing the relatively recent preference for museum workers with university credentials, MacIntosh insisted that Bailey would restrict himself to white-collar work. He furthermore implied that the young man lacked the masculine physicality necessary for curatorial positions. According to the director, the ideal museum man was virile and enterprising, disregarding physical comfort to do whatever work was required. This ideal resembles nineteenth-century descriptions of those amateur collectors and employees of the geological survey who struggled to overcome the rugged terrain of New Brunswick in order to gain economic control of it, as described in chapter 1.

Webster's vision of the ideal curator avoided discussions of physicality, associating flesh exclusively with what he considered the 'lower' orders. In *The Distressed Maritimes*, he disdained the way in which the uneducated population embraced what he called 'the pleasures of the flesh,' spending money on cars and other trifles rather than historic sites or museums.[62] In contrast, Webster depicted literature, history, and theatre as primarily concerning the mind rather than the body. His classification conforms to what Bourdieu describes as the 'aesthetic disposition,' entailing an emotional and bodily distance from culture in distinction from the working classes' direct engagement with it.[63] In his studies of sport and recreation, Bourdieu finds additional distinctive understandings of the body: the working classes historically emphasize the bodily signs associated with physical labour, such as increased muscle mass, whereas the middle and upper classes tend to cultivate the body as an end in itself, pursuing such projects as 'inner peace' that are apparently removed from material necessity.[64] According to Bourdieu's research, MacIntosh supported a working-class image for the museum curator, wanting to see the visible signs of productive labour, while Webster favoured an aristocratic curator who displayed intellectual acumen by reading, writing, and publishing books.

A report issued in 1917 by the American Association of Museums portrayed the curator as a figure on display, meant to be looked at by audiences. It asserted that museum staff should be physically fit, disqualifying anyone with 'unpleasant physical peculiarities' from engaging with the public.[65] The report suggests that an attractive appearance was required of museum personnel, while specifically mentioning the necessity of their 'cleanliness and orderliness of body and raiment' as importantly reflecting the congruent orderliness of art.[66] Although clearly discussing the staff of art galleries rather than natural history museums, the report positions the person of the curator or museum worker as representing the museum itself. MacIntosh's image of the curator is quite distinct, invoking a curator who disregards his appearance and 'raiment' by pushing up his sleeves and getting down on the floor. This curator is absorbed in his work, and he does not consider what others think even as his labour is visible while he serves, but does not necessarily represent, the museum. In contrast, the American Association of Museums report features a well-groomed museum worker who strives to please cultivated museum patrons, while potentially providing an image for the 'lower' orders to emulate.[67]

These discussions indicate a growing emphasis on the personal presentation of the curator, an issue potentially considered as important as the duties he actually performed. The tasks undertaken by Bailey had indeed changed – notably with a greater emphasis on research and publication – but in other ways had remained the same, including public service and lectures, as well as manual labour, despite MacIntosh's claims to the contrary. Webster exaggerated other differences between Bailey and MacIntosh, for although Bailey held more legitimate university degrees, he too had learned museum work on the job. MacIntosh was in some ways more highly trained than Bailey, given his long years of museum work and his efforts to visit as many museums as possible. This situation suggests that the professionalization of museums entailed more than reshaping the curator's job description and interaction with objects in the collection. It also included recasting the curator as an embodied representation of the museum and its goals. The gendered nature of this embodied work has already been alluded to in MacIntosh's insistence on a particular kind of masculinity, but more can be said about this topic. MacIntosh's prone stance also alludes to custodial work, even housecleaning, a supposedly feminine occupation that can be considered more fully through an analysis of the efforts to hire professional female staff at the New Brunswick Museum.

The Ideal Museum Woman

Although women had worked in the Museum of the Natural History Society since its foundation in the 1860s – at first by assisting male administrators to clean and arrange the collections, and later as librarians and museum guides under the supervision of MacIntosh –none had received an official title. During the 1930s, Lusk Webster was the first woman to be designated curator, and she was named honorary curator of the Art Department, which she funded and managed. The male administrators of the New Brunswick Museum, including her husband, consistently placed her domain beneath the Departments of Canadian History and Natural Science. In January of 1940, Lusk Webster tried to alter this situation by asking the chair of the New Brunswick Museum's Management Committee for permission to hire a qualified young man or woman to take over her position, promising to provide a salary of $1,200 per year, at least initially. In her letter, Lusk Webster modestly claimed that she had 'gone as far as an amateur can go,' suggesting that an officially trained curator would both professionalize and raise the profile of the Art Department.[68] Assuming that members of the Management Committee would be unfamiliar with the duties of an art curator, Lusk Webster furnished them with a list. It included caring for the collections by cleaning, repairing, dating, labelling, and installing objects, preparing exhibitions of recent accessions and loan collections, providing docent services within the museum as well as educational talks at local high schools, and contributing to the educational loan program by producing visual aids and notes for teachers.[69] Using her economic capital rather directly, Lusk Webster attempted to construct and legitimate the role of a curator of fine art and decorative objects.

In this she was partially successful. Edith Hudson was hired to work at the New Brunswick Museum on a trial basis during the summer of 1940. Lusk Webster's selection of Hudson strengthened the female presence in the museum, recalling the employment by the Ladies' Auxiliary of young women to work as librarians and guides in the Museum of the Natural History Society during the late nineteenth and early twentieth centuries. Yet unlike the members of the Ladies' Auxiliary, Lusk Webster did not hire workers meant to be subordinate to a male curator, simply guiding the public through the exhibitions instead of creating the displays themselves. Rather, she insisted that her candidate be qualified and equipped with university degrees. Edith Hudson was an ideal applicant, for in addition to her BA and MA degrees, she had successfully applied for funding from the Canadian Museums Committee of the Carnegie Corporation, undertaking research for ten weeks at the National Gallery of Canada in 1936, and surveying museums and historic sites in France, Germany, and England in 1939.[70]

All the same, Lusk Webster felt that Hudson lacked the crucial element of hands-on museum experience, and so she decided to enroll her protégé in the apprenticeship program at the Newark Museum.[71] Begun in 1925 by the museum's founder, John Cotton Dana, the apprenticeship program strove to equip an intelligent workforce with an array of practical skills that could transform 'gloomy museums' into useful institutions providing concrete benefits to society.[72] Dana and his associates strove to avoid specialization by having the apprentices work in each department, receiving a salary of fifty dollars per week in return. The apprentices followed an eight-month program, beginning their training in the public library connected with the Newark Museum before undertaking between two and five weeks of practical work in the Education, Registration, Exhibitions, and Science Departments.[73] Instead of dividing museum staff into expert curators and those who performed unskilled labour such as guards, Dana's program was meant to create a new kind of practical worker situated somewhere in between. The founder of the Newark Museum and his followers argued that the most useful and important kind of museum worker would perform 'active service, no longer isolated from the everyday life, no longer existing chiefly for the pleasure and enlightenment of the student and the initiated.'[74]

When Lusk Webster informed Currelly of her decision to enroll Hudson in the apprenticeship program, he responded with dismay, insisting that Hudson receive her museum training from him in Toronto. He criticized the program in Newark, arguing that it was 'no better than that given to our school children here.'[75] He reported having visited the Newark Museum in the past and being 'bitterly disappointed' because there was 'very little in the way of a museum.'[76] The director of the Royal Ontario Museum of Archaeology defined museums in terms of the original and valuable objects in their collections. Dana, on the other hand, openly ridiculed the high cost of European oil paintings and ancient artifacts, arguing that exhibitions of useful objects, such as bathtubs, would be of greater interest to the populace of Newark, an industrialized American city. Currelly's disgust with the populist nature of the Newark Museum, however, did not sway Lusk Webster. In 1941 she provided a weak defence of Dana's program, explaining that she had set aside her 'own objections to Newark, for I know no place where contact with the public is so intimate, or where instruction is given to children in such an elementary form, and believe that doing odd jobs in a one horse museum, is just what she [i.e., Hudson] needs to counteract her academic tendencies and fit her to meet our requirements.'[77] Lusk Webster seems to have associated the Newark Museum with the kind of menial labour liable to take Hudson down a peg, preparing her for work at the relatively small and underfunded New Brunswick Museum.

This exchange between Currelly and Lusk Webster reveals contested visions of museum professionals. One vision, supported by Dana and his followers, affirmed that museum workers should possess the practical skills required to produce diverse exhibitions that served the public instead of showcasing elitist knowledge. The other, supported by Currelly and the members of the Canadian Museums Committee, involved training students with MAs or PhDs to undertake specialized museum research, classification, and curatorship. When he recommended that Hudson receive training at his museum in Toronto, Currelly endorsed the pedagogical practices of the Canadian Museums Committee, an organization that had already shaped Hudson's education by awarding her a fellowship. As noted above, in 1936 she had undertaken research at the National Gallery of Canada in Ottawa, reading a wide range of art history textbooks in addition to quizzing staff members about how to make slides and restore pictures, and had later travelled throughout Europe to see various artworks.[78] Other candidates, including Donald A. Taylor, had similarly used a travel grant from the Canadian Museums Committee to visit American museums. He additionally pursued both hands-on and academic museum work in geology and paleontology by working with the directors and staff of different museums at the Royal Ontario Museums for ten months in 1934.[79] Currelly likely had a similar plan for training Hudson at his institution, albeit in the fine art and craft objects that interested her. The training promoted by the Canadian Museums Committee overlapped with that of Dana's apprenticeship program to a certain degree – both provided hands-on experience and the opportunity to visit important museums and art galleries – but it was designed to create specialists of particular kinds of objects who would direct museums or work as professional curators, rather than become flexible staff able to serve a broad public.

Members of the Canadian Museums Committee endorsed a kind of apprenticeship training with museum experts in large part because there were no official museum training programs in Canada, and still very few in the United States – the program created by Sachs in 1921 was indeed exceptional. One fundamental goal of Committee members was to evaluate, exploit, and create educational opportunities that would produce professionalized museum staff. Their emphasis on museum education echoes the earlier attempts made by the Carnegie Corporation of New York to professionalize library workers, though in that case library schools were already in existence. After ceasing to fund library buildings in 1917, the Carnegie Corporation focused on library education, a policy change initiated by Henry Pritchett, executive of the Carnegie foundation for the advancement of teaching.[80] He commissioned a survey of libraries in 1916, which resulted in a report calling for trained and efficient librarians. According to historian Barbara Brand, the small library schools that had prepared women to work in Carnegie libraries were ignored, with attention paid to reforming the fifteen 'professional' library schools, including the Columbia Library School, then active in the United States.[81] The Carnegie report insisted that only instructors with adequate experience and college degrees should teach in these programs, which should accept only students who were already college graduates. According to the Carnegie report, within these programs a proper librarian would acquire a broad knowledge and professional attitude, with such practical work as filing, indexing, and typewriting allocated to female high-school graduates trained in classes to be offered by large libraries. This hierarchical plan was meant, Brand argues, to counteract the feminization of library work by raising its intellectual status and attracting more men into the field. Jacalyn Eddy agrees that formal library training was designed to counteract the fact that by 1920 90 per cent of America's librarians were women.[82] The gendered nature of librarianship is a subject of much discussion and debate in the literature on library history, with scholars like Brand and Eddy considering attempts to 'masculinize' library work and others producing accounts of how influential library women both conformed to and resisted these efforts.[83]

Despite the dominance of the so-called professional library schools, there was ongoing disagreement about what kind of education students should receive, a point in common with later discussions of museum training. In an 1887 article published in *Library Notes*, Melvil Dewey, an American librarian famous both for creating the Dewey decimal system of classification and founding the first library school in Albany, New York, in 1883, argued that bachelor's and master's programs in library science should be just as rigorous as other programs, and subject to strict examination procedures.[84] Yet, according to library historian Dee Garrison, Dewey emphasized technical skills in his own curriculum, incurring opposition from those who wished to raise the status of library work by linking it with intellectual rather than manual labour.[85] In 1923 the president of the American Libraries Association, Charles C. Williamson, for example, criticized library education that included such clerical skills as cataloguing and typewriting.[86] Garrison argues that the service-oriented aspect of public libraries associated them with a docile kind of femininity that was, and remains, devalued in Western culture, an association that prompted attempts to distinguish library work from skills considered to be women's work. Addressing the same issue, Roma Harris bluntly argues that librarianship maintained a lowly status because of its association with both women and service.[87] Those striving to professionalize librarians therefore tried to achieve a more rational and scientific identity for them, shifting their identities away from providing direct service to the public and toward pursuing autonomous research.

In some ways, the Canadian Museums Committee sought to professionalize museum work along the same lines, focusing on research more than service. The stated goal of the Committee, however, was to displace amateurs, not women per se. When Hudson was appointed curator of the Art Department of the New Brunswick Museum in 1942, for instance, she replaced her 'amateur' benefactor, Alice Lusk Webster.[88] The gendered connotations of museum professionalization can nevertheless be addressed by taking a closer look at Hudson's career. It provides an important example of museum professionalization because she was trained by both the Canadian Museums Committee and the Newark Museum, combining the two contested models of museum staff. One reason Hudson was able to blend the two visions of museum workers into a single person was her sex. The Newark Museum training program primarily attracted female candidates. Records housed at the Newark Museum indicate that between 1925 and 1941 the apprenticeship program enrolled 217 students: 204 of them were women, and only 13 were men.[89] This statistic is partly explained by the gendered divisions of work and identity during the first half of the twentieth century. Dana's program envisioned the ideal museum worker as flexible and practical, dedicated to serving the public and educating children, roles then coded as feminine. Official publications released by the Newark Museum explicitly recognized that the apprenticeship program would appeal more to women than men, arguing that a man would want to specialize and make a name for himself, whereas a woman was 'like Lord Bacon,' taking 'all knowledge for her province.'[90] Women were thus naturally suited to work in museums, a point reinforced when apprentices received advice from representatives of large department stores in Newark, who informed the young women about what an employer would demand in terms of personal appearance, personality, and conduct.[91] The ideal museum worker favoured by Dana and his followers was an accommodating, pleasant, and attractive young woman, who would be 'fleet of foot, supple of wrist, accurate of eye, deft of hand, in good health, and merry. She is in practice a learner of a number of subjects. She has, probably, one or more foreign languages, some use of accurate, even elegant, English, the habit of doing more-or-less what she is told.'[92] This obedient woman would also be 'a bargain,' willing (or obliged) to work for half the wages a man would demand, an added bonus for underfunded institutions.[93] While the ideal female museum worker promoted by Dana's program focused on appearance in keeping with the 1917 report of the American Association of Museums, the Newark graduate was meant to please the public rather than wealthy art collectors and potential donors.

In contrast to the highly gendered image of the desired museum worker presented by the Newark Museum, the specialized museum curator or director pursued by the Canadian Museums Committee was not exclusively identified with either men or women. Between 1933 and 1938 the Committee funded some 26 students, including 12 women and 14 men.[94] It might therefore seem that the Canadian Museums Committee was devoted to the principle of gender equality, given that its members supported the education of female curators. Evaluating this possibility remains difficult because the surviving documentation related to the candidates who received Carnegie funding contains few details, simply listing the persons selected and their course of study. Yet, unlike Currelly, key members of the Canadian Museums Committee did not entirely dismiss Dana's apprenticeship program, and even enrolled three of their protégés in it, all of them women. In 1934, H.O. McCurry argued that the Newark Museum provided 'the best general training in museum work possible.'[95] He thereby emphasized generalized training for some women in contrast to the specialization officially endorsed by the Committee. It is striking that only male recipients of Carnegie funding, including Bailey and Taylor, were described in official reports as future directors of museums. Overall, then, the members of the Canadian Museums Committee seem to have pursued the production of specialized and credentialed 'masculine' museum personnel able to manage the collections, not subservient female staff members devoted to the public.

Unlike her male colleagues at the New Brunswick Museum, Hudson was trained to be both a specialist and a generalist, both a leader and a follower, both a professional and an underpaid servant of the public. She did not embrace all of these roles equally, a point that annoyed even Lusk Webster, her strongest supporter. Despite completing her apprenticeship in Newark, Hudson resented the servile work she performed for the school-service program at the New Brunswick Museum. In 1942 she wrote to Ruth Home, a lecturer who organized educational programs at the Royal Ontario Museums, complaining that she was spending too much of her time 'spoon-feeding' notes to rural schoolteachers in New Brunswick.[96] Hudson also openly rebelled against the gender distinctions enforced by her institution. In 1942 she remarked that although a new director was desperately needed, the Management Committee would wait until the war was over to begin its search because 'women aren't considered very able in these parts.'[97] By 1945, Hudson had announced her intention to find a new position, claiming that the 'Board refuses to grant equal status to male and female workers, regardless of training, qualifications, or anything else,' and noting that her annual salary was $1,800 though it 'should be $2,400, if I were paid the same as the male curator on the staff.'[98] Hudson was clearly not a submissive employee willing to be paid less than a man. Nor was she willing to accrue symbolic rather than economic capital. In the end, Hudson returned to the Newark Museum, working in the Registrar's Office for a starting salary of $2,000 per year, a fact which suggests that the obedient and poorly paid female museum worker described in the museum's apprenticeship pamphlet of 1928 did not necessarily pan out in practice.[99]

Although Lusk Webster consistently defended Hudson, she argued that her protégé had been too assertive at the New Brunswick Museum. This point was made by Lusk Webster in 1947, when she informed the curator hired to replace Hudson that his predecessor had angered male administrators by 'over-stepping the mark,' whereas Lusk Webster strove to maintain good relationships with them by displaying friendly and accommodating behaviour.[100] Lusk Webster stressed the importance of performing traditional 'feminine' qualities within the museum, implying that acting like the ideally servile and self-effacing museum worker described in the apprenticeship pamphlet could function as a survival mechanism for ambitious women, as well as for men engaged in the 'feminine' role of managing an art department. Although such gendered expectations about appropriate behaviour were and remain commonplace in the Western workplace, references to the confident personality of Hudson suggest that gender was central to debates about the shifting status of museum workers, affecting the professionalization of museums. Her refusal to 'spoon-feed' or otherwise perform domestic labour contrasts with Lusk Webster's proud assertion of her role in unpacking, arranging, and cleaning objects, as well as tidying the exhibition spaces of the Art Department, noted in chapter 3.[101] Lusk Webster regularly referred to herself as a housewife, particularly when giving talks to local women's groups in New Brunswick, emphasizing her bodily labour within the museum in common with that of MacIntosh. When the director of the New Brunswick Museum affirmed that rolling up his sleeves and getting down on his hands and knees were an essential part of his occupation, he invoked the kind of household labour typically associated with women. This association could have been enhanced when MacIntosh presided as curator of the Museum of the Natural History Society because this institution was located in a transformed house that he lived in and cared for. The model of curatorship supported by both MacIntosh and Lusk Webster involved an engaged and passionate kind of caregiving, the kind increasingly associated with 'amateur' natural historians and traditionally associated with women's domestic labour.

According to art historian Craig Clunas, during the twentieth century the institutional status of museums was defined against what was done in the home. Focusing on the installation of Asian visual culture, Clunas argues that curators increasingly used taxonomical classifications, particularly in relation to items of luxury consumption originally designed for the Chinese domestic market. He contends that by organizing Asian clothing, ceramics, wine jars, and personal religious items, museum curators strove to undermine their strong association with femininity and domestic use, erasing the function of Chinese art by placing it within an art-historical narrative.[102] Lusk Webster clearly participated in this re-evaluation of Asian material culture, committing herself to both the academic identity and professionalization of the New Brunswick Museum. Drawing on the latest scholarly publications and guided by Currelly, she wrote labels that were brief and factual, neglecting to mention her patronage.[103] The Mandarin coats and priests' robes that Lusk Webster had acquired hung lifeless in carefully arranged cases; they did not adorn her body as she welcomed visitors in the manner of a hostess at the Oriental Exhibition of 1924 discussed in chapter 3. All the same, she continued to foreground her physical labour, linking her activities with the earlier and potentially more 'feminine' kind of curating embodied by MacIntosh. In the end, then, Webster may have had more in common with MacIntosh than with Hudson, parting ways with her husband's efforts to associate museum work exclusively with intellectual activities.

Conclusions

The careers of Bailey and Hudson exemplify the extended process of defining professionalization in a Canadian museum, before the triumph of a more academic and credentialed version of curatorship. The discussion of MacIntosh also represents this contested period, suggesting that such elites as J.C. Webster and Lusk Webster could not simply commandeer the New Brunswick Museum, forcing their values and identities on those who had long supported the Museum of the Natural History Society. Nor were these elites homogeneous, untouched by considerations of gender and educational capital, as indicated by my contention that Lusk Webster's approach both overlapped with and differed from that of her husband. Even the Carnegie Corporation was not strictly unified, for although it endorsed elite culture, its focus on public education enabled MacIntosh to flourish longer than he otherwise might have. Carnegie influence was contradictory, promoting the establishment of professional cultural authorities as Brison has argued, but allowing the 'old guard' to continue the public education programs begun during the late nineteenth century. In the 1930s and 1940s, competing visions of the New Brunswick Museum existed side by side: former members of the Natural History Society insisted that the institution serve the general public by improving the educational and economic prospects of the province, while newcomers like J.C. Webster affirmed that the museum should become an enviable example of elite culture, run by equally cultivated administrators.

In addition to issues of class and education, gender clearly informed constructions of the identity of museum workers during the 1930s and 1940s in Canada and the United States. John Cotton Dana's ideal museum worker was a compliant woman, while the image promoted by the members of the Canadian Museums Committee was that of a highly specialized, masculine leader able to undertake intellectual research. Caught between these competing visions, Edith Hudson found her position at the New Brunswick Museum untenable. In some ways, MacIntosh was equally situated between these two ideals, albeit at the end rather than the beginning of his career. He continued to associate curatorship with physical labour in addition to the collection and arrangement of objects. His description of the curator who rolled up his sleeves was in keeping with conventional notions of masculine physicality, but also potentially linked with housekeeping and the generalized service increasingly considered feminine, at least by those arguing for more intellectually oriented and research-oriented curators. The absorbed and active male body described by MacIntosh was at odds with the cultivated body of the curator envisioned by the American Association of Museums and the welcoming female staff member promoted by the Newark Museum's apprenticeship program. It is striking that these different images of ideal staff members were informed by correspondingly different understandings of the museum's function. For Dana and his followers, museums were to be open and accessible, serving a diverse public staffed by attractive and pleasant women. According to Sachs, the American Association of Museums, Lusk Webster, J.C. Webster, and the members of the Canadian Museums Committee, museums were rightly bastions of elite culture, able to enlighten as well as cultivate the lower classes, and run by well-trained curators who identified with wealthy patrons. This more hierarchical version of the museum and its staff ostensibly won the battle, but has been consistently challenged, particularly within the last decade.

Current debates about the proper identity of museum curators – should they respond to the demands of the public, or focus on producing knowledge about the objects held in the museum's collections? – do not simply mirror these earlier discussions but can be enlightened and challenged by them. Some recent scholarship seems to conflate the definition of the curator with that of the museum, perhaps accepting the historically specific idea that curators embody or at least represent the institution. Young, for instance, fears that the recent movement away from research-oriented curators to those who provide public service amounts to an attack on the museum itself. In her account of what she calls the 'post-museum,' Eilean Hooper-Greenhill echoes Clifford by encouraging a more service-oriented role for curators but similarly assumes that moving them from a position of authority toward one of facilitation marks a kind of 'end' of the modern museum.[104] These discussions may also invoke historical conceptions of class, however unwittingly. Clifford's vision of curators who enable the use of collections is closer to the 'working-class model' endorsed by members of the Natural History Society of New Brunswick and Dana – despite their own largely middle-class identities – and Young's position resembles that of Webster, who saw elite culture disseminated by experts producing knowledge for the good of the public, even if that public did not always appreciate it. Reassertions of the gendered nature of museum work are more difficult to detect in recent publications, but scholars who are opposed to the museum becoming a public resource as envisaged by Dana may express covert anxieties about curators losing the symbolic capital, status, and masculine aura that many of them finally managed to achieve. It is worth considering whether or not criticisms of the so-called decline of the modern museum are ultimately underpinned by fears that it will become a 'feminine' space dedicated to unrigorous play rather than carefully managed educational experiences.

Conclusion

The current website of the New Brunswick Museum conveys some anxiety about the continuing transformation of the institution. An overview of the museum's impressive history ends with the following statement: 'In April 1996, the New Brunswick Museum officially opened its Exhibition Centre in leased space in uptown Saint John. The museum now offers three floors and 60,000 square feet of exhibition spaces and a wide range of public programs.'[1] The commercial nature of the new location in Market Square, a renovated shopping mall, is never mentioned. The website of Market Square – not linked to that of the museum – promotes the 'distinctive blend of shopping, entertainment and dining' provided by the fast-food outlets, luggage store, pub, and Saint John Free Public Library housed alongside the New Brunswick Museum.[2] The site portrays both the library and the museum as entertaining services, conflating the two institutions in a way that would worry some critics discussed in the introduction to this book while reinforcing what cultural theorist Alan Bryman calls the dedifferentiation of consumption, when such cultural practices as shopping, viewing exhibitions, and eating become indistinguishable.[3] Most visible at Disney theme parks and Las Vegas casinos, this relatively recent marketing trend was adopted to a lesser degree in Saint John both to reshape the harbourfront area and attract more local as well as international visitors to the underfunded museum. If steadily increasing attendance numbers can measure success, then the plan is working. In May of 2009, New Brunswick Museum chief executive officer Jane Fullerton announced that the total number of visitors had increased by 30 per cent to 67,313 from 2008 to 2009, noting that 'we were very gratified by this significant increase in attendance.'[4]

Yet administrators were clearly concerned by the potential loss of the museum's distinct status and identity when contemplating the relocation of its exhibition spaces. In 1996, Richard Oland, then president of the New Brunswick Museum, claimed that the board of directors decided to 'make the new museum look like the old one from the outside,' by having representations of sandstone blocks, pillars, and cornices painted on the façade inside the shopping mall. According to him, the image would 'remind visitors that this new facility is part of a museum tradition reaching all the way back to 1842.'[5] The painted architectural elements were meant to create a visual link between the two building sites, while insisting on a continuous heritage that ultimately stemmed from the nineteenth century. Scholars Carol Duncan and Alan Wallach explain that the typically classical façades of museums mark an important threshold, signalling to visitors that they are passing from the everyday world into an important and even sacrosanct museum space freed from the practical concerns of the present.[6] The flat 'storefront' inside the Market Square is nevertheless more decorative and less tangible than the majestic, three-dimensional façade of the 1930s building, suggesting that the new exhibition spaces offer a diminished sense of materiality, authority, and independence – possibilities that worry critics who perceive a broad movement away from object-centred museum policies and toward info-tainment.[7]

At the same time, the new location makes historical associations that the administrators of the New Brunswick Museum may have overlooked. As indicated in my discussion of the Ladies' Auxiliary of the Natural History Society of New Brunswick in chapter 3, engaging in consumer practices and eating in proximity to museum exhibits is nothing new; it recalls the nineteenth- and early twentieth-century social traditions primarily fostered by women within the previous museum buildings in Saint John. Material consumption was featured by the museum women who organized the Oriental Exhibition in 1924, for example, but economic interests were also fundamental to the foundation of the collections that were ultimately amalgamated by the New Brunswick Museum, including those of Abraham Gesner, the Mechanics' Institute, and the Natural History Society. In chapter 2, I explained that the latter organization formed a museum to promote the industrial development of the province by increasing the public's knowledge of its natural resources. The combination of consumption, display, and economic goals in the new exhibition spaces could thus be considered old-fashioned, rather than a recent alteration that threatens the museum's integrity. The location of the public library within the same building as the museum could be considered another return to tradition, though this combination of resources was for the most part an unrealized goal of the members of the Natural History Society as well as the other early museum-building societies compared in chapter 4. The relocation of these public institutions to the Market Square complex might nevertheless fulfill the dream of early museum founders by allowing visitors to compare and contrast material and written forms of knowledge, while encouraging administrators to work together toward common ends.

All the same, there are significant departures from the past in the new exhibition spaces. Among other things, the shifting nature of the economy, the image of New Brunswick, and gender dynamics have had an impact on the New Brunswick Museum. For example, Market Square is managed for profit and includes private businesses, whereas the nineteenth-century events were fundraisers or social occasions. The consumption featured at Market Square is often corporate, consisting of standardized products rather than locally produced goods or spectacles offered as a form of charitable donation. The New Brunswick Museum is now considered by government as a tool of urban development that can enhance tourism, not exclusively as a method of promoting natural resources. In fact, the current installations celebrate the past industrialization of New Brunswick, especially nineteenth-century forestry and shipbuilding; they do not portray the province as undeveloped and ripe for future economic expansion. And, as indicated by the previous reference to Jane Fullerton, women are now positioned in authoritative roles at the New Brunswick Museum, including that of CEO, although others continue to function in a volunteer capacity as docents and fundraisers.

While recognizing these historical changes, I want to intervene in critical museum theory by emphasizing continuities rather than only differences. Much literature about contemporary museums highlights change by either implying or explicitly arguing that early museums were authoritative institutions primarily devoted to education. What scholars see as the sheer difference of the current situation – museums aim to please the public, are more corporate, promote travelling 'blockbuster' exhibitions, and strive to produce profit – is perceived either as a loss of purpose and public utility, or welcomed as a move toward a newfound flexibility and openness.[8] I contend that a more complex picture of the museum's past undermines both positions while encouraging the formation of new questions in relation to current institutions.

Instead of bemoaning or praising the public orientation of many contemporary museums, for instance, critics could ask: Exactly how do recent forms of museum consumption diverge from the multi-sensory exhibitions featured in nineteenth- and early twentieth-century institutions? Is dedifferentiation really a new concept? Do gendered assumptions underpin some critiques of the corporate museum? Do they betray the fear that an implicitly authoritative and masculine museum structure could be replaced by the bodily pleasures conventionally linked with women, thereby causing a decline in the cultural status of museums? Was the early museum created more by exchanging objects than preserving them? Has the professionalization of museums ever really been achieved, or has it remained a domain of continual contestation? Can the strategies of long-lived organizations – as indicated in chapter 4, they collected a diverse array of objects rather than specializing in a single kind, employed curators who were non-specialists devoted to physical labour and caring for objects as well as public education, held popular social events that were enjoyed by the public, encouraged a high degree of female participation, and remained committed to the international exchange of objects and ideas, as well as to research and publication – inspire or inform current museum policy? Instead of being prescriptive, my goal in *Defining the Modern Museum* has been to open up the debate, asking those engaged in critical museum theory to reflect on the past in order to rethink the present.

My book has adopted a case study approach in order to make original contributions to critical museum theory. At the most basic level, this book has offered new information based on extensive archival research, documenting Canadian institutions that had not been extensively studied, particularly the New Brunswick Museum and its precursors. This methodology revealed the international exchanges promoted first by the male members of the Natural History Society and later by Alice Lusk Webster, the loan collections and events meant to teach the public how to see, the extent of female participation in the institutions, the varying interactions between the museums and library collections, and the battle to define curatorship during the early twentieth century. The latter discussion of curators was especially crucial because very little has been written about the early curatorship of natural history and other diverse museums, with most recent literature focusing on contemporary curators of art exhibitions and international biennials.[9] More importantly, however, *Defining the Modern Museum* offers a new way to think about museums by emphasizing their interrelationships and relationships with other institutions. Instead of a static museum formed primarily by collecting, preserving, and exhibiting objects, this book has presented the museum as a process of continual exchange and the relational construction of values. The ideal museum, conceived of differently by a range of reformers, including J.C. Webster and John Cotton Dana, was never fully achieved. Recognizing that early museums were ultimately impossible can highlight what is distinctive about contemporary museums without creating a simplified vision of early museums to either defend or discard.

This conclusion has leaped from the 1940s, where chapter 5 left off, to the contemporary New Brunswick Museum, a move that may seem sudden, especially to historians. In some ways, this historical gap was determined by privacy policies and archival documents, but it was also deliberate on my part, designed to avoid constructing a tidy, chronological narrative that attempted to explain all the transitions experienced by the institution. I wanted to emphasize the messiness of this and other museums. For even when early administrators strove to organize and catalogue museum collections, the objects often remained unlabelled, with exhibitions failing to achieve coverage, and storage areas filled with discarded or duplicate material. This point provides another link between the past and most institutions today. The storage areas of the New Brunswick Museum are fascinating, cluttered with a diverse array of carefully identified, unknown, pristine, and broken objects. My overall ambition was to avoid creating another impossibly perfect museum in this text, an ambition that might also inevitably result in failure.

Notes

Introduction

1 Michael O'Hanlon, Foreword to *Knowing Things: Exploring the Collections at the Pitt Rivers Museum, 1884–1945*, by Chris Gosden and Frances Larson (Oxford: Oxford University Press, 2007), xvii.

2 Gosden and Larson, *Knowing Things*, 11.

3 See, for example, Pierre Bourdieu and Alain Darbel, *L'Amour de l'art: Les Musées européens et leur public* (Paris: Minuit, 1969), English trans. *The Love of Art: European Art Museums and Their Public*, trans. Caroline Beattie and Nick Merriman (Stanford: Stanford University Press, 1990); Carol Duncan and AlanWallach, 'The Museum of Modern Art as Late Capitalist Ritual,' *Marxist Perspectives*, Winter 1978, pp. 28–51, and their 'The Universal Survey Museum,' *Art History* 3 (Dec. 1980): 447–69; and Tony Bennett, *The Birth of the Museum: History, Theory, Politics* (New York: Routledge, 1995).

4 See, for example, Michael Ames, *Cannibal Tours and Glass Boxes: The Anthropology of Museums* (Vancouver: University of British Columbia Press,1991); Mieke Bal, *Double Exposures: The Subject of Cultural Analysis* (New York: Routledge, 1996); Barbara Kirshenblatt-Gimblett, *Destination Culture: Tourism, Museums, and Heritage* (Berkeley: University of California Press, 1998); and Moira Simpson, *Making Representations: Museums in the Post-Colonial Era* (New York: Routledge, 1996).

5 Stephen Bann, 'Art History and Museums,' in *The Subjects of Art History: Historical Objects in Contemporary Perspective*, ed. Mark A. Cheetham, Michael Ann Holly, and Keith Moxey (Cambridge: Cambridge University Press, 1998), 241; Ruth Phillips, *Trading Identities: The Souvenir in Native North American Art from the Northeast, 1700–1900* (Seattle: University of Washington Press, 1998), 69; and Andrew McClellan, ed., *Art and Its Publics: Museum Studies at the Millennium* (Oxford: Blackwell, 2003), xviii.

6 Steven Conn, *Do Museums Still Need Objects?* (Philadelphia: University of Pennsylvania Press, 2010),15. Andrea Witcomb, in *Re-imagining the Museum: Beyond the Mausoleum* (London: Routledge, 2003), 12, argues that her book aims to 'balance the attack on museums.'

7 James Cuno, Introduction to *Whose Muse? Art Museums and the Public Trust*, ed. James Cuno (Princeton: Princeton University Press, 2004), 21.

8 See, for example, Nick Prior, 'Having One's Tate and Eating It: Transformations of the Museum in a Hypermodern Era,' in McClellan, ed., *Art and Its Publics: Museum Studies at the Millennium*, 64; and John H. Falk, *Identity and the Museum Visitor Experience* (Walnut Creek, CA: Left Coast Press, 2009), 37.

9 Robert R. Janes, *Museums in a Troubled World: Renewal, Irrelevance or Collapse?* (London: Routledge, 2009), 184; and Danielle Rice, 'Museums: Theory, Practice, and Illusion,' in McClellan, ed., *Art and Its Publics*, 93.

10 Though Didier Maleuvre's *Museum Memories: History, Technology, Art* (Stanford: Stanford University Press, 1999) is an admirable book, it provides an example of this phenomenon.

11 Carol Duncan, *Civilizing Rituals: Inside Public Art Museums* (London: Routledge, 1995).

12 Timothy W. Luke, in *Museum Politics: Power Plays at the Exhibition* (Minneapolis: University of Minnesota Press, 2002), discusses the Holocaust Memorial Museum and the exhibition 'The West as America' at the National Museum of Art in Washington, DC, which have both received multiple published interpretations.

13 See, for example, Karsten Schubert, *The Curator's Egg: The Evolution of the Museum Concept from the French Revolution to the Present Day* (London: Ridinghouse, 2009), 57.

14 Eilean Hooper-Greenhill, *Museums and the Interpretation of Visual Culture* (London: Routledge, 2000), 151–4.

15 This criticism is now almost a truism. See, for example, Brian Young, *The Making and Unmaking of a University Museum: The McCord, 1921–1996* (Montreal and Kingston: McGill-Queen's University Press, 2000), 3 and 123; Luke, *Museum Politics*, 15–16; and Maurice Berger, 'The "Corporate" Museum,' in *Museums of Tomorrow: A Virtual Discussion*, ed. Maurice Berger (New York: Distributed Art Publishers, 2004), 47–80.

16 Juris Dilevko and Lisa Gottlieb, *The Evolution of Library and Museum Partnerships: Historical Antecedents, Contemporary Manifestations, and Future Directions* (Westport, CT: Libraries Unlimited, 2004), 1–10.

17 Kate Hill, *Culture and Class in English Public Museums, 1850–1914* (Aldershot: Ashgate, 2005).

18 Dipesh Chakrabarty, *Provincializing Europe: Postcolonial Thought and Historical Difference* (Princeton: Princeton University Press, 2000).
19 Chakrabarty, *Provincializing Europe*, 43.
20 Jacques Derrida, *Archive Fever: A Freudian Impression* (Chicago: University of Chicago Press, 1996).
21 Appendix to the Catalogue of Gesner's Museum, 1842–1843, Natural History Society [NHS] fonds, S128A, F133, Archives of the New Brunswick Museum [ANBM].
22 Antoinette Burton, ed., *Archive Stories: Fact, Fictions, and the Writing of History* (Durham, NC: Duke University Press, 2005); Carolyn Hamilton et al., eds, *Refiguring the Archive* (Dordrecht: Kluwer Academic Publishers, 2002); and Judith Halberstam, *In a Queer Time and Place: Transgender Bodies, Subcultural Lives* (New York: New York University Press, 2005).
23 Ben Dibley, 'The Museum's Redemption: Contact Zones, Government and the Limit of Reform,' *International Journal of Cultural Studies* 8.1 (2005): 5–27. See also Bennett, *The Birth of the Museum*; and James Clifford, 'Museums as Contact Zones,' in *Routes: Travel and Translation in the Late Twentieth Century* (Cambridge: Harvard University Press, 1997), 188–219.
24 Witcomb, *Re-imagining the Museum*, 169.
25 T.W. Acheson, *Saint John: The Making of a Colonial Urban Community* (Toronto: University of Toronto Press, 1985); and Judith Fingard, *Jack in Port: Sailortowns of Eastern Canada* (Toronto: University of Toronto Press, 1982).
26 New Brunswick Museum, 'New Brunswick Museum Identifies Architectural Firm,' Media Release, 15 September 2006.
27 See the official website of the New Brunswick Museum, www.nbm-mnb.ca/index.php?option=com_content&view=article&id=59&Itemid=251 (accessed 10 April 2011).
28 Allison Mitcham, *Prophet of the Wilderness: Abraham Gesner* (Hantsport, NS: Lancelot Press, 1995).
29 Mitcham, *Prophet of the Wilderness*, 75.
30 Evelyn P. Costello, 'A Report on the Saint John Mechanics' Institute, 1838–1890' (MA thesis, University of New Brunswick, 1974).
31 NHS General Minutes, 1862–90, 29 January 1862, NHS fonds, S127, F40, ANBM.
32 LeBaron Botsford, 'Annual Address,' *Bulletin of the Natural History Society of New Brunswick* 9 (1890): 5.
33 NHS General Minutes, 1862–90, 29 January 1862.
34 Eileen Diana Mak, 'Patterns of Change, Sources of Influence: An Historical Study of the Canadian Museum and the Middle Class, 1850–1950' (PhD

diss., University of British Columbia, 1996), 36–42; Eilean Hooper-Greenhill, *Museums and the Shaping of Knowledge* (London: Routledge, 1992), 168; and Susan Sheets-Pyenson, *Cathedrals of Science: The Development of Colonial Natural History Museums during the Late Nineteenth Century* (Kingston, ON: Queen's University Press, 1988).

35 William MacIntosh, 'Curator's Report,' *Bulletin of the Natural History Society of New Brunswick* 27 (1909): 155; and NHS General Minutes, 1912–20, 26 October 1915, NHS fonds, S127, F42, ANBM.

36 Mak, 'Patterns of Change, Sources of Influence,' 201.

37 Sir Henry A. Miers and S.F. Markham, *A Report on the Museums of Canada to the Carnegie Corporation of New York* (Edinburgh: T. and A. Constable, 1932), 42.

38 In 1881, the NHS resolved to create an associate class of membership for women, available for a fee of one dollar per year. Women would be allowed to participate in all public business of the NHS, but not its Council (NHS Council Minutes, 1862–1901, 9 May 1881, NHS fonds, S127, F37, ANBM).

39 See, for example, Ladies' Auxiliary Minutes, 1893–1905, 6 November 1900, NHS fonds, S128A, F114, ANBM; and NHS General Minutes, 1890–1911, 2 February 1909, NHS fonds, S127, F41, ANBM. See also chapter 3 of this book.

40 NHS General Minutes, 1890–1911, 3 January 1910.

41 Ladies' Auxiliary Minutes, Annual Report, 17 October 1910, NHS fonds, S128A, F115, ANBM.

42 For a detailed discussion of these women, see my article 'Strategic Donations: Women and Museums in New Brunswick, 1862–1930,' *Journal of Canadian Studies* 42.2 (Spring 2008): 1–24.

43 Board and Executive Committee and Management Committee of the New Brunswick Museum [NBM] Minutes, 1 October 1930, microfilm NBM–Board and Executive Committee Minutes, 1929–1967, ANBM.

44 Gerald Thomas, 'John C. Webster: Applying Material History – Developing the New Brunswick Museum,' in *Studies in History and Museums*, ed. Peter E. Rider (Hull, PQ: Canadian Museum of Civilization, 1994), 33–55.

45 For the Websters' Asian art collection, see the John Clarence Webster Collection [JCW] fonds, S200, F639–642, ANBM.

46 For Lusk Webster's biography, see 'Progress and Permanence: Women and the New Brunswick Museum, 1880–1980,' an interactive website about the history of more than fourteen women who donated objects to the Museum of the NHS and the NBM, created with Shawna Stairs Quinn, launched 18 January 2007, www.unbf.ca/womenandmuseum. Reviewed by Bonnie Huskins for *The Public Historian* 31 (Feb. 2009): 129–36.

47 Alice Lusk Webster's working files, drafts of speeches, etc., Art Department Records, NBM fonds, F545, ANBM.
48 For the trade, see Records of the Registration Department, Royal Ontario Museum, and 'Museum Exhibits Swelled by Gifts Valued at $25,000,' *Telegraph Journal*, 31 July 1934, p. 12.
49 Alice Lusk Webster's working files, drafts of speeches, etc., Art Department Records, NBM fonds, F545, ANBM.
50 Attempts to professionalize the museum are discussed in chapter 5 of this book.
51 Oliver Impey and Arthur MacGregor, eds, *The Origins of Museums: The Cabinet of Curiosities in Sixteenth- and Seventeenth-Century Europe* (Oxford: Clarendon Press, 1985); Joy Kenseth, '"A World of Wonders in One Closet Shut,"' in *The Age of the Marvelous*, ed. Joy Kenseth (Hanover, NH: Hood Museum of Art, Dartmouth College, 1991), 81–101; and Paula Findlen, *Possessing Nature: Museums, Collecting, and Scientific Culture in Early Modern Italy* (Berkeley: University of California Press, 1994).
52 For the move to the grammar school, see NHS Scrapbook, 1862–96, 16 March 1868, NHS fonds, S129, F120; and Botsford, 'Annual Address,' 5. See also Lianne McTavish and Joshua Dickison, 'William MacIntosh, Natural History and the Professionalization of the New Brunswick Museum, 1898–1940,' *Acadiensis: Journal of the History of the Atlantic Region* 36.2 (Spring 2007): 72–90.
53 Arjun Appadurai, *The Social Life of Things: Commodities in Cultural Perspective* (Cambridge: Cambridge University Press, 1986), 4.
54 Jordanna Bailkin, 'Picturing Feminism, Selling Liberalism: The Case of the Disappearing Holbein,' in *Museum Studies: An Anthology of Contexts*, ed. Bettina Messias Carbonell (Oxford: Blackwell, 2003), 261.
55 John Cotton Dana, 'The Gloom of the Museum,' in *The New Museum: Selected Writings by John Cotton Dana*, ed. William A. Peniston (Newark, NJ: Newark Museum, 1999), 55.

1. Exchanging Values in the Nineteenth-Century Museum Marketplace

1 Sean Markey, 'World's Oldest Shark Fossil Found,' *National Geographic News*, 1 Oct. 2003, pp. 1–2, news.nationalgeographic.com/news/2003/10/1001_031001_sharkfossil.html (accessed 12 April 2011).
2 Randall Miller, e-mail message to author, 15 March 2007.
3 Government of New Brunswick, Department of Wellness, Culture and Sport, Heritage Conservation Act, www.gnb.ca/0131/HeritageConservationAct/index,asp (accessed 12 April 2011).

4 New Brunswick Museum Press Release, 'Saint John Could Become First Geopark in North America,' 6 February 2008, www.nbm-mnb.ca/mnb.ca/index.php?option=com_content&view=article&id=230&Itemid=561 (accessed 11 April 2011).

5 Randall Miller, e-mail message to author, 28 February 2011. For the Global Geoparks Network, see www.unesco.org/new/en/natural-sciences/environment/earth-sciences/geoparks/global-geoparks-network (accessed 13 April 2011).

6 Natural History Society [NHS] General Minutes, 1862–90, 29 January 1862, NHS fonds, S127, F40, Archives of the New Brunswick Museum [ANBM].

7 NHS General Minutes, 1890–1911, letter read aloud to members on 2 June 1896, NHS fonds, S127, F41, ANBM.

8 See, for example, Enid Schildkrout and Curtis A. Keim, eds, *The Scramble for Art in Central Africa* (Cambridge: Cambridge University Press, 1998); and Barbara Lawson, 'Collecting Cultures: Canadian Missionaries, Pacific Islanders, and Museums,' in *Canadian Missionaries, Indigenous Peoples: Representing Religion at Home and Abroad*, ed. Alvyn Austin and Jamie S. Scott (Toronto: University of Toronto Press, 2005), 235–61.

9 Cited in Martin J.S. Rudwick, *Bursting the Limits of Time: The Reconstruction of Geohistory in the Age of Revolution* (Chicago: University of Chicago Press, 2005), 39–40.

10 Simon J. Knell, *The Culture of English Geology, 1815–1851: A Science Revealed through Its Collecting* (Aldershot: Ashgate, 2000), 116–18; and Rudwick, *Bursting the Limits of Time*, 40. For the culture of geology in England, see also Ludmilla Jordanova and Roy Porter, eds, *Images of the Earth: Essays in the History of the Environmental Sciences* (St Giles, UK: British Society for the History of Science, 1979).

11 Marcel Mauss, *The Gift: The Form and Reason for Exchange in Archaic Societies*, trans. W.D. Halls (New York: Routledge, 2002).

12 See, for example, Moira McLoughlin, *Museums and the Representation of Native Canadians: Negotiating the Borders of Culture* (New York: Routledge, 1999). Samuel J.M.M. Alberti in 'Acquisition: Collecting Networks and the Museum,' in *Nature and Culture: Objects, Disciplines and the Manchester Museum* (Manchester: Manchester University Press, 2009), 91–122, provides a recent discussion but does not exclusively or extensively focus on exchanges.

13 Wolfgang Ernst, 'Archi(ve)textures of Museology,' in *Museums and Memory*, ed. Susan A. Crane (Stanford: Stanford University Press, 2000), 17–34.

14 Krzysztof Pomian, *Collectors and Curiosities: Paris and Venice, 1500–1800*, trans. Elizabeth Wiles-Portier (Cambridge: Polity Press, 1990), 20, 31, and 71.

15 Jean Baudrillard, 'The System of Collecting,' in *The Cultures of Collecting*, ed. John Elsner and Roger Cardinal (Cambridge: Harvard University Press, 1994), 7.
16 Suzanne Zeller, *Inventing Canada: Early Victorian Science and the Idea of a Transcontinental Nation* (Toronto: University of Toronto Press, 1987), 49.
17 Gerald J. Cassidy, 'George Frederic Matthew: Invertebrate Paleontologist,' *Geoscience Canada* 15.2 (1988): 157.
18 Morris Zaslow, *Reading the Rocks: The Story of the Geological Survey of Canada, 1842–1972* (Toronto: Macmillan, 1975), 55–7.
19 See, for example, the advertisement in the *Morning News* [Saint John, NB], 3 January 1842, p. 4.
20 Abraham Gesner, *Synopsis of the Contents of Gesner's Museum of Natural History, at Saint John, N.B. Opened the Fifth Day of April, 1842* (Saint John, NB: Henry Chubb, 1842), 47.
21 For Gesner's biography, see Allison Mitcham, *Prophet of the Wilderness: Abraham Gesner* (Hantsport, NS: Lancelot Press, 1995).
22 Gesner, *Synopsis of the Contents of Gesner's Museum of Natural History*, back cover.
23 NHS Scrapbook, 1862–96, report in December 1890, 149, NHS fonds, S129, F120, ANBM.
24 Randall Miller, e-mail to author, 12 March 2007.
25 NHS Scrapbook, 1893–9, circular pasted on page 28, NHS fonds, S129, F121, ANBM.
26 NHS Council Minutes, 1862–1901, 13 September 1867, NHS fonds, S127, F37, ANBM.
27 Ibid., 10 October 1863.
28 NHS Scrapbook, 1862–96, handwritten list of specimens sent to the Buffalo Society of Natural History, March 1865.
29 NHS Council Minutes, 1862–1901, 11 December 1868.
30 NHS Scrapbook, 1893–9, letter from Samuel Kain to the Public Museum in Milwaukee, Wisconsin, 18 March 1895, 161.
31 Ibid.
32 Record of Artifacts Donated to the NHS, 1889–1912, 10 March 1898, NHS fonds, S128A, F134, ANBM.
33 Ibid., exchanged to NHS May 1889 for Japanese bird skins sent August 1898.
34 For a biography of Matthew, see Randall F. Miller, 'Matthew, George Frederic,' *Dictionary of Canadian Biography Online*, Vol. 15 (University of Toronto / Université de Laval, and Library and Archives Canada, 2000), www.biographi.ca (accessed 13 April 2011).

35 See Randall F. Miller, 'George Frederic Matthew's Contribution to Precambrian Paleobiology,' *Geoscience Canada* 30.1 (2003): 1–8.
36 NHS Scrapbook, 1893–9, letter from F.J.V. Skiff to Samuel Kain, 6 January 1896, 198.
37 Record of Artifacts Donated to the NHS, 1889–1912, 29 May 1896.
38 NHS Scrapbook, 1893–9, letter from F.J.V. Skiff to Samuel Kain, 16 May 1896, 215.
39 Mauss, 'The Exchange of Gifts and the Obligation to Reciprocate (Polynesia),' in *The Gift*, 11–23.
40 Maurice Godelier, *The Enigma of the Gift*, trans. Nora Scott (Chicago: University of Chicago Press, 1996), 14.
41 Christopher Gregory, *Gifts and Commodities* (London: Academic Press, 1982), 43.
42 Mauss, *The Gift*, 14–15. For critiques of his theories, see Godelier, *The Enigma of the Gift*, 17–18 and 48–55.
43 NHS Scrapbook, 1893–9, letter from Mr Kirkland to Geoffrey Stead, 16 September 1897, 267.
44 Ibid., letter from George F. Dawson to Samuel Kain, 13 August 1896, 220.
45 Ibid., letter to Percy Hall from G. Brown Goode, 13 June 1896, 228.
46 Godelier, *The Enigma of the Gift*, 12.
47 NHS Scrapbook, 1893–9, letter to Percy Hall from F.J.V. Skiff, 3 September 1896, 223.
48 For efforts to increase access to the collections, see NHS Council Minutes, 1862–1901, 22 November 1873; for field meetings, see 5 April 1874.
49 Ibid., 5 July 1880.
50 Doris Phillips, 'Nova Scotia's Aid for the Sufferers of the Great Saint John Fire (June 20th, 1877),' *Nova Scotia Historical Quarterly* 7.4 (1977): 351–66; and Ronald Rees, 'Changing St. John: The Old and the New,' *Canadian Geographical Journal* 90.5 (1975): 12–17.
51 For the Loyalist and historical clubs, see Greg Marquis, 'Commemorating the Loyalists in the Loyalist City: Saint John, New Brunswick, 1883–1934,' *Urban History Review* 33.1 (2004): 24–33.
52 These events are described in the *Bulletin of the Natural History Society of New Brunswick* 1 (1882): 5–8; 3 (1884): 42–5; 4 (1885): 103–9; 5 (1886): 37–42; 6 (1887): 76–8; and 7 (1888): 75–6. For the women's contributions, see NHS Council Minutes, 1862–1901, 6 June 1881, and 13 June 1881. I discuss the contributions of these women at length in chapter 3 of this book.
53 Kendra Kennedy, anthropology intern at the Field Museum of Natural History, e-mail to author, 27 July 2000.
54 Knell, *The Culture of English Geology*, 121.

55 NHS Scrapbook, 1893–9, letter to Professor Cory from Samuel Kain, 14 June 1898, 298.
56 Field Columbian Museum of Chicago, Historical File, 'Natural History Society of New Brunswick,' letter sent to F. J.V. Skiff from Samuel Kain, 1 July 1899, sides 3A, 3B, File D-556, Field Museum of Natural History Museum Archives [FMNHMA].
57 Ibid., letter sent to Professor Charles B. Cory from F.J.V. Skiff, 7 February 1899.
58 Ibid., letter sent to F. J.V. Skiff from Samuel Kain, 1 July 1899, side 3B.
59 Ibid., letter sent to George A. Dorsey from F. J.V. Skiff, 7 March 899.
60 Record of Artifacts Donated to the NHS, 1889–1912, 5 April 1898, August 1898, and May 1899. The May entry notes that the Paraguayan material came from Dr Emil Hassler, a specialist in Paraguayan ethnography.
61 For standard definitions of a commodity, see *The Free Dictionary by Farlex*, www.thefreedictionary.com/commodity (accessed 13 April 2011); and *The Merriam-Webster Online Dictionary*, www.meriam-webster.com/dictionary/commodity (accessed 13 April 2011).
62 Cited in Arjun Appadurai, *The Social Life of Things: Commodities in Cultural Perspective* (Cambridge: Cambridge University Press, 1986), 12.
63 NHS Council Minutes, 1862–1901, 13 September 1867.
64 See, for example, NHS Correspondence, 1868–1932, letter to NHS from G.D. Harris of Cornell University demanding specimens, letter 22, 19 November 1909, NHS fonds, S127, F3, ANBM.
65 Appadurai, *The Social Life of Things*, 4.
66 Ibid., 13.
67 James Clifford, 'On Collecting Art and Culture,' in *The Predicament of Culture: Twentieth-Century Ethnography, Literature, and Art* (Cambridge: Harvard University Press, 1988), 215–51.
68 Jonathan Culler, *Saussure* (Glasgow: Collins, 1976), 48.
69 Carol Duncan and Alan Wallach, 'The Universal Survey Museum,' *Art History* 3 (Dec. 1980): 447–69.
70 See, for example, Joy Kenseth, '"A World of Wonders in One Closet Shut,"' in *The Age of the Marvelous*, ed. Joy Kenseth (Hanover, NH: Hood Museum of Art, Dartmouth College, 1991), 81–101; and Stephen Greenblatt, 'Resonance and Wonder,' in *Exhibiting Cultures: The Poetics and Politics of Museum Display*, ed. Ivan Karp and Steven D. Lavine (Washington, DC: Smithsonian Institution Press, 1991), 42–56.
71 William MacIntosh, 'Curator's Report,' *Bulletin of the Natural History Society of New Brunswick* 27 (1909): 154–5.
72 Jacques Derrida, *The Truth in Painting*, trans. Geoff Bennington and Ian McLeod (Chicago: University of Chicago Press, 1987), 63.

73 NHS Scrapbook, 1862–96, exchange list in October 1893, 174; for the number of bulletins printed, see Samuel W. Kain, 'Report of the Council,' *Bulletin of the Natural History Society of New Brunswick* 11 (1893): 45.
74 M. Chamberlain, Robert Chalmers, and George U. Hay, 'Advertisement,' *Bulletin of the Natural History Society of New Brunswick* 1 (1882): 3.
75 William J. Wilson, Recording Secretary, 'Report of the Council,' *Bulletin of the Natural History Society of New Brunswick* 5 (1886): 41–2.
76 William J. Wilson, Recording Secretary, 'Report of the Council,' *Bulletin of the Natural History Society of New Brunswick* 4 (1885): 109.
77 William F. Ganong, 'On the Economic Mollusca of Acadia,' *Bulletin of the Natural History Society of New Brunswick* 8 (1889): 3–116.
78 George U. Hay, James Vroom, and John Brittain, 'Report of the Botanical Committee,' *Bulletin of the Natural History Society of New Brunswick* 6 (1887): 79.
79 NHS Scrapbook, 1862–96, Second Annual Report of 1863. They continued to lobby government; for example, see NHS Council Minutes, 1901–20, 6 October 1908, and Treasurer's Reports, NHS fonds, S128, F54, ANBM.
80 Zaslow, *Reading the Rocks*, 123.
81 Knell, *The Culture of English Geology*, 7. The Canadian survey had similar motivations. Zaslow, in *Reading the Rocks*, 48 and 55–7, argues that the head of the Geological Survey of Canada, Sir William Logan, planned to 'put our economic specimens conspicuously forward' in both a national museum and at international exhibitions. According to Nancy Christie, in 'Sir William Logan's Geological Empire and the "Humbug" of Economic Utility,' *Canadian Historical Review* 75. 2 (June 1994): 161–81, Logan merely feigned an interest in economic utility to pacify government officials while he pursued his real interest in less practical scientific research.
82 Loring Woart Bailey, *Report on the Mines and Minerals of New Brunswick* (Fredericton, NB: G.E. Fenety, 1864), 3. The geological work done by Bailey is discussed in Zaslow, *Reading the Rocks*, 95 and 180.
83 Bailey, *Report on the Mines and Minerals of New Brunswick*, 4.
84 Zaslow, *Reading the Rocks*, 125.
85 Ibid., 55; and Knell, *The Culture of English Geology*, 308.
86 Zaslow, *Reading the Rocks*, 143–4.
87 NHS Scrapbook, 1862–96, handwritten annual report, 17 January 1881, 192.
88 Percy G. Hall, Secretary to Council, 'Report of the Council,' *Bulletin of the Natural History Society of New Brunswick* 17 (1899): 177. See also Loring Woart Bailey, *Descriptive Catalogue of a Collection of Economic Minerals of New Brunswick Prepared for the Toronto Exhibition on behalf of the New Brunswick Government* (n.l., 1908).

89 Martin J.S. Rudwick, *The Meaning of Fossils: Episodes in the History of Palaeontology* (London: Macdonald and Company, 1972), 14.
90 Bailey, *Report on the Mines and Minerals of New Brunswick*, 15. According to Zaslow (*Reading the Rocks*, 93), Logan liked to hire amateurs who 'were well versed in local situations.' For the importance of fieldwork, see Rudwick, *Bursting the Limits of Time*, 41–2; and Martin J.S. Rudwick, *The Great Devonian Controversy: The Shaping of Scientific Knowledge among Gentlemanly Specialists* (Chicago: University of Chicago Press, 1985), 40–1.
91 Bailey, *Report on the Mines and Minerals of New Brunswick*, 15.
92 Rudwick, *The Great Devonian Controversy*, 424. For an excellent discussion of how stratigraphical analysis produced a geological way of seeing nature, visualizing the land as governable, see Bruce Braun, 'Producing Vertical Territory: Geology and Governmentality in Late Victorian Canada,' *Ecumene* 7.1 (2000): 7–46.
93 For the fashionable status of geology, see Knell, *The Culture of English Geology*, 35; and Rudwick, *The Meaning of Fossils*, 201.
94 William R. Brice and Silvia F. de M. Figueirôa, 'Charles Frederick Hartt – a Pioneer of Brazilian Geology,' *GSA Today*, March 2003, pp. 18–19.
95 George F. Matthew, *Report on the Superfcial* [sic] *Geology of Southern New Brunswick, 1878* (Montreal: Dawson Brothers, 1879).
96 Miller, 'George Frederic Matthew's Contribution to Precambrian Paleobiology,' 1–8.
97 NHS Correspondence, 1868–1932, letter to George F. Matthew from Spencer F. Baird, letter 4-1, 9 February 1884, NHS fonds, S127, F1, ANBM.
98 Roy Porter, 'Gentlemen and Geology: The Emergence of a Scientific Career, 1660–1920,' *Historical Journal* 21.4 (Dec. 1978): 809–36. See also Knell, *The Culture of English Geology*, 7.
99 Knell, *The Culture of English Geology*, 5 and 37. See also Rudwick, *The Great Devonian Controversy*, 40.
100 Knell, *The Culture of English Geology*, 123.
101 Ibid., 20 and 27; and Zaslow, *Reading the Rocks*, 26, 42, and 45. Mark Lawrence Hineline, in 'The Visual Culture of the Earth Sciences, 1863–1970' (PhD diss., University of California, San Diego, 1993), 378, refers to the 'appeal to the rock' to explain how researchers relied on specimens as evidence.
102 NHS Council Minutes, 1862–1901, 9 July 1888; and NHS General Minutes, 1862–90, 19 July 1888. The minutes indicate that Sir Leonard Tilley, the Society's patron, was also in attendance.
103 See, for example, NHS General Minutes, 1862–90, 2 January 1865.
104 Noted entomologist Caroline Heustis, for example, appears as a mem-

ber of the standing committee on invertebrates over fifteen years before women were admitted as associate members in 1881. She continued to serve on various committees, including the entomology committee. See www.unbf.ca/womenandmuseum for more information.

105 Rudwick, *Bursting the Limits of Time*, 68.

106 Knell, *The Culture of English Geology*, 29–30.

107 For sportsmen who fished and hunted in New Brunswick, see William Parenteau, 'A "Very Determined Opposition to the Law": Conservation, Angling Leases, and Social Conflict in the Canadian Atlantic Salmon Fishery, 1867–1914,' *Environmental History* 9.3 (July 2004): 436–63. According to Knell (*Reading the Rocks*, 294), England was considered fully mapped and no longer linked with adventure.

108 Noah Heringman, *Romantic Rocks, Aesthetic Geology* (Ithaca, NY: Cornell University Press, 2004), 10.

109 Zaslow, *Reading the Rocks*, 43.

110 Bailey, *Report on the Mines and Minerals of New Brunswick*, 4–5; and Matthew, *Report on the Superfcial* [sic] *Geology of Southern New Brunswick, 1878*, 18–21.

111 Loring Woart Bailey, *Report on the Geology of Northern New Brunswick* (Montreal: Dawson Brothers, 1881), 4.

112 See, for example, Brian Young, *The Making and Unmaking of a University Museum: The McCord, 1921–1996* (Montreal: McGill-Queen's University Press, 2000), 3 and 123; Timothy Luke, *Museum Politics: Power Plays at the Exhibition* (Minneapolis: University of Minnesota Press, 2002), 15–16; and Maurice Berger, 'The "Corporate" Museum,' in *Museums of Tomorrow: A Virtual Discussion*, ed. Maurice Berger (New York: Distributed Art Publishers, 2004), 47–80.

113 For Charles Saatchi's 'Sensation' exhibition in 1997, see Elaine A. King, 'So, What's the Price – *The PM Principle* – Power, People, and Money,' in *Ethics and the Visual Arts*, ed. Elaine A. King and Gail Levin (New York: Allworth Press, 2006), 1–17; and L. Rosenbaum, 'The Battle of Brooklyn Ends, the Controversy Continues,' *Art in America* 88.6 (June 2000): 39–43.

2. Learning to See: Vision, Visuality, and Material Culture, 1862–1929

1 Hal Foster, ed., *Vision and Visuality* (Seattle: Bay Press, 1988), ix.

2 Jonathan Crary, *Techniques of the Observer: On Vision and Modernity in the Nineteenth Century* (Cambridge, MA: MIT Press, 1990). See also his *Suspensions of Perception: Attention, Spectacle, and Modern Culture* (Cambridge, MA: MIT Press, 1999). For some of the burgeoning literature on visuality,

see Teresa Brennan and Martin Jay, eds, *Vision in Context: Historical and Contemporary Perspectives on Sight* (New York: Routledge, 1996); Robert S. Nelson, ed., *Visuality before and beyond the Renaissance: Seeing as Others Saw* (Cambridge: Cambridge University Press, 1997); and Craig Clunas, *Pictures and Visuality in Early Modern China* (Princeton: Princeton University Press, 1997).

3 For a critique of Crary's account of early modern vision, see David Summers, review of *Suspension of Perception*, by Jonathan Crary, *Art Bulletin* 83.1 (March 2001): 57–61. For studies that extend Crary's analysis, see Elizabeth Ann Wiatr, 'Seeing American: Visual Education and the Making of Modern Observers, 1900–1935' (PhD diss., University of California, Irvine, 2003); and Peter John Brownlee, '"The Economy of the Eyes": Vision and the Cultural Production of the Market Revolution, 1800–1860' (PhD diss., George Washington University, 2004).

4 Tony Bennett, *The Birth of the Museum: History, Theory, Politics* (New York: Routledge, 1995), 61.

5 Ibid., 19. See also Michel Foucault, *Discipline and Punish: The Birth of the Prison*, trans. Alan Sheridan (New York: Vintage Books, 1979).

6 Ruth Phillips, *Trading Identities: The Souvenir in Native North American Art from the Northeast, 1700-1900* (Seattle: University of Washington Press, 1998), 69.

7 See, for example, the official website of the New Brunswick Museum, www.nbm-nmb.ca (accessed 10 April 2011). For Gesner, see Allison Mitcham, *Prophet of the Wilderness: Abraham Gesner* (Hantsport, NS: Lancelot Press, 1995).

8 Austin Squires, *The History and Development of the New Brunswick Museum* (Saint John: New Brunswick Museum, 1945).

9 See, for example, Brian Young, *The Making and Unmaking of a University Museum: The McCord, 1921-1996* (Kingston and Montreal: McGill-Queen's University Press, 2000), 123; and Timothy Luke, *Museum Politics: Power Plays at the Exhibition* (Minneapolis: University of Minnesota Press, 2002), 15–16.

10 Crary, *Techniques of the Observer*, 5 (italics in the original).

11 The use of the magic lantern is noted in the Natural History Society [NHS] Council Minutes, 1862–1901, 1 December 1896, NHS fonds, S127, F37, Archives of the New Brunswick Museum [ANBM].

12 NHS General Minutes, 1862-90, 29 January 1862, NHS fonds, S127, F40, ANBM.

13 LeBaron Botsford, 'Annual Address,' *Bulletin of the Natural History Society of New Brunswick* 9 (1890): 25.

14 NHS Council Minutes, 1862-1901, 23 February 1899.

15 William MacIntosh, 'Curator's Report,' *Bulletin of the Natural History Society of New Brunswick* 27 (1909): 153–4.
16 Ibid., 157.
17 For an analysis of dioramas, see Donna Haraway, 'Teddy Bear Patriarchy: Taxidermy in the Garden of Eden, New York City, 1908–1986,' in *Primate Visions: Gender, Race, and Nature in the World of Modern Science* (New York: Routledge, 1989), 26–58.
18 For a description of the scientific approach to nature inspired by Sir Francis Bacon (1561–1626), see W.A. Waiser, *The Field Naturalist: John Macoun, the Geological Survey, and Natural Science* (Toronto: University of Toronto Press, 1989), 10; and Suzanne Zeller, 'George Lawson: Victorian Botany, the Origin of the Species and the Case of Nova Scotian Heather,' in *Profiles of Science and Society in the Maritimes prior to 1914*, ed. Paul A. Bogaard (Fredericton: Acadiensis Press, 1990), 53–4.
19 Cited in Waiser, *The Field Naturalist*, 7.
20 Steven Conn, *Museums and American Intellectual Life, 1876–1926* (Chicago: University of Chicago Press, 1998), 32–73.
21 Mary P. Winsor, *Reading the Shape of Nature: Comparative Zoology at the Agassiz Museum* (Chicago: University of Chicago Press, 1991), 12–14.
22 Members of the Society occasionally sent specimens to Harvard to be identified by Agassiz. See NHS Correspondence, 1868–99, letter 1, 3 June 1868, S127, F1, ANBM.
23 NHS Scrapbook, 1862–1896, annual report of 1863, NHS fonds, S129, F120, ANBM. See George F. Matthew, 'Charles Frederick Hartt,' *Bulletin of the Natural History Society of New Brunswick* 9 (1890): 1–18 for a biography.
24 NHS Council Minutes, 1862–1901, 6 March 1894. See also NHS Scrapbook, 1862–96, 20 August 1896, where it is noted that a teacher, Miss M.E.S. Leat, was presented with bamboo, ores, and fossils for use in her school.
25 'Natural History Society to Lend Collections to Schools,' *Daily Telegraph*, 11 May 1907, p. 10.
26 William MacIntosh, 'Curator's Report,' *Bulletin of the Natural History Society of New Brunswick* 27 (1909): 155; NHS General Minutes, 1912–20, William MacIntosh's Curator's Report, 26 October 1915, NHS fonds, S127, F42, ANBM.
27 Museum School Service CB, uncatalogued and undated boxes kindly supplied by archivists, ANBM.
28 Squires, *The History and Development of the New Brunswick Museum*.
29 Outside Activities/Organizations, New Brunswick Museum, Saint John, 1933–9, undated loan collection lists, Carnegie Corporation [CC] fonds, Box 294, File 1, 7.4C, National Gallery of Canada Library and Archives [NGCLA].

30 According to semiotician Charles Sanders Peirce, diagrams support the conceptual processes of those who use them and enable the creation of new ideas. See Charles Sanders Peirce, *Collected Papers*, vol. 4, ed. Charles Hartshorne and Paul Weiss (Cambridge, MA: Belknap Press of Harvard University Press, 1931–5), 87.

31 Statistical Reports, Report of 11 October 1934, NHS fonds, S128, F53, ANBM. The Carnegie Corporation awarded $9,000, payable $3,000 annually for three years beginning 1934–5, from its British Dominions and Colonies Fund to the New Brunswick Museum exclusively toward the support of its educational program.

32 MacIntosh sent the life history of the polyphemus moth to a teacher in Clark's Corner, Queens County, New Brunswick (NHS Correspondence, 1906–9, letter 4–10, 10 April 1911, NHS fonds, S128, F60, ANBM). For his description of Reiker mounts, see NHS General Minutes, 1912–20, 20 October 1914.

33 For a sample lesson on beetles, see the file at the NGCLA as per note 29 above. A few lessons survive because MacIntosh sent them to National Gallery of Canada director H.O. McCurry, then secretary of the Carnegie Corporation.

34 William MacIntosh, 'Injurious and Other Insects of New Brunswick,' *in Report on Agriculture for the Province of New Brunswick* (Fredericton: Department of Agriculture, 1913), 268–71.

35 For a biography of George U. Hay, see Stephen R. Clayden, 'Hay, George Upham,' *Dictionary of Canadian Biography Online*, Vol. 14 (University of Toronto / Université de Laval, and Library and Archives Canada, 2000), www.biographi.ca (accessed 20 April 2011).

36 George Upham Hay Botany Series, lecture 3, 'A Study of the Environment of Plants,' nd, 21–2, NHS fonds, S128, F92, ANBM.Ibid., 33.

37 *Educational Review* 1.1 (June 1887): 1; Alexander H. MacKay, 'Ferndale School, No. 1, A Cocoon,' *Educational Review* 1.1 (June 1887): 5–8.

38 Anonymous, 'Ferndale School, No. 3, Olisiocampa,' *Educational Review* 1.3 (Aug. 1887): 51–3. For another natural history drawing lesson, see Anonymous, 'Ferndale School, No. 5, An Apple Tree Borer,' *Educational Review* 1.5 (1887): 91.

39 Matthew, 'Charles Frederick Hartt,' 3.

40 George Upham Hay Botany Papers 1887–1904, lecture 2, 'Plant Life,' 19 July 1888, 5, NHS fonds, S128, F90, ANBM.

41 Reverend E. Thring, 'Thinking in Shape and Pictorial Teaching,' *Educational Review* 1.2 (July 1887): 37.

42 Anonymous, 'Art Studies and Drawing in Schools,' *Educational Review* 11.7 (Dec. 1897): 111. A short, untitled article contends, 'Only a few lines of

chalk, and from the black surface there rises in apparent relief, a winged butterfly' (*Educational Review* 1.8 [Jan. 1888]: 146).

43 Clive Ashwin, 'Pestalozzi and the Origins of Pedagogical Drawing,' *British Journal of Education Studies* 29.2 (June 1981): 138–51.

44 Cited in Ashwin, 'Pestalozzi and the Origins of Pedagogical Drawing,' 148; Kate Silber, *Pestalozzi: The Man and His Work* (London: Routledge and Kegan Paul, 1976), 119–50.

45 Katherine F.C. MacNaughton, *The Development of the Theory and Practice of Education in New Brunswick 1784–1900* (Fredericton: University of New Brunswick Historical Studies, 1947), 110–11.

46 Cited in Ashwin, 'Pestalozzi and the Origins of Pedagogical Drawing,' 140.

47 NHS General Minutes, 1862–90, 29 January 1862.

48 Suzanne Zeller, *Land of Promise, Promised Land: The Culture of Victorian Science in Canada* (Ottawa: Canadian Historical Association, 1996), 3.

49 Suzanne Zeller, *Inventing Canada: Early Victorian Science and the Idea of a Transcontinental Nation* (Toronto: University of Toronto Press, 1987), 49.

50 NHS General Minutes, 1890–1911, Report of the Orinthology Committee, 19 October 1909, NHS fonds, S127, F41, ANBM. See also the entry of 2 April 1907, where 'so called sportsmen' are condemned for causing the extinction of shore birds.

51 Richard W. Judd, *Common Lands, Common People: The Origins of Conservation in Northern New England* (Cambridge: Harvard University Press, 1997), 6–7.

52 For the park, see NHS General Minutes, 1890–1911, 5 March 1901. For the creosoting timber plant, see NHS Scrapbook, 1893–9, letter to the minister of public works, 1893, 222, NHS fonds, S129, F121, ANBM; and a letter from Office of the Minister of Public Works, 7 September 1896, 224. See also the letter of 20 February 1897, 251, stating why Saint John would be a good location for the plant.

53 For the dispute between Muir and Giffard, see Robert W. Righter, *The Battle over Hetch Hetchy: America's Most Controversial Dam and the Birth of Modern Environmentalism* (New York: Oxford University Press, 2005).

54 Outside Activities/Organizations, New Brunswick Museum, Saint John, 1933–9, undated lesson. Red Rose Tea was founded by Theodore Estabrooks in 1861, and sold by him in 1932.

55 David J. Rhees, 'Corporate Advertising, Public Relations, and Popular Exhibits: The Case of Du Pont,' in *Industrial Society and Its Museums, 1890–1990: Social Aspirations and Cultural Politics*, ed. Brigitte Schroeder-Gudehus (Paris: Harwood Academic Publishers, 1993), 67–75.

56 William MacIntosh, 'Curator's Report,' *Bulletin of the Natural History Society of New Brunswick* 27 (1909): 153.

57 A lengthy letter submitted to Saint John's *Telegraph* in March 1907 argued that the NHS promoted 'educational and other useful purposes.' See NHS Scrapbook, Newspaper Clippings, 1893–1902, for 'NHS to lend collection to schools,' *Daily Telegraph* 11 May 1907, NHS fonds, S128A, F117, ANBM. MacIntosh argued that a collection of game and fur-bearing animals was of great value to tourists and sportsmen. The NHS Council Minutes, 1901–20, 18 February 1915 (NHS fonds, S127, F38, ANBM) affirms the NHS will 'continue to admit the public free to its museum every week day from 2 to 5 o'clock.'

58 NHS General Minutes, 1862–90, 21 January 1896; Samuel Kain, 'Secretary's Report,' *Bulletin of the Natural History Society of New Brunswick* 17 (1899): 176–7; William MacIntosh, 'Curator's Report,' *Bulletin of the Natural History Society of New Brunswick* 30 (1913): 484; NHS General Minutes, 1912–20, 17 October 1916.

59 A lesson on linoleum is preserved at the NGCLA (Outside Activities/ Organizations, New Brunswick Museum, Saint John, 1933–9, undated lesson). MacIntosh noted the display of economic woods of New Brunswick within the Museum of the NHS (NHS General Minutes, 1912–20, 20 October 1914).

60 NHS Correspondence, 1902–7, letter 46, 21 March 1907, NHS fonds, S127, F2, ANBM; NHS Correspondence, 1908–9, letter 26, NHS fonds, S127, F3, ANBM; Department of Agriculture Correspondence, 1910–11, letter 3, 2 April 1910, NHS fonds, S127, F7, ANBM; Department of Agriculture Correspondence, 1910–11, letter of 25 November 1911. See the many letters sent to MacIntosh in the NHS fonds, S127, F7BF10, ANBM.

61 NHS General Minutes, 1912–20, 20 October 1914.

62 Ibid. MacIntosh was also the provincial entomologist at this time.

63 MacIntosh, 'Injurious and Other Insects of New Brunswick,' 269.

64 Anonymous, 'Ferndale School, No. 2, A Beetle,' *Educational Review* 1.2 (July 1887): 26–8.

65 Timothy Lewis, 'Agrarian Idealism and Progressive Agriculture in Maritime Canada: Agricultural Leadership in New Brunswick, 1895–1929' (PhD diss., University of New Brunswick, 2003).

66 T.W. Acheson, 'The National Policy and the Industrialization of the Maritimes, 1880–1910,' *Acadiensis* 1.2 (Spring 1972): 6.

67 Patricia A. Thornton, 'The Problem of Out-Migration from Atlantic Canada, 1871–1921: A New Look,' *Acadiensis* 15.1 (Autumn 1985): 20.

68 R.P Steeves, *Nature Study and Agricultural Course for Use in the Public Schools of New Brunswick* (nl, 1914; 1st edn, 1908), 24. J.V., 'Nature Study,' *Educational Review* 16.5 (1902): 87, also discusses teaching children to appreciate the beauty of landscape.

69 Hay and Matthew described the summer camp held at Bocabec, Charlotte County, in August 1883, with seventeen members in attendance (NHS General Minutes, 1862–90, 4 September 1883). Ganong wished to renew the summer camps in 1885 (NHS Council Minutes, 1862–1901, 31 March 1885).

70 In 1881the NHS resolved to create an associate class of membership for women, available for a fee of one dollar per year. Women would be allowed to participate in all public business of the NHS, but not its Council (NHS Council Minutes, 1862–1901, 9 May 1881). The Junior Society for boys between twelve and eighteen years of age was described as 'revived' in the NHS Council Minutes, 1862–1901, 3 March 1885. The first mention of the Junior Associate Branch for girls aged ten to twenty-one occurs in the annual report in the *Bulletin of the Natural History Society of New Brunswick* 27 (1909): 171.

71 NHS General Minutes, 1890–1911, 19 October 1909.

72 David Matless, 'Visual Culture and Geographical Citizenship: England in the 1940s,' *Journal of Historical Geography* 22.4 (1996): 425.

73 For discussions of the links between natural history and nationalism, see R. Dunlap, *Nature and the English Diaspora: Environment and History in the United States, Canada, Australia, and New Zealand* (Cambridge: Cambridge University Press, 1999), 26; Curtis M. Hinsley, '"Magnificent Intentions": Washington, D.C., and American Anthropology in 1846,' in *Museum Studies: An Anthology of Contexts*, ed. Bettina Messias Carbonell (Malden, MA: Blackwell, 2004), 163; and Zeller, *Inventing Canada*, 34.

74 Carl Berger, *Science, God, and Nature in Victorian Canada* (London: University of Toronto Press, 1983), xiii, 10, 17, 31–2, 45.

75 In addition to the religious Hay, an exception was Senator John V. Ellis, who expounded on the relationship between God and nature in, for example, the *Bulletin of the Natural History Society of New Brunswick* 23 (1905), and 24 (1906).

76 William F. Ganong, 'The Echinodermata of New Brunswick,' *Bulletin of the Natural History Society of New Brunswick* 7 (1888): 13.

77 NHS General Minutes, 1890–1911, 19 October 1909.

78 Keith Thomas, *Man and the Natural World: A History of the Modern Sensibility* (New York: Pantheon Books, 1983), 17–41.

79 Steeves, *Nature Study and Agricultural Course for Use in the Public Schools of New Brunswick*. In Province of New Brunswick, *Summer Rural Science School for Teachers at the Fisher Vocational School, Woodstock* (nl, 1914), 4, it is noted that each student must have a separate plot in the garden, which would provide a basis for independent observation and record-keeping.

80 Anonymous, 'School Grounds,' *Educational Review* 4.7 (Dec. 1890): 111.

81 Cited in *Educational Review* 7.11 (April 1894): 206. Zeller (*Inventing Canada*,

207) claims school grounds were often a source of utility and national pride.

82 John Brittain, *Elementary Agriculture and Nature Study* (Toronto: Educational Book Co., 1911), 181–4.

83 F.E. MacDiarmid et al., *Science and Agriculture for New Brunswick Schools* (Toronto: Copp Clark Co., 1942), 55–60.

84 Thornton, 'The Problem of Out-Migration from Atlantic Canada,' 8.

85 George Upham Hay Botany Papers, lecture 2, untitled botanical lecture, nd, 14, NHS fonds, S128, F93, ANBM.

86 Ganong, 'The Echinodermata of New Brunswick,' 13.

87 For a good discussion of early modern natural history collections, see Paula Findlen, *Possessing Nature: Museums, Collecting, and Scientific Culture in Early Modern Italy* (Berkeley: University of California Press, 1994). For the political messages of modern collections, see Christopher Looby, 'The Constitution of Nature: Taxonomy as Politics in Jefferson, Peale, and Bartram,' in Carbonell, ed., *Museum Studies*, 143–57.

88 In 1893, Lieutenant-Governor John Boyd, for example, agreed to act as patron of the NHS (NHS Council Minutes, 1862–1901, 3 October 1893).

89 William Parenteau, 'A "Very Determined Opposition to the Law": Conservation, Angling Leases, and Social Conflict in the Canadian Atlantic Salmon Fishery, 1867–1914,' *Environmental History* 9.3 (July 2004): 436–63.

90 NHS General Minutes, 1862–1890, 20 November 1863.

91 George Upham Hay Education Papers, lecture 3, 'Nature Study No. VII,' nd, np, NHS fonds, S128A, F95, ANBM; and NHS General Minutes, 1862–1890, Annual Report, 21 January 1896.

92 NHS General Minutes, 1912–1920, 14 October 1914.

93 Berger, *Science, God, and Nature in Victorian Canada*, 17–18. For the 'Oriental' exhibition held in 1924, see chapter 3 of this book.

94 Michel Foucault, *The History of Sexuality*, vol. 1, trans. Robert Hurley (New York: Vintage, 1990), 95: 'Where there is power, there is resistance, and yet, or rather consequently, this resistance is never in a position of exteriority in relation to power.'

95 Young, *The Making and Unmaking of a University Museum*, 118–24; and Luke, *Museum Politics*, 3.

96 I thank my former colleague at the University of New Brunswick, Steve Turner, for suggesting this interpretation.

3. Offering Orientalism: Women and the Gift Economy of the Museum, 1880–1940

1 Letter from Alice Lusk Webster to C.T. Currelly, dated only 1934, Records

of the Registration Department, Royal Ontario Museum [ROM]. All material from the Records of the Registration Department of the ROM in this and following endnotes is located in one large, unmarked file, uncategorized and unnumbered.

2 For the Webster's Asian art collection, see the John Clarence Webster [JCW] fonds, S200, F639–F 642, Archives of the New Brunswick Museum [ANBM].

3 For different kinds of capital, see Pierre Bourdieu, *Distinction: A Social Critique of the Judgement of Taste*, trans. Richard Nice (Cambridge, MA: MIT Press, 1994).

4 See, for example, David Carrier, 'Isabella Stewart Gardner's Museum,' in *Museum Skepticism: A History of the Display of Art in Public Galleries* (Durham, NC: Duke University Press, 2006), 110–25; Gaby Porter, 'Seeing through Solidity: A Feminist Perspective on Museums,' in *Museum Studies: An Anthology of Contexts*, ed. Bettina Messia Carbonell (Oxford: Blackwell, 2004), 104–16; Isabella Stewart Gardner Museum, *Cultural Leadership in America: Art Matronage and Patronage* (Boston: Trustees of the Isabella Stewart Gardner Museum, 1997); S. Hyde, *Exhibiting Gender* (Manchester: Manchester University Press, 1997); Janice B. Yablonski, *Museum Women: A Century of Women's Employment in Art Museums* (New York: Columbia University, 1992); and Carol Duncan, *Aesthetics and Power* (Cambridge: Cambridge University Press, 1993).

5 Brian Young, *The Making and Unmaking of a University Museum: The McCord, 1921–1996* (Montreal and Kingston: McGill-Queen's University Press, 2000), 80–111.

6 For a lengthy discussion of these women, see Lianne McTavish, 'Strategic Donations: Women and Museums in New Brunswick, 1862–1930,' *Journal of Canadian Studies* 42.2 (Spring 2008): 1–24.

7 Edward Said, *Orientalism* (London: Penguin, 2003).

8 Sarah Cheang, 'Consuming the Exotic Other,' *Critical Studies in Mass Communication* 12 (1995): 263–86; Mari Yoshihara, *Embracing the East: White Women and Orientalism* (Oxford: Oxford University Press, 2003), 6; and Stacey Loughrey Sloboda, 'Making China: Design, Empire, and Aesthetics in Britain, 1745–1851' (PhD diss., University of Southern California, 2004).

9 Natural History Society [NHS] Council Minutes, 1862–1901, 9 May 1881, NHS fonds, S127, F37, ANBM.

10 Ibid., 5 July 1880.

11 Ibid., 1 June 1886.

12 'Annual Report of the Council,' *Bulletin of the Natural History Society of New*

Brunswick 5 (1886): 39; 'Annual Report of the Council,' *Bulletin of the Natural History Society of New Brunswick* 30 (1912): 481; NHS Council Minutes, 1924–42, 30 September 1925, NHS fonds, S127, F39, ANBM.

13 NHS General Minutes, 1862–90, 2 January 1865, NHS fonds, S127, F40, ANBM.

14 NHS Council Minutes, 1862–1901, 28 February 1882.

15 Ibid., 15 January 1884 and 1 March 1892.

16 Ladies' Auxiliary Treasurer's Reports, 1916–26, 1925, NHS fonds, S128A, F104, ANBM.

17 Harriet B. Holman fonds, CB DOC, ANBM.

18 Ladies' Auxiliary Treasurer's Reports, 1916–26, 1922.

19 Ladies' Auxiliary Minutes, 1926–32, 6 December 1927, NHS fonds, S128A, F116, ANBM.

20 Ladies' Auxiliary Minutes, 1893–1905, 6 November 1900, NHS fonds, S128A, F114, ANBM; and NHS General Minutes, 1890–1911, 2 February 1909, NHS fonds, S127, F41, ANBM.

21 Ladies' Auxiliary Minutes, 1906–10, 28 February 1906, NHS fonds, S128A, F115, ANBM.

22 NHS General Minutes, 1890–1911, 1 May 1906.

23 Cecilia Morgan, *Public Men and Virtuous Women: The Gendered Languages of Religion and Politics in Upper Canada, 1791–1850* (Toronto: University of Toronto Press, 1996), 203–7.

24 Lynne Marks, *Revivals and Roller Rinks: Religion, Leisure, and Identity in Late Nineteenth-Century Small-Town Ontario* (Toronto: University of Toronto Press, 1996), 65–7, 75.

25 Kathleen D. McCarthy, *Women's Culture: American Philanthropy and Art, 1830–1930* (Chicago: University of Chicago Press, 1991), 261.

26 Alice Taylor, 'Trading in Abolitionism: The Commercial, Material and Social World of the Boston Antislavery Fair, 1834–1858' (PhD diss., University of Western Ontario, 2007).

27 Marcel Mauss, *The Gift: The Form and Reason for Exchange in Archaic Societies*, trans. W.D. Halls (New York: Routledge, 2002), 11–23.

28 NHS Council Minutes, 1862–1901, 16 September 1898 and 3 April 1894.

29 William MacIntosh, 'Curator's Report,' *Bulletin of the Natural History Society of New Brunswick* 26 (1908): 61.

30 NHS General Minutes, 1890–1911, 3 January 1910.

31 NHS Scrapbook, Newspaper Clippings, 1921–34, 3, S128A, F124, ANBM.

32 E.A. Heaman, *The Inglorious Arts of Peace: Exhibitions in Canadian Society during the Nineteenth Century* (Toronto: University of Toronto Press, 1999), 262–3.

33 'Exhibit of Gay Little Dolls at the Oriental Display in the N. H. S. Hall,' *Saint John Globe*, 10 January 1924.

34 For Dr Travis, see 'Progress and Permanence: Women and the New Brunswick Museum: 1880–1980,' a website created by Lianne McTavish and Shawna Stairs Quinn: www.unbf.ca/womenandmuseum/btravis.htm.

35 For Dr Hanington, see 'Natural History Society of New Brunswick Missionaries,' a website created by Andrea Kirkpatrick: website.nbm-mnb.ca/wow/online/natural_history_society-missionaries-china-hanington.asp (accessed 23 April 2011).

36 NHS Scrapbook, Newspaper Clippings, 1921–34, 20A, 'To Have Exhibition of Oriental Curios' (January 1924). For Loretta Shaw, see Andrea Kirkpatrick, 'Loretta L. Shaw,' *Dictionary of Canadian Biography* (forthcoming). I thank Andrea Kirkpatrick for sharing her research with me. See also Stairs Quinn, 'Progress and Permanence': www.unbf.ca/womenandmuseum/bshaw.htm.

37 Andrea Kirkpatrick, e-mail message to author, 23 July 2009.

38 See note 36 above.

39 Among Florence Ayscough's many publications, see *A Chinese Mirror: Being Reflections of the Reality behind Appearance* (London: Jonathan Cape, 1925), and *Chinese Women Yesterday and Today* (London: Jonathan Cape, 1938).

40 See, for example, Anthony David Edwards, *The Role of International Exhibitions in Britain, 1850–1910: Perceptions of Economic Decline and the Technical Education Issue* (Amherst, NY: Cambria, 2008); Cristina Della Coletta, *World's Fairs Italian Style: The Great Exhibitions in Turin and Their Narratives, 1860–1915* (Toronto: University of Toronto Press, 2006); Matthew F. Bokovoy, *The San Diego World's Fairs and Southwestern Memory, 1880–1940* (Albuquerque: University of New Mexico Press, 2005); John E. Findling, *Chicago's Great World's Fairs* (Manchester: Manchester University Press, 1994); and Robert W. Rydell and Nancy E. Gwinn, *Fair Representations: World's Fairs and the Modern World* (Amsterdam: VU University Press, 1994).

41 See, for example, Bernth Lindfors, *Africans on Stage: Studies in Ethnological Show Business* (Bloomington: Indiana University Press, 1999); Zeynep Çelik, *Displaying the Orient: Architecture of Islam at Nineteenth-Century World's Fairs* (Berkeley: University of California Press, 1992); and Annie E. Coombes, 'Museums and the Formation of National and Cultural Identities,' *Oxford Art Journal* 11 (1988): 57–68.

42 For accounts of an exhibition at the Mechanics' Institute in 1842, see the *New Brunswick Courier*, 21 May 1842, p. 2, and 20 August 1842, p. 2; for a larger exhibition in 1883, see the *Saint John Globe*, 10 October 1883, p. 2. The first provincial exhibition was held in Fredericton in October of 1882, while

in 1878 the first such exhibition was hosted by the Department of Agriculture.

43 See the column in Saint John's *Morning News* (19 August 1842).

44 Ibid.

45 For accounts of New Brunswick goods at the Great Exhibition in 1862, see Saint John's *Morning News*, 9 July 1862, p. 2, and the *Saint John Globe*, 13 June 1862, n.pag.

46 Heaman, *The Inglorious Arts of Peace*, 259–84.

47 Ladies' Auxiliary Treasurer's Reports, 1916–26, 1922.

48 Tony Bennett, *The Birth of the Museum: History, Theory, Politics* (New York: Routledge, 1995), 102–5.

49 *The Living Message* (December 1925; March 1926; June 1930; October 1931). Undated clipping found in the NHS Scrapbook, 1862–1921, 1899, NHS fonds, S128A, F126, ANBM.

50 Catherine Mackenzie, 'Florence Wheelock Ayscough's Niger Reef Tea House,' *Journal of Canadian Art History* 23.1-2 (2002): 41.

51 Ibid., 39.

52 NHS General Minutes, 1890–1911, 6 March 1894.

53 Ladies' Auxiliary Scrapbook, 1903–9, 7 February 1908, NHS fonds, S128A, F113, ANBM.

54 NHS General Minutes, 1912–1920, typed sheets dated October 1915, NHS fonds, S127, F42, ANBM.

55 See chapter 1 for a discussion of these publications.

56 The presidential address given by Katherine Matthew in 1907 was, for example, reprinted in the *Saint John Globe*.

57 Sloboda, 'Making China,' 122.

58 Juliet Kinchin, 'Interiors: Nineteenth-Century Essays on the "Masculine" and the "Feminine" Room,' in *The Gendered Object*, ed. Pat Kirkham (Manchester: Manchester University Press, 1996), 18.

59 Beverly Lemire, verbal communication to author, 2 May 2008; Sarah Cheang, 'Turning Chinese: Fashion, Chinoiserie and Cross-Cultural Masquerade in 1920s Britain,' unpublished paper presented at the symposium 'Fashion, Community and Culture: Explorations of the Material World,' held at the Material Culture Institute, University of Alberta, 2 May 2008.

60 Sarah Cheang, 'What's in a Chinese Room? 20th Century Chinoiserie, Modernity and Femininity,' in *Chinese Whispers: Chinoiserie in Britain 1650–1930*, ed. David Beevers (Brighton and Hove: The Royal Pavilion and Museums, 2008), 75–7.

61 Susan R. Fernsebner, 'Material Modernities: China's Participation in World's Fairs and Expositions, 1876–1955' (PhD diss., University of Cali-

fornia, San Diego, 2002), 171–3, reproduces an image from the *San Francisco Chronicle*, 4 July 1915.

62 Cheang, 'What's in a Chinese Room?' 77.

63 Walter Davis, verbal communication to author, 15 May 2008.

64 Andrea Kirkpatrick, e-mail to author, 25 July 2009. See also http://website.nbm-mnb.ca/wow/online/natural_history_society-missionaries-china-hanington.asp.

65 Yoshihara, *Embracing the East*, 78.

66 Ibid., 79.

67 Noel Fahden Briceño, 'The Chinoiserie Revival in Early Twentieth-Century American Interiors' (MA thesis, University of Delaware, 2008), 15–16.

68 Yoshihara, *Embracing the East*, 35–6.

69 Ibid., 99.

70 Briceño, 'The Chinoiserie Revival in Early Twentieth-Century American Interiors,' 18.

71 Cheang, 'Consuming the Exotic Other,' 275–80.

72 For the concept of domestic feminism in relation to the public and cultural activities of nineteenth-century middle-class white women, see Karen J. Blair, *The Torchbearers: Women and Their Amateur Arts Associations in America, 1890–1930* (Bloomington: Indiana University Press, 1994).

73 Shawna Stairs Quinn, 'Loretta Shaw,' in 'Progress and Permanence,' www.unbf.ca/womenandmuseum/bshaw.htm.

74 See website.nbm-mnb.ca/wow/online/search.asp?txtsearch=hanington.

75 'Chinese Finery Is Given N. H. S.,' *Saint John Globe*, 8 November 1923. Found in NHS Scrapbook, Newspaper Clippings, 1921–34, 16a.

76 Fernsebner, 'Material Modernities,' 124–5.

77 Janice Mary Cook, 'Child Labour in Saint John, New Brunswick and the Campaign for Factory Legislation' (MA thesis, University of New Brunswick, 1994), 82.

78 Veronica Strong-Boag, 'The Roots of Modern Canadian Feminism: The National Council of Women, 1893–1921,' *Canada* 3.2 (1975): 22–33.

79 Ladies' Auxiliary, Various Reports and Speeches, 1915–31, 30 September 1920, NHS fonds, S128A, F105, ANBM.

80 'Women's Auxiliary Plans Program: To Undertake Work for New Brunswick Museum,' *Telegraph-Journal* [Saint John], 21 October 1930, p. 7.

81 New Brunswick Museum [NBM] Minutes of the Board and Executive Committee and Management Committee, 1 October 1930, ANBM. The committee claimed to need 'about $410,000.'

82 Ibid., 20 August 1929.

83 For discussions of the building and its site, see NBM Minutes of the Board

and Executive Committee and Management Committee, 27 June 1929.

84 Outside Activities/Organizations, Individuals, Bailey, Alfred (1934–9), letter from John C. Webster to H.O. McCurry, 20 September 1937, CC fonds, RG 7.4C, Box 296, F17, National Gallery of Canada Library and Archives [NGCLA].

85 Outside Activities/Organizations, Individuals, Webster, J. Clarence (1929–36, 1938–42, 1944–53, 1974), letter from John C. Webster to H.O. McCurry, 11 September 1934, CC fonds, RG 7.4W, Box 330, F4, NGCLA.

86 Letter from Alice Lusk Webster to C.T. Currelly, marked answered 16 July 1934, Records of the Registration Department, ROM.

87 Letter from Alice Lusk Webster to C.T. Currelly, 23 June 1941, Records of the Registration Department, ROM.

88 Alice Lusk Webster's Working Files, drafts of speeches etc., Art Department Records [ADR], NBM fonds, F545, ANBM. For rough notes that indicate the dimensions and weight of the boxes sent from Toronto to Saint John, see the undated and unclassified file in the Records of the Registration Department, ROM.

89 Letter from Alice Lusk Webster to Miss Greenaway, marked received 26 December 1939, Records of the Registration Department, ROM.

90 Letter from Alice Lusk Webster to C.T. Currelly, undated but likely 1946, Records of the Registration Department, ROM.

91 Letter from Alice Lusk Webster to C.T. Currelly, marked received 16 July 1934, Records of the Registration Department, ROM.

92 Letter from Alice Lusk Webster to C.T. Currelly, 20 October 1937, Records of the Registration Department, ROM.

93 Craig Clunas, 'China in Britain: The Imperial Collections,' in *Grasping the World: The Idea of the Museum*, ed. Donald Preziosi and Claire Farago (Aldershot: Ashgate, 2004), 464.

94 Alice Lusk Webster's Working Files, drafts of speeches etc., ADR, NBM fonds, F546, ANBM.

95 Package containing nineteen black-and-white photographs, with extensive notations, sent by Alice Lusk Webster to C.T. Currelly, stamped 3 July 1935, Records of the Registration Department, ROM.

96 Clunas, 'China in Britain,' 468.

97 Stacey Pierson, *Collectors, Collections and Museums: The Field of Chinese Ceramics in Britain, 1560–1960* (Bern: Peter Lang, 2007), 140–1.

98 Letter from Alice Lusk Webster to C.T. Currelly, 20 October 1937, Records of the Registration Department, ROM.

99 Alice Lusk Webster's Working Files, drafts of speeches etc., ADR, NBM fonds, F546.

100 Some of Lusk Webster's rough lecture notes (undated) are stored in the ADR, NBM fonds, F545. See also a description of one of her tours in *Maritime Art* 1.5 (June 1941): 30. Thanks to Kirk Neirgarth for providing this reference.

101 Sigmund Freud, *The Interpretation of Dreams* (1900), vols 4-5 of *The Complete Psychological Works of Sigmund Freud, The Standard Edition*, ed. and trans. James Strachey (Harmondsworth: Penguin, 1976); and Sigmund Freud, 'Repression (1915),' in *The Complete Psychological Works of Sigmund Freud, The Standard Edition*, vol. 14, 141–58.

102 Charles Trick Currelly, *I Brought the Ages Home* (Toronto: Royal Ontario Museum, 1956).

103 *Evening Times-Globe* [Saint John], 17 October 1940. See also 'Pottery of Today Compared to That of Ancient Times: Interesting Display in the Museum Is Arranged by Mrs. J.C. Webster,' *Times-Globe* [Saint John], 12 July 1935.

104 Alice Lusk Webster's Working Files, drafts of speeches etc., ADR, NBM fonds, F545.

105 Ibid.,F546.

106 Ibid.

107 Alice Lusk Webster's Working Files, drafts of letters, ADR, NBM fonds, F544. ANBM.

108 Letter from Alice Lusk Webster to C.T. Currelly, marked answered 29 March 1935, Records of the Registration Department, ROM.

109 Letter from Alice Lusk Webster to C.T. Currelly, 1939, Records of the Registration Department, ROM.

110 Letter from Alice Lusk Webster to C.T. Currelly, 22 July 1938, Records of the Registration Department, ROM.

111 Letter from Alice Lusk Webster to C.T. Currelly, marked answered 29 March 1935, Records of the Registration Department, ROM.

112 Letter sent by Alice Lusk Webster to C.T. Currelly, 23 June 1941, Records of the Registration Department, ROM.

113 'Mrs. J. Clarence Webster,' *Evening Times-Globe* [Saint John], 16 December 1953, p. 4.

114 www.nbm-mnb.ca/index.php?option=com_content&view=article&id=115&Itemid=231 (accessed 23 April 2011).

115 Letter from Alice Lusk Webster to C.T. Currelly, marked received 16 July 1934, Records of the Registration Department, ROM; letter from J.C. Webster to C.T. Currelly, 26 September 1936, Records of the Registration Department, ROM.

116 Letter from Alice Lusk Webster to C.T. Currelly, marked received 16 July 1934, Records of the Registration Department, ROM.

117 Letter from Alice Lusk Webster to C.T. Currelly, marked received 16 July

1934, Records of the Registration Department, ROM; letter from Alice Lusk Webster to C.T. Currelly, marked answered 9 March 1937, Records of the Registration Department, ROM.

118 Maurice Berger, 'The "Corporate" Museum,' in *Museums of Tomorrow: A Virtual Discussion*, ed. Maurice Berger (New York: Distributed Art Publishers, 2004), 47–80; Timothy Luke, *Museum Politics: Power Plays at the Exhibition* (Minneapolis: University of Minnesota Press, 2002), 15–16; and Young, *The Making and Unmaking of a University Museum*, 3, 23.

4. Libraries and Museums: Shifting Relationships, 1830–1940

1 Ian E. Wilson, 'Biographical Notes,' www.collectionscanada.gc.ca/about-us/012-201-e.html (accessed 2 December 2008). Wilson has since been replaced by Daniel J. Caron, but similar rhetoric is used in the vision and mandate of Library and Archives Canada: www.collectionscanada.gc.ca/about-us/012-413-e.html (accessed 26 April 2011).

2 Tony Bennett, *The Birth of the Museum: History, Theory, Politics* (London: Routledge, 1995), 18. See also Pierre Bourdieu and Alain Darbel, *L'Amour de l'art: Les Musées européens et leur public* (Paris: Minuit, 1969); and Carol Duncan, *Civilizing Rituals: Inside Public Art Museums* (London: Routledge, 1995).

3 Bennett, *The Birth of the Museum*, 65–6.

4 The literature produced about specific provincial and local societies, as opposed to national organizations, has mostly been narrative and celebratory. See, for example, Peter Corley-Smith, *White Bears and Other Curiosities … The First 100 Years of the Royal British Columbia Museum* (Victoria, BC: Royal British Columbia Museum 1989).

5 Abigail A. Van Slyck, *Free to All: Carnegie Libraries and American Culture, 1890–1920* (Chicago: University of Chicago Press, 1995), 22.

6 Haynes McMullen, *American Libraries before 1876* (Westport, CT: Greenwood Press, 2000), 15.

7 George S. Bobinski, *Carnegie Libraries: Their History and Impact on American Public Library Development* (Chicago: American Library Association, 1969), 260. See also Robert Sidney Martin, *Carnegie Denied: Communities Rejecting Carnegie Construction Grants, 1898–1925* (Westport, CT: Greenwood Press, 1993).

8 Juris Dilevko and Lisa Gottlieb, *The Evolution of Library and Museum Partnerships: Historical Antecedents, Contemporary Manifestations, and Future Directions* (Westport, CT: Libraries Unlimited, 2004), 121–2.

9 Ibid., 1–12; Ray Lester, 'The Convergence of Museums and Libraries?' *Alexandria* 13 (March 2001): 183–91.

10 See, for example, Brian Young, *The Making and Unmaking of a University Museum: The McCord, 1921–1996* (Montreal and Kingston: McGill-Queen's Press, 2000).
11 Natural History Society [NHS] General Minutes, 1862–90, 29 January 1862, NHS fonds, S127, F40, Archives of the New Brunswick Museum [ANBM].
12 See chapter 1 for a discussion of this bulletin, esp. note 73.
13 MacIntosh sent, for example, the life history of the polyphemus moth to a teacher in Clark's Corner, Queens County, New Brunswick (NHS Correspondence 1911, letter 4-10, from William MacIntosh, 10 April 1911, NHS fonds, S128, F60, ANBM). For a sample lesson on beetles, see the progress report sent by MacIntosh to H.O. McCurry, 17 May 1937 (Outside Activities/Organizations, New Brunswick Museum, Saint John, 1933–9, Carnegie Corporation [CC]fonds, RG 7.4C, Box 294, File 1, National Gallery of Canada Library and Archives [NGCLA]).
14 William MacIntosh, 'Curator's Report,' *Bulletin of the Natural History Society of New Brunswick* 26 (1908): 59.
15 Stanley Brice Frost, 'Science Education in the Nineteenth Century: The Natural History Society of Montreal, 1827–1925,' *McGill Journal of Education* 17.1 (Winter 1982): 31.
16 Natural History Society of Montreal [NHSM] Minutes of the Proceedings of the Society, from its formation in May 1827 until the 20th of October 1829, 16 May 1827, Special Collections of the McGill University Library Rare Books and Special Collections [MURBSC].
17 Ibid., 16 May 1827.
18 Ibid., 29 October 1827.
19 Ibid., 29 October 1827.
20 See, for example, NHSM Minutes of the Proceedings of the Society, commencing 18th May 1830, ending 27th February 1832, 28 March 1831, MURBSC.
21 NHSM Minutes of the Proceedings of the Society, from its formation in May 1827 until the 20th of October 1829, 28 April 1828.
22 Ibid., 24 November 1828.
23 Ibid., 29 October 1827.
24 Ibid., 23 February 1829.
25 Ibid., 24 November 1828.
26 Ibid., 28 April 1828.
27 Oliver C. Farrington, 'On the Ideal Relations of Public Libraries, Museums, and Art Gallery to the City' [early 1900s], in *Museum Origins: Readings in Early Museum History and Philosophy*, ed. Hugh H. Genoways and Mary Anne Andrei (Walnut Creek, CA: Left Coast Press, 2008), 80.

28 NHSM Minutes of the Proceedings of the Society, commencing 30th November 1829, ending 20th April 1830, 18 April 1830, MURBSC.
29 NHS Council Minutes, 1862–1901, 3 October 1882, 21 January 1897, and 2 February 1897, NHS fonds, S127, F37, ANBM. See also NHS Correspondence, 1868–99, letter 14, from J.W. Lawrence, president of the New Brunswick Historical Society, to LeBaron Botsford, president of the NHS, 3 October 1882, NHS fonds, S127, F1, ANBM.
30 NHSM Minutes of the Proceedings of the Society, commencing 18th May 1830, ending 27th February 1832, 30 May 1831.
31 I thank Harry Kuntz for sharing his research on this matter with me (e-mail to author, 25 January 2010).
32 The Society's financial woes are discussed throughout the minutes, but see a newspaper clipping in the *Montreal Gazette* (23 August 1923) for a report of the Society selling its properties for about $100,000–$150,000 to cover outstanding debts, with no plans to buy another property.
33 NHSM Minutes of the Proceedings of the Society, commencing 30th July 1844, ending 31st August 1857, 11 May 1853, MURBSC.
34 NHSM Council Minutes, 1853–90, 22 December 1864, MURBSC. Joseph Frederick Whiteaves was a British paleontologist who studied geology in Quebec before becoming the curator of the Museum of the Montreal NHS from 1863 to 1875, when he joined the Geological Survey of Canada.
35 For William MacIntosh as the curator of the Museum of the NHS of New Brunswick, see Lianne McTavish and Joshua Dickison, 'William MacIntosh, Natural History and the Professionalization of the New Brunswick Museum, 1898–1940,' *Acadiensis: Journal of the History of the Atlantic Region* 36.2 (Spring 2007): 81.
36 NHS Council Minutes, 1862–1901, 22 February 1898.
37 NHSM Minutes of the Proceedings of the Society, commencing 31st May 1858, ending 28th May 1888, 29 April 1867, MURBSC.
38 NHSM Council Minutes, 1894–1922, undated insert listing committees of 1909, MURBSC.
39 For biographical information, see *Dictionary of Canadian Biography Online*, Vol. 11 (for McCord) and Vol. 10 (for Bethune), ed. John English and Réal Bélanger (Toronto and Laval: University of Toronto and Université Laval, 1959), www.biographi.ca/009004-119.01 (accessed 24 April 2011).
40 Ibid., Vol. 8.
41 Hervé Gagnon, 'The Natural History Society of Montreal's Museum and the Socio-Economic Significance of Museums in 19th-Century Canada,' *Scientia Canadensis: Canadian Journal of the History of Science, Technology and Medicine* 18.2 (1994): 115.

42 The constitution and by-laws published by the NHSM in 1852 note that the collections were open to the public only on particular holidays. The NHSM minutes of 31 August 1857 report that when the museum was open to the public from 12 to 19 August, some 173 persons signed the museum's guest book, while hundreds of mineral specimens appeared to be missing (NHMS Minutes of the Proceedings of the Society, commencing 30th July 1844, ending 31st August 1857).
43 NHSM Council Minutes, May 1827–May 1830, 23 February 1829, MURBSC. See also Gagnon, 'The Natural History Society of Montreal's Museum and the Socio-Economic Significance of Museums in 19th-Century Canada,' 118, for the regulations of 1829 and the annual government grant that had been fixed at $1000 since 1860.
44 NHSM Council Minutes, 1853–90, 26 May 1866, outlines these rules in relation to the opening hours of the museum over the next seven months.
45 Ibid., 20 November 1866.
46 Bennett, *The Birth of the Museum*, 24.
47 *Act of Incorporation and Constitution and By-Laws of the Historical and Scientific Society of Manitoba* [HSSM] (Winnipeg: Manitoba Free Press, 1896; first published 1879), Collections of the Manitoba Legislative Library [MLL].
48 Natural History Society of Manitoba [NHSM] Reports, Minutes, Constitution, 1920–69, Revised Constitution, November 1932, Manitoba Naturalists Society [MNS] fonds, Box P5070, Archives of Manitoba [AM]. See also the minutes of 1 May 1922 for a speech given by its director, Dr H.M. Speechly, entitled 'The Natural History Society of Manitoba, 1920 to 1940,' which notes that in 1932 the Civic Auditorium Commissioners invited the formation of a museum in the West Gallery of the Auditorium Building, and that the NHS participated in a museum sub-committee, ultimately forming the Manitoba Museum Association. This group included women in administrative positions from its foundation. It organized field trips to local sites and held lectures in various rooms at the University of Manitoba but, unlike the organizations in Montreal and Saint John, did not invest in a building to house its own collections. Instead it donated specimens to the provincial museum, which opened in 1932, while occasionally arranging temporary exhibitions in downtown storefronts.
49 For the Manitoba Historical Society, see the website www.mhs.mb.ca (accessed 24 April 2011).
50 For the biography of Chief Justice Wood, see the website www.mhs.mb.ca/docs/people/wood_eb.shtml (accessed 24 April 2011).
51 HSSM, *Transactions and Proceedings, from its organization in 1879 till the close of the Society's year 1902–1903; being transactions nos. 1 to 66, and annual*

reports for the years 1880 to 1903 (Winnipeg: The Voice Publishing Co., 1904), 'Annual Report,' 1888, MLL.

52 *Act of Incorporation and Constitution and By-Laws of the HSSM* includes a printed library catalogue from 1884.

53 *Act of Incorporation and Constitution and By-Laws of the HSSM*, 'Librarian,' Article XIII, 25 June 1879.

54 Ibid. For Miss Inkster, see HSSM, *Transactions and Proceedings*, 'Annual Report,' 1888.

55 *Act of Incorporation and Constitution and By-Laws of the HSSM* includes 'Catalogue of 340 Specimens from the Collection of the Historical and Scientific Society, Winnipeg. Comprising Geology, Mineralogy, Ethnology, and History of the Canadian Northwest, Forming a portion of the exhibit sent to the Dominion and Centennial Exhibition held at St. John, New Brunswick, October, 1883.' See also HSSM, *Transactions and Proceedings*, 'Annual Report,' 1884.

56 HSSM, *Transactions and Proceedings*, 'Annual Report, 1884.

57 Ibid., 'Annual Report,' 1887.

58 Ibid., 'Annual Report,' 1890.

59 Ibid., 'Annual Report,' 1903.

60 Ibid., 'Annual Report,' 1905.

61 Ibid., 'Annual Report,' 1884.

62 Ibid., 'Annual Report,' 1883.

63 For Bryce's biography, see the website www.mhs.mb.ca/docs/people/bryce_m.shtml (accessed 24 April 2011).

64 *Constitution of the Art, Historical and Scientific Association* [AHSA] *of Vancouver, 1894* (Vancouver: The Association, 1894), 5, MSS 336, Vancouver Museums and Planetarium Association [VMPA] fonds, Series: Constitutions, agreements, and other legal establishment records, 1894–1986, 546-E-4, file 1, City of Vancouver Archives [CVA]. A separate Natural History Society [NHS] of Vancouver was established by John Davidson in 1918, and its archives are also located at the CVA. After reading them thoroughly and researching this organization further, I decided not to include it as there was surprisingly little connection between it and the AHSA. The NHS was devoted to field trips and collecting, and was more open to a broader public than was the AHSA.

65 Secretary's Annual Report of 1904, MSS 336, VMPA fonds, Series: Minutes, Subseries: Board of Trustees Minutes, Board Minutes, 546-E-5, file 2, CVA.

66 See Ruth Phillips, *Trading Identities: The Souvenir in Native North American Art from the Northeast, 1700-1900* (Seattle: University of Washington Press, 1998).

67 Douglas Cole, *Captured Heritage: The Scramble for Northwest Coast Artifacts* (Vancouver: University of British Columbia Press, 1995) describes the scramble for northwest coast artifacts, canoes, and bones, among many other items, from the late nineteenth to the early twentieth century. In 1886 the Royal British Columbia Museum was founded in Victoria immediately after thirty elite citizens urged the provincial government to preserve the native objects being removed by foreigners. Most early museums in Canada, including those formed in Montreal, Saint John, and Winnipeg, began as private enterprises aligned with a local society that struggled to receive even minimal amounts of government funding. In Victoria, the Natural History Society of British Columbia was established in 1890, holding its first meeting at the museum, its mandate specifying that the group would 'promote a more extended knowledge of the Natural History of the Province ... [acting] as an independent auxiliary to the Provincial Museum.' In this unusual case, Society members took up a secondary position in relation to an existing museum, while engaging in the kind of collecting trips and lecture series supported by other natural history groups. See *Revised Constitution and List of Members of the Natural History Society of British Columbia* (Victoria, BC: Colonist Presses, 1913; orig. 1909), 3; and Corley-Smith, *White Bears and Other Curiosities*, 17, 26.

68 The history of the Association, beginning with the Art Association, is recounted by Noel Robinson, in 'The Years Between,' in *Vancouver City Museum Golden Jubilee 1894–1944* (Vancouver: Art, Historical and Scientific Association, 1944). After moving its collections to two other temporary locations on Granville Street, in 1895 members relocated the exhibition to an elementary school before returning to the use of rented rooms in the downtown area. See also the publication produced by the AHSA, *Museum Notes* 1.2 (1926): 5-6, for a discussion of the various accommodations used to display the collections.

69 Secretary's Annual Report of 1901, MSS 336, VMPA fonds, Series: Minutes, Subseries: Board of Trustees Minutes, Board Minutes, 546-E-5, file 1, CVA.

70 Cited in 'Vancouver Museum,' www.vancouver profile.com/artsculture/content.php/id/130 (accessed 24 April 2011).

71 Bennett, *The Birth of the Museum*, 17–21.

72 *Constitution of the Art, Historical and Scientific Association of Vancouver, 1894*, 5.

73 Secretary's Annual Report of 1900, MSS 336, VMPA fonds, Series: Minutes, Subseries: Board of Trustees Minutes, Board Minutes, 546-E-5, file 1, CVA.

74 See the newspaper clippings about the various events pasted into the file cited in note 73.

75 Charles Hill-Tout, *Later Prehistoric Man in British Columbia* (Ottawa: Transactions of the Royal Society of Canada, Section II, 1895).
76 See the newspaper clippings about the various events pasted into the file cited in note 73.
77 For McLagan's biography, see *Museum Notes* 1.2 (1926): 9–10.
78 Secretary's Annual Report of 1911, MSS 336, VMPA fonds, Series: Minutes, Subseries: Board of Trustees Minutes, Board Minutes, 546-E-5, file 3, CVA.
79 The first mention of the possibility of accommodations within the Carnegie library is in the Secretary's Annual Report of 1902, MSS 336, VMPA fonds, Series: Minutes, Subseries: Board of Trustees Minutes, Board Minutes, 546-E-5, file 2, CVA.
80 For the history of the Vancouver public libraries, see the website www.vpl.vancouver.bc.ca/about/cat/C401/#van_read (accessed 24 April 2011). See also E.S. Robinson, 'The Vancouver Public Library, 1869-1927,' *Museum Notes* 12.4 (1926): 9–12.
81 Paul Whitney, 'A Refuge and a Sanctuary: Vancouver's Carnegie Library as Civic Space,' in *Last One Out Turn Off the Lights: Is This the Future of American and Canadian Libraries?* ed. Susan E. Cleyle and Louise M. McGillis (Lanham, MD: Scarecrow Press, 2005), 64–72.
82 A copy of this agreement, dated 26 August, is appended to the Secretary's Annual Report of 1903, MSS 336, VMPA fonds, Series: Minutes, Subseries: Board of Trustees Minutes, Board Minutes, 546-E-5, file 2, CVA.
83 Secretary's Annual Report of 1912, MSS 336, VMPA fonds, Series: Minutes, Subseries: Board of Trustees Minutes, Board Minutes, 546-E-5, file 3, CVA.
84 Secretary's Annual Report of 1904.
85 See, for example, 'Vancouver's Museum,' *Daily News Advertiser*, 20 April 1905, p. 2.
86 *Constitution of the Art, Historical and Scientific Association of Vancouver, 1894*, 5.
87 Secretary's Annual Report of 1904.
88 Secretary's Annual Report of 1905, MSS 336, VMPA fonds, Series: Minutes, Subseries: Board of Trustees Minutes, Board Minutes, 546-E-5, file 2, CVA.
89 Secretary's Annual Report of 1916, MSS 336, VMPA fonds, Series: Minutes, Subseries: Board of Trustees Minutes, Board Minutes, 546-E-5, file 3, CVA.
90 Art, Historical and Scientific Association, *The Museum* (Vancouver: The Association, 1915).
91 Secretary's Annual Report of 1905.
92 Secretary's Annual Report of 1909, MSS 336, VMPA fonds, Series: Minutes, Subseries: Board of Trustees Minutes, Board Minutes, 546-E-5, file 3, CVA.

93 Secretary's Annual Report of 1911.
94 Report of the Annual Meeting of 1924, MSS 336, VMPA fonds, Series: Minutes, Subseries: Board Minutes, 546-F-1, CVA.
95 Robinson, 'The Years Between,' 5.
96 Ibid.
97 Secretary's Annual Report of 1915.
98 Letter from William Ferris to Secretary, Carnegie Corporation of New York, 30 July 1921, MSS 336, VMPA fonds, Series: Correspondence, Subseries: Applications for non-civic grants, 547-B-1, file 6, CVA.
99 'Museum to Be Ousted,' *Sun*, 12 December 1924, MSS 336, VMPA fonds, Series: Correspondence, Subseries: Association activities, 547-B-1, file 7, CVA.
100 Letter from Edgar Robinson to Robert M. Lester, Secretary, Carnegie Corporation of New York, 24 January 1940, MSS 336, VMPA fonds, Series: Correspondence, Subseries: Applications for non-civic grants.
101 Letter from Robert M. Lester, Secretary, Carnegie Corporation of New York, to Edgar Robinson, 26 January 1940, MSS 336, VMPA fonds, Series: Correspondence, Subseries: Applications for non-civic grants.
102 Cited in Jacalyn Eddy, '"We Have Become Too Tender-Hearted": The Language of Gender in the Public Library, 1880–1920,' in *Libraries as Agencies of Culture*, ed. Thomas Augst and Wayne Wiegand (Lawrence, KS: American Studies, 2001), 161.
103 Christopher Dewolf, 'What Makes a Good library?' *Spacing Montreal*, 26 November 2007, spacingmontreal.ca/2007/11/26/what-makes-a-good-library (accessed 24 April 2011).

5. Gendered Professionals: Debating the Ideal Museum Worker during the 1930s and 1940s

1 Pierre Bourdieu and Alain Darbel, *L'Amour de l'art: Les Musées européens et leur Public* (Paris: Minuit, 1969).
2 For a biography of Dana, see Kevin Mattson, 'The Librarian as Secular Minister to Democracy: The Life and Ideas of John Cotton Dana,' *Libraries and Culture* 33.4 (Fall 2000): 514–34. See also William A. Peniston, ed., *The New Museum: Selected Writings by John Cotton Dana* (Newark, NJ: Newark Museum, 1999).
3 'Canadian Committee on Canadian Museums Progress Report,' 26 August 1936, 15, Outside Activities/Organizations, General, Carnegie Corporation [CC] fonds, RG 7.4 C, Box 291, file 5, National Gallery of Canada Archives [NGCA].

4 Rudi Volti, 'Professions and Professionalization,' in *An Introduction to the Sociology of Work and Occupations* (Thousand Oaks, CA: Pine Forge Press, 2008), 97–116; and Gregg Scott, 'The Complex History of Credentialism,' in *The Professionalization of Work*, ed. Merle Jacobs and Stephen E. Bosanac (Whitby, ON: de Sitter Publications, 2006), 252–81.
5 For the history of the Canadian Museums Association, see the website www.museums.ca/About/History/?n=12-104 (accessed 29 April 2011).
6 Letters from J.C. Webster to H.O. McCurry, 20 and 22 September 1937, Outside Activities/Organizations, Individuals, Bailey, Alfred (1934–9), CC fonds, RG 7.4 C, Box 296, NGCA.
7 James Clifford, 'Museums as Contact Zones,' in *Routes: Travel and Translation in the Late Twentieth Century* (Cambridge: Harvard University Press, 1997), 188–219.
8 James Cuno, ed., *Whose Muse? Art Museums and the Public Trust* (Princeton: Princeton University Press, 2004). See also Peter White, ed., *Naming a Practice: Curatorial Strategies for the Future* (Banff, AB: Walter Phillips Gallery, 1996); Paul O'Neill, ed., *Curating Subjects* (London: Open Editions, 2007); Carolee Thea and Thomas Micchelli, eds, *On Curating: Interviews with Ten International Curators* (New York: Distributed Art Publishers, 2009).
9 Barbara Maria Stafford, 'Spectacle of Nature,' in *Artful Science: Enlightenment Entertainment and the Eclipse of Visual Education* (Cambridge, MA: MIT Press, 1999), 217–79; and Tony Bennett, 'Pedagogic Objects, Clean Eyes, and Popular Instruction: On Sensory Regimes and Museum Didactics,' *Configurations* 6.3 (Fall 1998): 345–71.
10 For Hunter, see Natural History Society of Montreal [NHSM] 'Annual Report of 1859,' 8, *Printed Annual Reports Delivered by the Council of the Natural History Society of Montreal at the Annual Meeting of the Society, 1854–63* (Montreal: Montreal Gazette Office, 1863), McGill University Rare Books and Special Collections [MURBSC]; and Minutes of the Council of the NHSM, commencing May 1853, ending March 1922, 22 January 1867, MURBSC.
11 For Whiteaves, see Minutes of the Council of the NHSM, commencing May 1853, ending March 1922, letters from Whiteaves dated 25 February 1863 and 4 March 1863; and NHSM Clippings and Correspondence pertaining to J.F. Whiteaves, 1871–1907, MURBSC.
12 For receipts related to MacIntosh's salary, see the Natural History Society [NHS] Business Accounts 1862–1933, NHS fonds, S127, F19–F25, Archives of the New Brunswick Museum [ANBM].
13 NHS Council Minutes, 1901–20, 1 June 1912, NHS fonds, S127, F38, ANBM; and NHS Correspondence 1902–7, letter to MacIntosh from William F. Ganong, 11 October 1907, 20, NHS fonds, S127, F2, ANBM.

14 UNB Honorary Degree Recipients, University of New Brunswick Archives, www.lib.unb.ca/archives/honrary/hon3.html (accessed 21 August 2006). No records were found identifying the nominators of MacIntosh, or the reasons why he received the honorary degrees. For Whiteaves's education, see Susan Sheets-Pyenson, 'Whiteaves, Joseph Frederick,' *Dictionary of Canadian Biography Online*, Vol. 13 (University of Toronto and Université de Laval, 2000), www.biographi.ca (accessed 29 April 2011).

15 See, for example, Lynn L. Merrill, *The Romance of Victorian Natural History* (Oxford: Oxford University Press, 1989). See also Lianne McTavish and Joshua Dickison, 'William MacIntosh, Natural History and the Professionalization of the New Brunswick Museum, 1898-1940,' *Acadiensis: Journal of the History of the Atlantic Region* 36.2 (Spring 2007): 72–90.

16 For a description of the scientific approach to nature inspired by Sir Francis Bacon (1561–1626), see W.A. Waiser, *The Field Naturalist: John Macoun, the Geological Survey, and Natural Science* (Toronto: University of Toronto Press, 1989), 10; Suzanne Zeller, 'George Lawson: Victorian Botany, the Origin of the Species and the Case of Nova Scotian Heather,' in *Profiles of Science and Society in the Maritimes prior to 1914*, ed. Paul A. Bogaard (Sackville, NB: Centre for Canadian Studies, Mount Allison University, 1990), 53–4; and Suzanne Zeller, *Land of Promise, Promised Land: The Culture of Victorian Science in Canada* (Ottawa: Canadian Historical Association, 1996), 3.

17 Waiser, *The Field Naturalist*, 7.

18 Norman Criddle (1875–1933), P4661–P4665, Provincial Archives of Manitoba.

19 Robert E. Kohler, *All Creatures: Naturalists, Collectors, and Biodiversity, 1850–1950* (Princeton: Princeton University Press, 2006), 207.

20 Ibid., 208–15.

21 Merrill, *The Romance of Victorian Natural History*, 75–106.

22 See chapter 2 of this book.

23 NHS Council Minutes, 1924–42, 1 April 1924, 2 December 1924, and 5 November 1929, NHS fonds, S127, F39, ANBM.

24 New Brunswick Museum [NBM] Minutes of the Board and Executive Committee and Management Committee, 23 January 1934, ANBM.

25 In 'Museum Exhibits Swelled by Gifts Valued at $25,000,' *Telegraph Journal*, 31 July 1934, p. 12, MacIntosh explained that various art works would be 'occupying the hall originally intended for the natural history objects of the province.' In a letter of 20 November 1934, W.F. Ganong wrote to J.C.Webster that MacIntosh was 'lukewarm' about the art collection because he feared it might impose on his 'pet N.B. animals room' (Correspondence June–December 1934, William Francis Ganong [WFG] fonds, S218, F115, ANBM).

26 NBM Minutes of the Board and Executive Committee and Management Committee, 17 January 1947, indicates that the third floor was not yet constructed.
27 Outside Activities/Organizations, Individuals, Bailey, Alfred (1934–9), letter from J.C. Webster to H.O. McCurry, 20 September 1937.
28 Ibid., 31 March 1935.
29 John Clarence Webster, *The Distressed Maritimes: A Study of Educational and Cultural Conditions in Canada* (Toronto: Ryerson Press, 1926), 12.
30 M.H. Long, 'The Historic Sites and Monuments Board of Canada,' Presidential Address of the Canadian Historical Association, delivered in 1954, website of the Canadian Historical Association, www.health.library.mcgill.ca/osler/archives/detail.cfm?FondID=1 (accessed 12 September 2008).
31 Nancy Benn, personal communication to Joshua Dickison, 15 August 2006.
32 Webster, *The Distressed Maritimes*, 13; Lawrence Levine, *Highbrow/Lowbrow: The Emergence of a Cultural Hierarchy in America* (Cambridge: Harvard University Press, 1988).
33 Eileen Diana Mak, 'Patterns of Change, Sources of Influence: An Historical Study of the Canadian Museum and the Middle Class, 1850–1950' (PhD diss., University of British Columbia, 1996).
34 Tony Bennett, *The Birth of the Museum: History, Theory, Politics* (New York: Routledge, 1995), 14, 19; Eilean Hooper-Greenhill, *Museums and the Shaping of Knowledge* (London: Routledge, 1992).
35 Ruth Phillips, *Trading Identities: The Souvenir in Native North American Art from the Northeast, 1700–1900* (Seattle: University of Washington Press, 1998), 69.
36 Jeffrey D. Brison, *Rockefeller, Carnegie, and Canada: American Philanthropy and the Arts and Letters in Canada* (Montreal and Kingston: McGill-Queen's University Press, 2005), 122.
37 Henry Alexander Miers and S.F. Markham, *A Report on the Museums of Canada* (Edinburgh: Constable, 1932).
38 Brison, *Rockefeller, Carnegie, and Canada*, 125.
39 See the collection of newspaper clippings from 1926 in Boards and Committees, John Clarence Webster [JCW] fonds, S193, F103, ANBM.
40 Letter to McCurry from J.C. Webster, 21 February 1933, Outside Activities/Organizations, General, CC fonds, RG 7.4 C, Box 290, file 6, NGCA.
41 Pierre Bourdieu, *Distinction: A Social Critique of the Judgement of Taste*, trans. Richard Nice (Cambridge: Harvard University Press, 1984), esp. 11–96.
42 C. Mary Young, 'Loring Woart Bailey,' *Dictionary of Canadian Biography Online*, Vol. 15, www.biographi.ca (accessed 29 April 2011).
43 'Canadian Committee on Canadian Museums Progress Report,' 26 August

1936, 15–16, Outside Activities/Organizations, General, CC fonds, RG 7.4 C, Box 291, file 5, NGCA.

44 Sally Anne Duncan, 'Harvard's "Museum Course" and the Making of America's Museum Profession,' *Archives of American Art Journal* 42.1-2 (2002): 2–16.

45 Carnegie Corporation Funds Administered by Canadian Committee for Museum Development, Training Plan in Effect 1933–1939, 1, Outside Activities/Organizations, General, CC fonds, RG 7.4 C, Box 291, file 5, NGCA.

46 NHS Scrapbook, Newspaper Clippings 1934–6, 'Dr. Webster's Gifts Notable Feature in Museum Display,' NHS fonds, S128A, F125, ANBM. See also Gerald Thomas, 'John C. Webster: Applying Material History – Developing the New Brunswick Museum,' in *Studies in History and Museums*, ed. Peter E. Rider (Hull, PQ: Canadian Museum of Civilization, 1994), 42–5.

47 Alfred Bailey, 'Report to the Canadian Carnegie Committee on Work Done under a Grant, by Alfred G. Bailey, Ph.D., at the New Brunswick Museum, from Sept. 1st, 1935, to May 7th, 1936 (Eight Months),' Outside Activities/Organizations, Individuals, Bailey, Alfred (1934–9).

48 'Carnegie Corporation Scholarships,' Report of 30 April 1935, 1, Outside Activities/Organizations, General, CC fonds, RG 7.4 C, Box 290, file 8, NGCA.

49 Ibid.

50 Correspondence 1938–41, letter from J.C. Webster to W.F. Ganong, 7 December 1938, WFG fonds, S218, F118, ANBM: 'At the last Board meeting Addy tried to push through the hiring of Sansom, Webster and the Governor postponed it.'

51 NBM Minutes of the Board and Executive Committee and Management Committee, letter from Macintosh to Wetmore, 24 November 1938.

52 Lusk Webster, in a letter of 17 October 1937 to Currelly, explains that McCurry agrees that a man with degrees should be trained to become curator of the Natural Science Division (Records of the Registration Department, Royal Ontario Museum [ROM]).

53 Letter from J.C. Webster to McCurry, 8 September 1937, Outside Activities/Organizations, Individuals, Bailey, Alfred (1934–9).

54 Miers and Markham, *A Report on the Museums of Canada*, 42.

55 MacIntosh's letters, reports and attachments are in Outside Activities/Organizations, New Brunswick Museum, Saint John, 1933–9, CC fonds, Box 294, File 1, NGCA.

56 Letter from Bailey to J.C. Webster, 8 September 1937, JCW fonds, S194, F237, ANBM.

57 Letter from J.C. Webster to McCurry, 11 April 1938, Outside Activities/Organizations, Individuals, Bailey, Alfred (1934–9).

58 Alfred G. Bailey, *The Conflict of European and Eastern Algonkian Cultures, 1504–1700: A Study in Canadian Civilization* (Toronto: University of Toronto Press, 1969). See also Bruce Trigger, 'Alfred G. Bailey – Ethnohistorian,' *Acadiensis* 18 (Spring 1989): 3–21.

59 Letter from J.C. Webster to McCurry, 20 September 1937, Outside Activities/Organizations, Individuals, Bailey, Alfred (1934–9).

60 Reports 1865–1932, William MacIntosh, 'Report of the Archaeological Committee,' 1919, NHS fonds, S128, F56, ANBM. See also the letter from Lusk Webster to Currelly, marked answered 26 August 1936, Records of the Registration Department, ROM: 'The truth is our friend the director, has the gift of speech, but cannot express himself on paper, and he is afraid that history and the arts will steal a march on natural history and the local interests that he represents.'

61 Alfred Goldsworthy Bailey, 'Saint John and the New Brunswick Museum in the Hungry Thirties, 1935–1938' (revised 1982), MS4.7.1.6, 4, University of New Brunswick Archives.

62 Webster, *The Distressed Maritimes*, 9.

63 Bourdieu, *Distinction*, 28–33.

64 Pierre Bourdieu, 'How Can One Be a Sports Fan?' in *The Cultural Studies Reader*, ed. Simon During (London: Routledge, 1993), 339–56.

65 College Art Association, 'Discussion of the Report of a Committee of American Association of Museums on Training of Museum Workers,' *Bulletin of the College Art Association of America* 1.3 (Nov. 1917): 26.

66 Ibid.

67 Bennett, *The Birth of the Museum*, 17–33.

68 Alice Lusk Webster to the Management Committee of the New Brunswick Museum, 10 January 1940, NBM fonds, ANBM.

69 Ibid.

70 Edith Hudson to McCurry, 1 October 1936, Outside Activities/Organizations, Individuals, Hudson, Edith A., CC fonds, RG 7.4 C, Box 297, file 18, NGCA.

71 Alice Lusk Webster to C.T. Currelly, 23 June 1941, Records of the Registration Department, ROM.

72 John Cotton Dana, 'The New Museum,' and 'The Gloom of the Museum,' in *The New Museum: Selected Writings by John Cotton Dana*, ed. William A. Peniston (Newark, NJ: Newark Museum, 1999), 42 and 55.

73 Records of the Apprenticeship School, 1925–81, Boxes 1–3 (unprocessed collection), Newark Museum Archives [NMA]; and E.T. Booth and John

Cotton Dana, *Apprenticeship in the Museum* (Newark, NJ: The Museum, 1928), 27.

74 Katherine Coffey, 'Apprenticeship Study for Museum Work' (paper presented at a conference in Detroit, May 1940), Records of the Director's Office, 1909–94, Box 3, Departments-Education, NMA.

75 Currelly to Lusk Webster, 30 June 1941, Records of the Registration Department, ROM.

76 Currelly to Lusk Webster, 9 May 1941, Records of the Registration Department, ROM.

77 Lusk Webster to Currelly, 23 June 1941, Records of the Registration Department, ROM.

78 Hudson to McCurry, 1 November 1938, Outside Activities/Organizations, Individuals, Hudson, Edith A.

79 'Carnegie Corporation Scholarships,' Report of 30 April 1935, 1, Royal Ontario Museum Minute Book, Education Committee, 1934, 22 October 1934, RG 26, Archives of the Royal Ontario Museum [AROM].

80 Barbara B. Brand, 'Pratt Institute Library School: The Perils of Professionalization,' in *Reclaiming the American Library Past: Writing the Women In*, ed. Suzanne Hildenbrand (Norwood, NJ: Ablex, 1996), 259.

81 Ibid., 251–75.

82 Jacalyn Eddy, '"We Have Become Too Tender-Hearted": The Language of Gender in the Public Library, 1880–1920,' in *Libraries as Agencies of Culture*, ed. Thomas Augst and Wayne Wiegand (Lawrence, KS: American Studies, 2001), 159.

83 See, for example, Kathleen Heim, ed., *The Status of Women in Librarianship: Historical, Sociological, and Economic Issues* (New York: Neal-Schuman, 1983); and Joanne Passet, 'Entering the Professions: Women Library Educators and the Placement of Female Studies, 1887–1912,' *History of Education Quarterly* 31.2 (Summer 1991): 207–28.

84 Melvil Dewey, 'Columbia's Library School,' *Library Notes* 1.4 (March 1887), reproduced in Rory Litwin, *Library Daylight: Tracings of Modern Librarianship, 1874–1922* (Duluth, MN: Library Juice Press, 2006), 63–9.

85 Dee Garrison, *Apostles of Culture: The Public Librarian and American Society, 1876–1920* (London: Collier Macmillan, 1979), 191.

86 Ibid.

87 Ibid., 189; and Roma Harris, *Librarianship: The Erosion of a Woman's Profession* (Norwood, NJ: Ablex Publishing, 1992), 18.

88 McTavish and Dickison, 'William MacIntosh,' 72–90.

89 Records of the Apprenticeship School, 1925–181, Box 1.

90 Booth and Dana, *Apprenticeship in the Museum*, 17.

91 Ibid., 43–7.
92 Ibid., 17.
93 Ibid., 16.
94 'Carnegie Corporation Funds Administered by Canadian Committee for Museum Development, Training Plan in Effect 1933–1939,' Outside Activities/Organizations, General, CC fonds, RG 7.4 C, Box 291, file 5, NGCA. The Commission also funded individual museums and such organizations as the Maritime Art Association.
95 McCurry to Webster, 2 October 1934, JCW fonds, S193, F97, ANBM.
96 Hudson to Home, 25 September 1942, letter 49, Art Department Records [ADR], NBM fonds, F4, ANBM.
97 Hudson to Beatrice Winser, director of the Newark Museum, 21 May 1945, Apprenticeship Program, 1909–1950s, 'Bishop, Mrs. Edith H.,' ANM.
98 Ibid.
99 See Edward P. Alexander, *The Museum in America: Innovators and Pioneers* (Walnut Creek: Altamira, 1997), 162, for an account of Beatrice Winser, the woman appointed director of the Newark Museum after Dana's death in 1929.
100 Lusk Webster to Avery Shaw, curator of the Art Department, 1947, letter 39, ADR, NBM fonds, F10, ANBM.
101 Alice Lusk Webster's Working Files, drafts of speeches etc., ADR, NBM fonds, F546, ANBM.
102 Craig Clunas, 'China in Britain: The Imperial Collections,' in *Grasping the World: The Idea of the Museum*, ed. Donald Preziosi and Claire Farago (Aldershot: Ashgate, 2004), 464.
103 Alice Lusk Webster's Working Files, drafts of speeches etc.
104 Clifford, 'Museums as Contact Zones,' 188–219; Young, *The Making and Unmaking of a University Museum*, 138–47; and Eilean Hooper-Greenhill, *Museums and the Interpretation of Visual Culture* (London: Routledge, 2000).

Conclusion

1 www.nbm-mnb.ca/index.php?option=com_content&view=article7id=59&Itemid=251 (accessed 30 April 2011).
2 www.marketsquaresj.com/Market/about.htm (accessed 1 May 2011).
3 Alan Bryman, 'The Disneyization of Society,' in *McDonaldization: The Reader*, ed. George Ritzer (Thousand Oaks: Pine Forge, 2002), 52–9.
4 www.nbm-mnb.ca/index.php?option=com_content&view=article&id=410&Itemid=561 (accessed 30 April 2011).

5 'From "Diamond in the Rough" to Uptown Jewel,' *Telegraph Journal* [Saint John], 24 April 1996.

6 Carol Duncan and Alan Wallach, 'The Museum of Modern Art as Late Capitalist Ritual,' *Marxist Perspectives*, Winter 1978, pp. 30–1.

7 See the Introduction to this book, especially notes 7, 15, and 16.

8 See the Introduction to this book, especially notes 13–15.

9 See, for example, Peter White, ed., *Naming a Practice: Curatorial Strategies for the Future* (Banff, AB: Walter Phillips Gallery, 1996); Paul O'Neill, ed., *Curating Subjects* (London: Open Editions, 2007); and Carolee Thea and Thomas Micchelli, eds, *On Curating: Interviews with Ten International Curators* (New York: Distributed Art Publishers, 2009).

Bibliography

Archival Sources

Archives of the Newark Museum
Records of the Apprenticeship School
Records of the Director's Office

Archives of the New Brunswick Museum
William Francis Ganong fonds
Harriet Holman fonds
Natural History Society fonds
New Brunswick Museum fonds
John Clarence Webster fonds

City Archives of Vancouver
Vancouver Museums and Planetarium Association fonds

Field Museum of Natural History
Museum Archives

McGill University Library Rare Books and Special Collections
Natural History Society of Montreal collections

National Gallery of Canada Library and Archives
Carnegie Corporation fonds

Provincial Archives of British Columbia
British Columbia Provincial Museum fonds
Newcombe Family Papers

Provincial Archives of Manitoba
Manitoba Naturalists Society fonds
Norman Criddle fonds

Provincial Archives of New Brunswick
Bulletin of the Natural History Society of New Brunswick, vols 1–24

Royal Ontario Museum
Records of the Registration Department

University of New Brunswick Archives
Alfred Goldsworthy Bailey, 'Saint John and the New Brunswick Museum in the Hungry Thirties, 1935–1938,' (revised 1982), MS4.7.1.6, 4.

Printed Sources

Acheson, T.W. 'The National Policy and the Industrialization of the Maritimes, 1880–1910.' *Acadiensis* 1.2 (Spring 1972): 3–28.

– *Saint John: The Making of a Colonial Urban Community*. Toronto: University of Toronto Press, 1985.

Alberti, Samuel J.M.M. *Nature and Culture: Objects, Disciplines and the Manchester Museum*. Manchester: Manchester University Press, 2009.

Alexander, Edward P. *The Museum in America: Innovators and Pioneers*. Walnut Creek: Altamira, 1997.

Ames, Michael. *Cannibal Tours and Glass Boxes: The Anthropology of Museums.* Vancouver: University of British Columbia Press, 1991.

Appadurai, Arjun. *The Social Life of Things: Commodities in Cultural Perspective.* Cambridge: Cambridge University Press, 1986.

Ashwin, Clive. 'Pestalozzi and the Origins of Pedagogical Drawing.' *British Journal of Educational Studies* 29.2 (June 1981): 138–51.

Aysough, Florence. *A Chinese Mirror: Being Reflections of the Reality behind Appearance*. London: Jonathan Cape, 1925.

– *Chinese Women Yesterday and Today*. London: Jonathan Cape, 1938.

Bailey, Alfred G. *The Conflict of European and Eastern Algonkian Cultures, 1504–1700: A Study in Canadian Civilization*. Toronto: University of Toronto Press, 1969.

Bailey, Loring Woart. *Report on the Geology of Northern New Brunswick: Embracing Portions of the Counties of Restigouche, Gloucester, and Northumerland.* Montreal: Dawson Brothers, 1881.

– *Report on the Mines and Minerals of New Brunswick*. Fredericton: G.E. Fenety, 1864.

Bailkin, Jordanna. 'Picturing Feminism, Selling Liberalism: The Case of the

Disappearing Holbein.' In *Museum Studies: An Anthology of Contexts*. Ed. Bettina Messias Carbonell. Oxford: Blackwell, 2003. 260–72.

Bal, Mieke. *Double Exposures: The Subject of Cultural Analysis*. New York: Routledge, 1996.

Bann, Stephen. 'Art History and Museums.' In *The Subjects of Art History: Historical Objects in Contemporary Perspective*. Ed. Mark A. Cheetham, Michael Ann Holly, and Keith Moxey. Cambridge: Cambridge University Press, 1998. 230–49.

Baudrillard, Jean. 'The System of Collecting.' In *The Cultures of Collecting*. Ed. John Elsner and Roger Cardinal. Cambridge: Harvard University Press, 1994. 7–24.

Bennett, Tony. *The Birth of the Museum: History, Theory, Politics*. New York: Routledge, 1995.

– 'Pedagogic Objects, Clean Eyes, and Popular Instruction: On Sensory Regimes and Museum Didactics.' *Configurations* 6.3 (Fall 1998): 345–71.

Berger, Carl. *Science, God, and Nature in Victorian Canada*. Toronto: University of Toronto Press, 1983.

Berger, Maurice. 'The "Corporate" Museum.' In *Museums of Tomorrow: A Virtual Discussion*. Ed. Maurice Berger. New York: Distributed Art Publishers, 2004. 47–80.

Blair, Karen J. *The Torchbearers: Women and Their Amateur Arts Associations in America, 1890–1930*. Bloomington: Indiana University Press, 1994.

Bobinski, George S. *Carnegie Libraries: Their History and Impact on American Public Library Development*. Chicago: American Library Association, 1969.

Bokovoy, Matthew F. *The San Diego World's Fairs and Southwestern Memory, 1880–1940*. Albuquerque: University of New Mexico Press, 2005.

Bourdieu, Pierre. *Distinction: A Social Critique of the Judgement of Taste*. Trans Richard Nice. Cambridge, MA: MIT Press, 1994.

– 'How Can One Be a Sports Fan?' In *The Cultural Studies Reader*. Ed. Simon During. London: Routledge, 1993. 339–56.

Bourdieu, Pierre, and Alain Darbel. *L'Amour de l'art: Les Musées européens et leur public*. Paris: Minuit, 1969. English trans. *The Love of Art: European Art Museums and Their Public*. Trans. Caroline Beattie and Nick Merriman. Stanford: Stanford University Press, 1990.

Brand, B., 'Pratt Institute Library School: The Perils of Professionalization.' In *Reclaiming the American Library Past: Writing the Women In*. Ed. Suzanne Hildenbrand. Norwood, NJ: Ablex, 1996. 251–78.

Braun, Bruce, 'Producing Vertical Territory: Geology and Governmentality in Late Victorian Canada.' *Ecumene* 7.1 (2000): 7–46.

Brennan, Teresa, and Martin Jay, eds. *Vision in Context: Historical and Contemporary Perspectives on Sight*. New York: Routledge, 1996.

Brice, William R., and Silvia F. de M. Figueirôa. 'Charles Frederick Hartt—a Pioneer of Brazilian Geology.' *GSA Today*, March 2003, pp. 18–19.

Briceño, Noel Fahden. 'The Chinoiserie Revival in Early Twentieth-Century American Interiors.' MA thesis, University of Delaware, 2008.

Brison, Jeffrey D. *Rockefeller, Carnegie, and Canada: American Philanthropy and the Arts and Letters in Canada.* Montreal and Kingston: McGill-Queen's University Press, 2005.

Brittain, John. *Elementary Agriculture and Nature Study.* Toronto: Educational Book Co., 1911.

Brownlee, Peter. '"The Economy of the Eyes": Vision and the Cultural Production of the Market Revolution, 1800–1860.' PhD diss., George Washington University, 2004.

Bryman, Alan, 'The Disneyization of Society.' In *McDonaldization: The Reader.* Ed. George Ritzer. Thousand Oaks: Pine Forge, 2002. 52–9.

Burton, Antoinette, ed. *Archive Stories: Fact, Fictions, and the Writing of History.* Durham, NC: Duke University Press, 2005.

Carbonell, Bettina Messias, ed. *Museum Studies: An Anthology of Contexts.* Oxford: Blackwell, 2003.

Carrier, David, 'Isabella Stewart Gardner's Museum.' In *Museum Skepticism: A History of the Display of Art in Public Galleries.* Durham, NC: Duke University Press, 2006. 110–25.

Cassidy, Gerald J. 'George Frederic Matthew: Invertebrate Paleontologist.' *Geoscience Canada* 15.2 (1988): 157–62.

Çelik, Zeynep. *Displaying the Orient: Architecture of Islam at Nineteenth-Century World's Fairs.* Berkeley: University of California Press, 1992.

Chakrabarty, Dipesh. *Provincializing Europe: Postcolonial Thought and Historical Difference.* Princeton: Princeton University Press, 2000.

Cheang, Sarah. 'Consuming the Exotic Other.' *Critical Studies in Mass Communication* 12 (1995): 263–86.

– 'What's in a Chinese Room? 20th Century Chinoiserie, Modernity and Femininity.' In *Chinese Whispers: Chinoiserie in Britain, 1650–1930.* Ed. David Beevers. Brighton and Hove: The Royal Pavilion and Museums, 2008. 74–81.

Christie, Nancy. 'Sir William Logan's Geological Empire and the "Humbug" of Economic Utility.' *Canadian Historical Review* 75.2 (June 1994): 161–81.

Clifford, James. 'Museums as Contact Zones.' In *Routes: Travel and Translation in the Late Twentieth Century.* Cambridge: Harvard University Press, 1997. 188–219.

– 'On Collecting Art and Culture.' In *The Predicament of Culture: Twentieth-Century Ethnography, Literature, and Art.* Cambridge: Harvard University Press, 1988. 215–51.

Clunas, Craig. 'China in Britain: The Imperial Collections.' In *Grasping the World: The Idea of the Museum.* Ed. Donald Preziosi and Claire Farago. Aldershot: Ashgate, 2004. 461–72.

– *Pictures and Visuality in Early Modern China.* Princeton: Princeton University Press, 1997.

Cole, Douglas. *Captured Heritage: The Scramble for Northwest Coast Artifacts.* Vancouver: University of British Columbia Press, 1995.

Coletta, Cristina Della. *World's Fairs Italian Style: The Great Exhibitions in Turin and Their Narratives, 1860–1915.* Toronto: University of Toronto Press, 2006.

Conn, Steven. *Do Museums Still Need Objects?* Philadelphia: University of Pennsylvania Press, 2010.

– *Museums and American Intellectual Life, 1876–1926.* Chicago: University of Chicago Press, 1998.

Cook, Janice Mary. 'Child Labour in Saint John, New Brunswick and the Campaign for Factory Legislation.' MA thesis, University of New Brunswick, 1994.

Coombes, Annie E. 'Museums and the Formation of National and Cultural Identities.' *Oxford Art Journal* 11 (1988): 57–68.

Corley-Smith, Peter. *White Bears and Other Curiosities … The First 100 Years of the Royal British Columbia Museum.* Victoria, BC: Royal British Columbia Museum, 1989).

Costello, Evelyn P. 'A Report on the Saint John Mechanics' Institute, 1838–1890.' MA thesis, University of New Brunswick, 1974.

Crary, Jonathan. *Suspensions of Perception: Attention, Spectacle, and Modern Culture.* Cambridge, MA: MIT Press, 1999.

– *Techniques of the Observer: On Vision and Modernity in the Nineteenth Century.* Cambridge, MA: MIT Press, 1990.

Culler, Jonathan. *Saussure.* Glasgow: Collins, 1976.

Cuno, James, ed. *Whose Muse? Art Museums and the Public Trust.* Princeton: Princeton University Press, 2004.

Currelly, C.T. *I Brought the Ages Home.* Toronto: Royal Ontario Museum, 1956.

Derrida, Jacques. *Archive Fever: A Freudian Impression.* Chicago: University of Chicago Press, 1996.

– *The Truth in Painting*. Trans. Geoff Bennington and Ian McLeod. Chicago: University of Chicago Press, 1987.

Dewey, Melvil. 'Columbia's Library School.' *Library Notes* 1.4 (March 1887). Reproduced in Rory Litwin. *Library Daylight: Tracings of Modern Librarianship,* 1874–1922. Duluth, MN: Library Juice Press, 2006. 63–9.

Dewolf, Christopher. 'What Makes a Good Library?' *Spacing Montreal,* 26 November 2007. spacingmontreal,ca/2007/11/26/what-makes-a-good-library. Accessed 24 April 2011.

Dibley, Ben. 'The Museum's Redemption: Contact Zones, Government and the Limit of Reform.' *International Journal of Cultural Studies* 8.1 (2005): 5–27.

Divelko, Juris, and Lisa Gottlieb. *The Evolution of Library and Museum Partnerships: Historical Antecedents, Contemporary Manifestations, and Future Directions.* Westport, CT: Libraries Unlimited, 2004.

Duncan, Carol. *Aesthetics and Power.* Cambridge: Cambridge University Press, 1993.

– *Civilizing Rituals.* London: Routledge, 1995.

Duncan, Carol, and Alan Wallach. 'The Museum of Modern Art as Late Capitalist Ritual.' *Marxist Perspectives,* Winter 1978, pp. 28–51.

– 'The Universal Survey Museum.' *Art History* 3 (Dec. 1980): 447–69.

Duncan, Sally Anne. 'Harvard's "Museum Course" and the Making of America's Museum Profession.' *Archives of American Art Journal* 42.1-2 (2002): 2–16.

Dunlap, R. *Nature and the English Diaspora: Environment and History in the United States, Canada, Australia, and New Zealand.* Cambridge: Cambridge University Press, 1999.

Eddy, Jacalyn. '"We Have Become Too Tender-Hearted": The Language of Gender in the Public Library, 1880–1920.' In *Libraries as Agencies of Culture.* Ed. Thomas Augst and Wayne Wiegand. Lawrence, KS: American Studies, 2001. 155–72.

Edwards, Anthony David. *The Role of International Exhibitions in Britain, 1850–1910: Perceptions of Economic Decline and the Technical Education Issue.* Amherst, NY: Cambria, 2008.

Ernst, Wolfgang. 'Archi(ve)textures of Museology.' In *Museums and Memory.* Ed. Susan A. Crane. Stanford: Stanford University Press, 2000. 17–34.

Falk, John H. *Identity and the Museum Visitor Experience.* Walnut Creek, CA: Left Coast Press, 2009.

Farrington, Oliver C. 'On the Ideal Relations of Public Libraries, Museums, and Art Gallery to the City.' In *Museum Origins: Readings in Early Museum History and Philosophy.* Ed. Hugh H. Genoways and Mary Anne Andrei. Walnut Creek, CA: Left Coast Press, 2008. 79–82.

Fernsebner, Susan R. 'Material Modernities: China's Participation in World's Fairs and Expositions, 1876–1955.' PhD diss., University of California, San Diego, 2002.

Findlen, Paula. *Possessing Nature: Museums, Collecting, and Scientific Culture in Early Modern Italy.* Berkeley: University of California Press, 1994.

Findling, John E. *Chicago's Great World's Fairs.* Manchester: Manchester University Press, 1994.

Fingard, Judith. *Jack in Port: Sailortowns of Eastern Canada.* Toronto: University of Toronto Press, 1982.

Foster, Hal, ed., *Vision and Visuality.* Seattle: Bay Press, 1988.
Foucault, Michel. *Discipline and Punish: The Birth of the Prison.* Trans. Alan Sheridan. New York: Vintage Books, 1979.
– *The History of Sexuality*. Vol. 1. Trans. Robert Hurley. New York: Vintage, 1990.
Freud, Sigmund. *The Interpretation of Dreams* (1900). In *The Complete Psychological Works of Sigmund Freud: The Standard Edition*. Vols 4–5. Trans. and ed. James Strachey. Harmondsworth: Penguin, 1976.
– 'Repression' (1915). In *The Complete Psychological Works of Sigmund Freud: The Standard Edition*. Vol. 14. Trans. and ed. James Strachey. Harmondsworth: Penguin, 1976. 141–58.
Frost, Stanley Brice. 'Science Education in the Nineteenth Century: The Natural History Society of Montreal, 1827–1925.' *McGill Journal of Education* 17.1 (Winter 1982): 31–43.
Gagnon, Hervé. 'The Natural History Society of Montreal's Museum and the Socio-Economic Significance of Museums in 19th-Century Canada.' *Scientia Canadensis: Canadian Journal of the History of Science, Technology and Medicine* 18.2 (1994): 103–35.
Garrison, Dee. *Apostles of Culture: The Public Librarian and American Society, 1876–1920*. London: Collier Macmillan, 1979.
Gesner, Abraham. *Synopsis of the Contents of Gesner's Museum of Natural History, at Saint John, N.B. Opened the Fifth Day of April, 1842*. Saint John, NB: Henry Chubb, 1842.
Godelier, Maurice. *The Enigma of the Gift*. Trans. N. Scott. Chicago: University of Chicago Press, 1996.
Gosden, Chris, and Frances Larsen. *Knowing Things: Exploring the Collections at the Pitt Rivers Museum, 1884–1945*. Oxford: Oxford University Press, 2007.
Greenblatt, Stephen. 'Resonance and Wonder.' In *Exhibiting Cultures: The Poetics and Politics of Museum Display*. Ed. Ivan Karp and Steven D. Lavine. Washington, DC: Smithsonian Institution Press, 1991. 42–56.
Gregory, Christopher. *Gifts and Commodities.* London: Academic Press, 1982.
Halberstam, Judith. *In a Queer Time and Place: Transgender Bodies, Subcultural Lives.* New York: New York University Press, 2005.
Hamilton, Carolyn, et al., eds. *Refiguring the Archive.* Dordrecht: Kluwer Academic Publishers, 2002.
Haraway, Donna. 'Teddy Bear Patriarchy: Taxidermy in the Garden of Eden, New York City, 1908–1986.' In *Primate Visions: Gender, Race, and Nature in the World of Modern Science.* New York: Routledge, 1989. 26–58.
Harris, Roma. *Librarianship: The Erosion of a Woman's Profession.* Norwood: Ablex Publishing, 1992.

Heaman, E.A. *The Inglorious Arts of Peace: Exhibitions in Canadian Society during the Nineteenth Century.* Toronto: University of Toronto Press, 1999.

Heim, Kathleen, ed. *The Status of Women in Librarianship: Historical, Sociological, and Economic Issues.* New York: Neal-Schuman, 1983.

Heringman, Noah. *Romantic Rocks, Aesthetic Geology.* Ithaca, NY: Cornell University Press, 2004.

Hill, Kate. *Culture and Class in English Public Museums, 1850–1914.* Aldershot: Ashgate, 2005.

Hill-Tout, Charles. *Later Prehistoric Man in British Columbia.* Ottawa: Transactions of the Royal Society of Canada, Section II, 1895.

Hineline, Mark Lawrence. 'The Visual Culture of the Earth Sciences, 1863–1970.' PhD diss., University of California, San Diego, 1993.

Hinsley, Curtis M., '"Magnificent Intentions": Washington, D.C., and American Anthropology in 1846.' In Carbonell, ed., *Museum Studies,* 159–74.

Hooper-Greenhill, Eilean. *Museums and the Interpretation of Visual Culture.* London: Routledge, 2000.

Huskins, Bonnie. 'Review of "Progress and Permanence: Women and the New Brunswick Museum, 1880–1980": www.unbf.ca/womenandmuseum.' *The Public Historian* 31 (Feb. 2009): 129–36.

Hyde, S. *Exhibiting Gender.* Manchester: Manchester University Press, 1997.

Impey, Oliver, and Arthur MacGregor, eds. *The Origins of Museums: The Cabinet of Curiosities in Sixteenth- and Seventeenth-Century Europe.* Oxford: Clarendon Press, 1985.

Isabella Stewart Gardner Museum. *Cultural Leadership in America: Art Matronage and Patronage.* Boston: Trustees of the Isabella Stewart Gardner Museum, 1997.

Janes, Robert R. *Museums in a Troubled World: Renewal, Irrelevance or Collapse?* London: Routledge, 2009.

Jordanova, Ludmilla, and Roy Porter, eds. *Images of the Earth: Essays in the History of the Environmental Sciences.* St Giles, UK: British Society for the History of Science, 1979.

Judd, Richard W. *Common Lands, Common People: The Origins of Conservation in Northern New England.* Cambridge: Harvard University Press, 1997.

Kenseth, Joy. '"A World of Wonders in One Closet Shut."' In *The Age of the Marvelous.* Ed. Joy Kenseth. Hanover, NH: Hood Museum of Art, Dartmouth College, 1991. 81–101.

Kinchin, Juliet. 'Interiors: Nineteenth-Century Essays on the "Masculine" and the "Feminine" Room.' In *The Gendered Object.* Ed. Pat Kirkham. Manchester: Manchester University Press, 1996. 12–29.

King, Elaine A. 'So, What's the Price—*The PM Principle*—Power, People, and

Money.' In *Ethics and the Visual Arts*. Ed. Elaine A. King and Gail Levin. New York: Allworth Press, 2006. 1–17.

Kirshenblatt-Gimblett, Barbara. *Destination Culture: Tourism, Museums, and Heritage*. Berkeley: University of California Press, 1998.

Knell, Simon J. *The Culture of English Geology, 1815–1851: A Science Revealed through Its Collecting*. Aldershot: Ashgate, 2000.

Kohler, Robert E. *All Creatures: Naturalists, Collectors, and Biodiversity, 1850–1950*. Princeton: Princeton University Press, 2006.

Lawson, Barbara. 'Collecting Cultures: Canadian Missionaries, Pacific Islanders, and Museums.' In *Canadian Missionaries, Indigenous Peoples: Representing Religion at Home and Abroad*. Ed. Alvyn Austin and Jamie S. Scott. Toronto: University of Toronto Press, 2005. 235–61.

Lester, R., 'The Convergence of Museums and Libraries?' *Alexandria* 13 (March 2001): 183–91.

Levine, Lawrence. *Highbrow/Lowbrow: The Emergence of a Cultural Hierarchy in America*. Cambridge: Harvard University Press, 1988.

Lewis, Timothy. 'Agrarian Idealism and Progressive Agriculture in Maritime Canada: Agricultural Leadership in New Brunswick, 1895–1929.' PhD diss., University of New Brunswick, 2003.

Lindfors, Bernth. *Africans on Stage: Studies in Ethnological Show Business*. Bloomington: Indiana University Press, 1999.

Looby, Christopher. 'The Constitution of Nature: Taxonomy as Politics in Jefferson, Peale, and Bartram.' In Carbonell, ed., *Museum Studies*, 143–57.

Luke, Timothy W. *Museum Politics: Power Plays at the Exhibition*. Minneapolis: University of Minnesota Press, 2002.

MacDiarmid, F.E., et al. *Science and Agriculture for New Brunswick Schools*. Toronto: Copp Clark Co., 1942.

MacIntosh, William. 'Injurious and Other Insects of New Brunswick.' In *Report on Agriculture for the Province of New Brunswick*. Fredericton: Department of Agriculture, 1913. 268-71.

MacKay, Alexander H. 'Ferndale School, No. 1, A Cocoon.' *Educational Review* 1.1 (June 1887): 5–8.

Mackenzie, Catherine. 'Florence Wheelock Ayscough's Niger Reef Tea House.' *Journal of Canadian Art History* 23.1-2 (2002): 34–65.

MacNaughton, Katherine F.C. *The Development of the Theory and Practice of Education in New Brunswick, 1784–1900*. Fredericton: University of New Brunswick Historical Studies, 1947.

Mak, Eileen Diana. 'Patterns of Change, Sources of Influence: An Historical Study of the Canadian Museum and the Middle Class, 1850–1950.' PhD diss., University of British Columbia, 1996.

Maleuvre, Didier. *Museum Memories: History, Technology, Art*. Stanford: Stanford University Press, 1999.

Marks, Lynne. *Revivals and Roller Rinks: Religion, Leisure, and Identity in Late Nineteenth-Century Small-Town Ontario*. Toronto: University of Toronto Press, 1996.

Marquis, Greg. 'Commemorating the Loyalists in the Loyalist City: Saint John, New Brunswick, 1883–1934.' *Urban History Review* 33.1 (2004): 24–33.

Martin, R.S. *Carnegie Denied: Communities Rejecting Carnegie Construction Grants, 1898–1925*. Westport, CT: Greenwood Press, 1993.

Matless, David. 'Visual Culture and Geographical Citizenship: England in the 1940s.' *Journal of Historical Geography* 22.4 (1996): 424–39.

Matthew, George F. *Report on the Superfcial* [sic] *Geology of Southern New Brunswick, 1878*. Montreal: Dawson Brothers, 1879.

Mattson, Kevin. 'The Librarian as Secular Minister to Democracy: The Life and Ideas of John Cotton Dana.' *Libraries and Culture* 33.4 (Fall 2000): 514–34.

Mauss, Marcel. *The Gift: The Form and Reason for Exchange in Archaic Societies*. Trans. W.D. Halls. New York: Routledge, 2002.

McCarthy, Kathleen D. *Women's Culture: American Philanthropy and Art, 1830-1930*. Chicago: University of Chicago Press, 1991.

McClellan, Andrew, ed. *Art and Its Publics: Museum Studies at the Millennium*. Oxford: Blackwell, 2003.

McLoughlin, Moira. *Museums and the Representation of Native Canadians: Negotiating the Borders of Culture*. New York: Routledge, 1999.

McMullen, Haynes. *American Libraries before 1876*. Westport, CT: Greenwood Press, 2000.

McTavish, Lianne. 'Strategic Donations: Women and Museums in New Brunswick, 1862–1930.' *Journal of Canadian Studies* 42.2 (Spring 2008): 1–24.

McTavish, Lianne, and Joshua Dickison. 'William MacIntosh, Natural History and the Professionalization of the New Brunswick Museum, 1898–1940.' *Acadiensis: Journal of the History of the Atlantic Region* 36.2 (Spring 2007): 72–90.

Merrill, Lynn L. *The Romance of Victorian Natural History*. Oxford: Oxford University Press, 1989.

Miers, Sir Henry A., and S.F. Markham. *A Report on the Museums of Canada to the Carnegie Corporation of New York*. Edinburgh: T. and A. Constable, 1932.

Miller, Randall F. 'George Frederic Matthew's Contribution to Precambrian Paleobiology.' *Geoscience Canada* 30.1 (2003): 1–8.

– 'Matthew, George Frederic.' *Dictionary of Canadian Biography Online*. University of Toronto / Université de Laval, and Library and Archives Canada, 2004. www.biographi.ca.

Mitcham, Allsion. *Prophet of the Wilderness: Abraham Gesner*. Hantsport, NS: Lancelot Press, 1995.

Morgan, Cecilia. *Public Men and Virtuous Women: The Gendered Languages of Religion and Politics in Upper Canada, 1791-1850*. Toronto: University of Toronto Press, 1996.

Nelson, Robert S., ed. *Visuality before and beyond the Renaissance: Seeing as Others Saw*. Cambridge: Cambridge University Press, 1997.

O'Neill, Paul, ed. *Curating Subjects*. London: Open Editions, 2007.

Parenteau, William. 'A "Very Determined Opposition to the Law": Conservation, Angling Leases, and Social Conflict in the Canadian Atlantic Salmon Fishery, 1867–1914.' *Environmental History* 9.3 (July 2004): 436–63.

Passet, Joanne. 'Entering the Professions: Women Library Educators and the Placement of Female Studies, 1887–1912.' *History of Education Quarterly* 31.2 (Summer 1991): 207–28.

Peirce, Charles Sanders. *Collected Papers*. Vol. 4. Ed. C. Hartshorne and P. Weiss. Cambridge: Belknap Press of Harvard University Press, 1931–5.

Peniston, William A., ed. *The New Museum: Selected Writings by John Cotton Dana*. Newark, NJ: Newark Museum, 1999.

Phillips, Doris. 'Nova Scotia's Aid for the Sufferers of the Great Saint John Fire (June 20th, 1877).' *Nova Scotia Historical Quarterly* 7.4 (1977): 351–66.

Phillips, Ruth. *Trading Identities: The Souvenir in Native North American Art from the Northeast, 1700–1900*. Seattle: University of Washington Press, 1998.

Pierson, Stacey. *Collectors, Collections and Museums: The Field of Chinese Ceramics in Britain, 1560–1960*. Bern: Peter Lang, 2007.

Pomian, Krzysztof. *Collectors and Curiosities: Paris and Venice, 1500–1800*. Trans. Elizabeth Wiles-Portier. Cambridge: Polity Press, 1990.

Porter, Gaby. 'Seeing through Solidity: A Feminist Perspective on Museums.' In Carbonell, ed., *Museum Studies*, 104–16.

Porter, Roy. 'Gentlemen and Geology: The Emergence of a Scientific Career, 1660–1920.' *Historical Journal* 21.4 (Dec. 1978): 809–36.

Prior, Nick. 'Having One's Tate and Eating It: Transformations of the Museum in a Hypermodern Era.' In McClellan, ed., *Art and Its Publics*, 51–76.

Rees, Ronald. 'Changing St. John: The Old and the New.' *Canadian Geographical Journal* 90.5 (1975): 12–17.

Rhees, David J. 'Corporate Advertising, Public Relations, and Popular Exhibits: The Case of Du Pont.' In *Industrial Society and Its Museums, 1890-1990: Social Aspirations and Cultural Politics*. Ed. Brigitte Schroeder-Gudehus. Paris: Harwood Academic Publishers, 1993. 67–75.

Rice, Danielle. 'Museums: Theory, Practice, and Illusion.' In McClellan, ed., *Art and Its Publics*, 77–96.

Righter, Robert W. *The Battle over Hetch Hetchy: America's Most Controversial Dam and the Birth of Modern Environmentalism*. New York: Oxford University Press, 2005.

Robinson, Noel. *Vancouver City Museum Golden Jubilee, 1894–1944*. Vancouver: The Art, Historical and Scientific Association, 1944.

Rosenbaum, L. 'The Battle of Brooklyn Ends, the Controversy Continues.' *Art in America* 88.6 (June 2000): 39–43.

Rudwick, Martin J.S. *Bursting the Limits of Time: The Reconstruction of Geohistory in the Age of Revolution*. Chicago: University of Chicago Press, 2005.

– *The Great Devonian Controversy: The Shaping of Scientific Knowledge among Gentlemanly Specialists*. Chicago: University of Chicago Press, 1985.

– *The Meaning of Fossils: Episodes in the History of Palaeontology*. London: Macdonald and Company, 1972.

Rydell, Robert W., and Nancy E. Gwinn. *Fair Representations: World's Fairs and the Modern World*. Amsterdam: VU University Press, 1994.

Said, Edward. *Orientalism*. London: Penguin, 2003.

Schildkrout, Enid, and Curtis A. Keim, eds. *The Scramble for Art in Central Africa*. Cambridge: Cambridge University Press, 1998.

Schubert, Karsten. *The Curator's Egg: The Evolution of the Museum Concept from the French Revolution to the Present Day*. London: Ridinghouse, 2009.

Scott, Gregg. 'The Complex History of Credentialism.' In *The Professionalization of Work*. Ed. Merle Jacobs and Stephen E. Bosanac.Whitby, ON: de Sitter Publications, 2006. 252–81.

Sheets-Pyenson, Susan. *Cathedrals of Science: The Development of Colonial Natural History Museums during the Late Nineteenth Century*. Kingston, ON: Queen's University Press, 1988.

Silber, Kate. *Pestalozzi: The Man and His Work*. London: Routledge and Kegan Paul, 1976.

Simpson, Moira. *Making Representations: Museums in the Post-Colonial Era*. New York: Routledge, 1996.

Sloboda, Stacey Loughrey. 'Making China: Design, Empire, and Aesthetics in Britain, 1745–1851.' PhD diss., University of Southern California, 2004.

Squires, Austin. *The History and Development of the New Brunswick Museum*. Saint John: New Brunswick Museum, 1945.

Stafford, Barbara Maria. 'Spectacle of Nature.' In *Artful Science: Enlightenment Entertainment and the Eclipse of Visual Education*. Cambridge, MA: MIT Press, 1999. 217–79.

Steeves, R.P. *Nature Study and Agricultural Course for Use in the Public Schools of New Brunswick*. N.l., 1914 [1st edn. 1908].

Strong-Boag, Veronica. 'The Roots of Modern Canadian Feminism: The National Council of Women, 1893–1921.' *Canada* 3.2 (1975): 22–33.

Summers, David. '*Suspension of Perception* (Book Review).' *Art Bulletin* 83.1 (March 2001): 57–61.

Taylor, Alice. 'Trading in Abolitionism: The Commercial, Material, and Social World of the Boston Antislavery Fair, 1834–1858.' PhD diss., University of Western Ontario, 2007.

Thea, Carolee, and Thomas Micchelli, eds. *On Curating: Interviews with Ten International Curators.* New York: Distributed Art Publishers, 2009.

Thomas, Gerald. 'John C. Webster: Applying Material History — Developing the New Brunswick Museum.' In *Studies in History and Museums.* Ed. Peter E. Rider. Hull, PQ: Canadian Museum of Civilization, 1994. 33–55.

Thomas, Keith. *Man and the Natural World: A History of the Modern Sensibility.* New York: Pantheon Books, 1983.

Thornton, Patricia A. 'The Problem of Out-Migration from Atlantic Canada, 1871–1921: A New Look.' *Acadiensis* 15.1 (Autumn 1985): 3–34.

Thring, Reverend E. 'Thinking in Shape and Pictorial Teaching.' *Educational Review* 1.2 (July 1887): 37.

Trigger, Bruce. 'Alfred G. Bailey – Ethnohistorian.' *Acadiensis* 18 (Spring 1989): 3–21.

Van Slyck, Abigail A. *Free to All: Carnegie Libraries and American Culture, 1890–1920.* Chicago: University of Chicago Press, 1995.

Volti, Rudi. 'Professions and Professionalization.' In *An Introduction to the Sociology of Work and Occupations.* Thousand Oaks, CA: Pine Forge Press, 2008. 97–116.

Waiser, W.A. *The Field Naturalist: John Macoun, the Geological Survey, and Natural Science.* Toronto: University of Toronto Press, 1989.

Webster, John Clarence. *The Distressed Maritimes: A Study of Educational and Cultural Conditions in Canada.* Toronto: Ryerson Press, 1926.

White, Peter, ed. *Naming a Practice: Curatorial Strategies for the Future.* Banff, AB: Walter Phillips Gallery, 1996.

Whitney, Paul. 'A Refuge and a Sanctuary: Vancouver's Carnegie Library as Civic Space.' In *Last One Out Turn Off the Lights: Is This the Future of American and Canadian Libraries?* Ed. Susan E. Cleyle and Louise M. McGillis. Lanham, MD: Scarecrow Press, 2005. 64–72.

Wiatr, Elizabeth Ann. 'Seeing American: Visual Education and the Making of Modern Observers, 1900–1935.' PhD diss., University of California, Irvine, 2003.

Winsor, Mary P. *Reading the Shape of Nature: Comparative Zoology at the Agassiz Museum.* Chicago: University of Chicago Press, 1991.

Witcomb, Andrea. *Re-imagining the Museum: Beyond the Mausoleum.* London: Routledge, 2003.

Yablonski, Janice B. *Museum Women: A Century of Women's Employment in Art Museums.* New York: Columbia University, 1992.

Yoshihara, Mari. *Embracing the East: White Women and Orientalism.* Oxford: Oxford University Press, 2003.

Young, Brian. *The Making and Unmaking of a University Museum: The McCord,1921–1996.* Montreal and Kingston: McGill-Queen's University Press, 2000.

Zaslow, Morris. *Reading the Rocks: The Story of the Geological Survey of Canada, 1842–1972.* Toronto: Macmillan, 1975.

Zeller, Suzanne. 'George Lawson: Victorian Botany, the Origin of the Species and the Case of Nova Scotian Heather.' In *Profiles of Science and Society in the Maritimes prior to1914.* Ed. Paul A. Bogaard. Fredericton: Acadiensis Press, 1990. 50–62.

– *Inventing Canada: Early Victorian Science and the Idea of a Transcontinental Nation.* Toronto: University of Toronto Press, 1987.

– *Land of Promise, Promised Land: The Culture of Victorian Science in Canada.* Ottawa: Canadian Historical Association, 1996.

Index

CULTURAL SPACES

Cultural Spaces explores the rapidly changing temporal, spatial, and theoretical boundaries of contemporary cultural studies. Culture has long been understood as the force that defines and delimits societies in fixed spaces. The recent intensification of globalizing processes, however, has meant that it is no longer possible – if it ever was – to imagine the world as a collection of autonomous, monadic spaces, whether these are imagined as localities, nations, regions within nations, or cultures demarcated by region or nation. One of the major challenges of studying contemporary culture is to understand the new relationships of culture to space that are produced today. The aim of this series is to publish bold new analyses and theories of the spaces of culture, as well as investigations of the historical construction of those cultural spaces that have influenced the shape of the contemporary world.

Books in the Series:

Peter Ives, *Gramsci's Politics of Language: Engaging the Bakhtin Circle and the Frankfurt School*

Sarah Brophy, *Witnessing AIDS: Writing, Testimony, and the Work of Mourning*

Shane Gunster, *Capitalizing on Culture: Critical Theory for Cultural Studies*

Jasmin Habib, *Israel, Diaspora, and the Routes of National Belonging*

Serra Tinic, *On Location: Canada's Television Industry in a Global Market*

Evelyn Ruppert, *The Moral Economy of Cities: Shaping Good Citizens*

Mark Coté, Richard J.F. Day, and Greg de Peuter, eds., *Utopian Pedagogy: Radical Experiments against Neoliberal Globalization*

Michael McKinnie, *City Stages: Theatre and the Urban Space in a Global City*

David Jefferess, *Postcolonial Resistance: Culture, Liberation, and Transformation*

Mary Gallagher, ed., *World Writing: Poetics, Ethics, Globalization*

Maureen Moynagh, *Political Tourism and Its Texts*

Erin Hurley, *National Performance: Representing Quebec from Expo 67 to Céline Dion*

Lily Cho, *Eating Chinese: Culture on the Menu in Small Town Canada*

Rhona Richman Kenneally and Johanne Sloan, eds, *Expo 67: Not Just a Souvenir*

Gillian Roberts, *Prizing Literature: The Celebration and Circulation of National Culture*

Lianne McTavish, *Defining the Modern Museum: A Case Study of the Challenges of Exchange*

www.ingramcontent.com/pod-product-compliance
Lightning Source LLC
LaVergne TN
LVHW090157080826
844660LV00013B/848/J

* 9 7 8 1 4 4 2 6 4 4 4 3 4 *